FALL OF THE MERCHANT-FARMER REPUBLIC

The Battle of Visby 1361 and the Danish Conquest of Gotland

Michael Fredholm von Essen

Helion & Company Limited
Unit 8 Amherst Business Centre
Budbrooke Road
Warwick
CV34 5WE
England
Tel. 01926 499 619
Email: info@helion.co.uk
Website: www.helion.co.uk
X (formerly Twitter): @Helionbooks
Facebook: @HelionBooks
Visit our blog https://helionbooks.wordpress.com/

Published by Helion & Company 2025
Designed and typeset by Mary Woolley, Battlefield Design (www.battlefield-design.co.uk)
Cover designed by Paul Hewitt, Battlefield Design (www.battlefield-design.co.uk)

Text © Michael Fredholm von Essen 2025
Photographs and illustrations as individually credited
Front cover, colour and pen artwork by Giorgio Albertini © Helion & Company 2025
Maps by George Anderson © Helion & Company 2025

Disclaimer: Illustrations attributed to Army Museum, Stockholm, Maritime Museum, Stockholm, and Gotland Museum, Visby, are reproduced under the Creative Commons license and derive from the website, https://digitaltmuseum.se. Illustrations attributed to Royal Armoury, Stockholm, are reproduced under the Creative Commons license and derive from the website, http://emuseumplus.lsh.se. Illustrations attributed to History Museum, Stockholm, are reproduced under the Creative Commons license and derive from the website, https://samlingar.shm.se, with special thanks to Helena Rosengren, curator at the museum, and Katarina Nimmervoll, image archivist. The photograph from Uppsala University is reprinted under the Creative Commons license with special thanks to the staff of the University's image archive. The photograph from Mästerby is reproduced with the permission of, and with special thanks to, Maria Lingström, the archaeologist in charge of the battlefield excavation. Other illustrations are reproduced under GNU Free Documentation License (GNU FDL) coupled with the Creative Commons Attribution Share-Alike License or derive from the author's personal collection. The artwork by the late Tommy Hellman is reproduced with the permission of his family. Photographs attributed to Medström are reproduced with the permission of this publisher.

Every reasonable effort has been made to trace copyright holders and to obtain their permission for the use of copyright material. The author and publisher apologize for any errors or omissions in this work and would be grateful if notified of any corrections that should be incorporated in future reprints or editions of this book.

ISBN 978-1-804518-29-8

British Library Cataloguing-in-Publication Data.
A catalogue record for this book is available from the British Library.

All rights reserved. No part of this publication may be reproduced, stored in a retrieval system, or transmitted, in any form, or by any means, electronic, mechanical, photocopying, recording or otherwise, without the express written consent of Helion & Company Limited.

For details of other military history titles published by Helion & Company Limited contact the above address or visit our website: http://www.helion.co.uk.

We always welcome receiving book proposals from prospective authors.

Dedication

Dedicated to the memory of Tommy Hellman (1945–2016), an accomplished expert on the arms and equipment of medieval and early modern soldiers, and Gunnar Thompson (1946–2017), a talented artist and scholar of early maps and maritime discovery. For Tommy, in memory of our many discussions from the 1970s onwards of the Battle of Visby and similar topics, and for Gunnar, in memory of our numerous discussions from the 1990s onwards of early contacts and trade between Scandinavia and America, and between East Asia and America

Contents

Introduction		vii
Chronology		ix
Prologue		xvii
1	The Scanian Herring Market	39
2	The Conquest of the Scanias	47
3	King Valdemar's Strategic Goals	51
4	King Valdemar's Invasion Army	58
5	The Gotland Rural Militia	77
6	The Visby Hanseatic League Burgher Militia	103
7	King Valdemar Conquers Oland	108
8	The Danish Fleet Lands on Gotland, 22 July	110
9	The Battle of Mästerby, 25 July	115
10	The Battle of Visby, 27 July	120
11	The Submission of Visby	129
12	The Battle of Fide, 10 August	135
13	King Valdemar Departs	138
14	The League Goes to War	141
15	Swedish Turmoil	147
16	The League Again Goes to War	152
17	The Kalmar Union	157
18	Piracy	159
19	The End of a Golden Age	165

Appendices:

I	Pictorial Description of Cuirasses Excavated at Visby	170
II	North European Currency	177

Colour Plate Commentaries	179
Further Reading	185
Bibliography	189

Introduction

This book describes and analyses the Battle of Visby in 1361, which was fought on the Baltic Sea island of Gotland between an invasion army under Danish King Valdemar Atterdag and the Gotland rural militia.

The battle was fought after King Valdemar's conquest of Scanian territories previously lost to Sweden and constituted the natural continuation of this campaign. Having recovered the lost territories, King Valdemar set out to conquer the islands of Öland and, yet more importantly, Gotland, the prosperous centre of the Baltic region's Eastern trade.

Gotland, the largest island in the Baltic Sea, was a semi-autonomous Swedish territory. Technically, Gotland consisted of two polities: the Gotland Republic of rural merchant-farmers and the heavily fortified city of Visby, the island's only major population centre, which was a leading member of the powerful Hanseatic League. Gotland suffered from tensions over trading rights between the traditional rural merchant-farmers, the Gotlanders, and the burghers, many of whom were of German origin. The Gotland merchant-farmers traded throughout the Baltic region, from England and the North Sea in the west to Novgorod, the Crimea, Constantinople, and the Black Sea in the east in direct competition with the wealthy and monopolistic Hanseatic League.

When King Valdemar landed on the island with Danish knights on horseback and experienced German mercenaries on foot, his chief adversary was the Gotland Republic's well-armed rural militia. While many merchant-farmers had the means to raise armed men, the militia was untrained. Defeated at Mästerby, the Gotlanders withdrew to Visby, expecting the city's burgher militia and mercenary garrison to join them against the invaders. By this time, the Gotlanders had raised all available men, young as well as old. Would the Visby burghers join the Gotlanders in the battle against the Danes?

The story of King Valdemar's invasion of Gotland contains everything that might strike us as archetypal of the Middle Ages. Predatory kings, battle-hardened knights, rambunctious mercenaries eager for coin, pious but learned churchmen, a certified but slanderous saint, rumours of witches, the walls and towers of proud cities, wealthy merchants with hoards of gold and silver, hard-fought battles, a ruthless massacre of thousands, even stories (although apocryphal and almost certainly false) about young, unrequited love and betrayal – all of which was set against the background of the Black Death and the Four Horsemen of the Apocalypse. But the story also contains industrious merchant-adventurers, travels to distant lands in search of trade, hard-working freeholders, a merchant-farmer republic, and acts of defiance and resistance that still resonates through the ages (not least in medieval-inspired festivals), even though the facts behind the events now often are forgotten.

We will see that Scandinavian power politics really were family affairs. Previous historians commonly regarded King Valdemar through the lens of the modern nation-state and assumed that the war was caused by the Danish King's desire for national reunification. King Valdemar would not have thought in such terms. To begin with, he habitually spoke Low German, not Danish. What can be termed national prejudices certainly existed in the Middle Ages, and local populations as well as provincial laws held that the people of other kingdoms, or for that matter, of other provinces, carried less value than themselves. The penalty for killing a stranger was always lower than for killing a fellow countryman. Yet, such sentiments hardly existed among the strongmen. The strongmen and nobles of Scandinavia were few in numbers. Most knew each other, and they frequently intermarried, or married into the royal families, the members of which typically held no more distinction than being the first among equals. It was common for the same family simultaneously to rule more than one kingdom, or for that matter, to shift from one kingdom to another. Kings were technically elected. Most kings attempted to nominate a son as successor, but this strategy did not always succeed. A display of military strength usually impressed more than mere royal birth when claiming the crown.

Yet, military power cost money. Successful kings found suitable sources of revenue. From an economic perspective, no Scandinavian king could compete with the powerful Hanseatic League, which produced revenue streams that northern kings only could dream of. Then, as now, money was a key source of conflict. For this reason, the present book describes a relentless military campaign with thousands of dead, but it is in equal measure the story of monetary revenues, and how trade decided the fortune of kingdoms.

In addition, this book describes the background and the events on Gotland during the Danish invasion and details the opposing armies. The Battle of Visby was only one of several battles that took place on Gotland during the campaign. Recent battlefield archaeological excavations have brought more information to light. This book presents new research on the arms, armour, and military organisation of the Gotland merchant-farmers, and explains the outcome and consequences of King Valdemar's invasion for Gotland and the burghers of Visby.

Chronology

1340   21 May: Emerging Hanseatic League of mercantile cities transfers its support to Danish Prince Valdemar in exchange for his confirming their future rights in the profitable Scanian herring market
24 June: Valdemar elected King of Denmark
1341   3 January: King Valdemar forced to renounce his right to Scania to the Swedish Crown, and also must sell South Halland province to Sweden; he loses the Scanian herring market
1342   King Valdemar goes to war against Sweden to recover Scania, but fails
1343   18 November: Treaty of Varberg; King Valdemar acknowledges King Magnus of Sweden as rightful suzerain of all the Scanias
1346   29 August: King Valdemar sells Estonia to the Teutonic Order
1347   King Valdemar goes on a pilgrimage to Jerusalem with several close friends
1348   King Magnus goes to war against the Novgorod Republic, embargoes trade in the Gulf of Finland; the war impacts negatively on the Gotland Republic which controls a trade factory in Novgorod and the Hanseatic Visby merchants, who derive much profit from the Novgorod trade
1349-1350   King Valdemar campaigns in Germany; Black Death devastates Germany
1350   Black Death devastates Sweden; King Magnus abandons the war against the Novgorod Republic
1356   17 October: King Magnus's eldest son Eric rebels against his father
1357   28 April: Negotiated settlement between father and son formally divides Sweden and kingship, with Eric crowned King of Scania; Swedish civil war ends
1358   20 January: Second Hanseatic Diet meeting; Hanseatic League acquires a formal identity and organisation
1359   Late winter: King Magnus visits King Valdemar; King Valdemar betroths his daughter Margaret to King Magnus's second son King Haakon of Norway
Spring: King Valdemar leads his army into Scania, where he confronts King Eric's men, and then withdraws
June: King Eric contracts the plague and dies
7 August: King Magnus breaks the betrothal between King Haakon and Margaret, enters into an alliance with Duke Albert of Mecklenburg

FALL OF THE MERCHANT-FARMER REPUBLIC

1360   24 May: King Valdemar acquires the consent of the Danish nobility to attempt the conquest of the Scanias

Late May or early June: King Valdemar informs the Hanseatic League that war is imminent, and that he cannot guarantee the security of League personnel or goods if they remain in the Scanias; in response, League representatives ask King Valdemar for a renewal of their Scanian market privileges after he has conquered Scania

Late June: King Valdemar invades Scania

26 June: Hanseatic envoys arrive in Copenhagen; King Valdemar already in Scania

4 July: King Valdemar seizes the mercantile centre of Malmö

10 July: King Valdemar lays siege to Helsingborg Castle

17 July: King Valdemar promises the League to protect their trade, after he has recovered Scania

10 August: Duke Albert of Mecklenburg defects to the Danish side and enters into an alliance with King Valdemar

24 August–9 October: Scanian herring market takes place under Danish control; King Valdemar remains in Scania

1 October (circa): Duke Albert of Mecklenburg contrives to give King Valdemar control over Helsingborg Castle, hence full control over the Scanias

1361   14 February: King Magnus writes to the City Council in Visby, ordering it to muster men and ships for the defence of the country

6 March: King Valdemar's ally, Duke Eric of Saxe-Lauenburg, concludes a non-aggression treaty with Lübeck, a leading Hanseatic city

Spring: King Valdemar musters his army and fleet on Zealand

2 May: King Magnus warns Visby of an imminent Danish attack

19 May: Hanseatic League meets to agree on how to divide the payment to King Valdemar for Scanian market privileges

June: King Magnus calls up the ledung fleet

Early July: King Valdemar lands his army on and seizes the island of Öland

22 July: King Valdemar lands his army on Gotland; initial skirmish with local rural militia who unsuccessfully oppose the landing

23 July: Confrontation or skirmish at Ajmund's Bridge between Danes and central Gotland militia, which prevents the Danes from crossing

24 July: Danish scouts locate an alternative route through Fjäle Fen, possibly followed by an immediate but unsuccessful Danish attack through the fen

25 July: Danes attack through the fen in force; Battle of Mästerby between Danes and Gotland militia; Danes are victorious; southern Gotland militia possibly returns south to protect their farmsteads

27 July: Battle of Visby between Danes and rural militia from central and northern Gotland; Danes win a decisive victory

1 August: Unsatisfied with already-concluded deal with King Valdemar over Scanian market privileges, the Wendish-Saxon cities

of the Hanseatic League embargo Danish ports three weeks before the market opens

3 August: King Valdemar signs Letter of Privilege for the Hanseatic city of Visby

10 August: Battle of Fide between Danes and southern Gotland militia; Danes are victorious

22 August: Swedish emissaries arrive in Lübeck to negotiate an alliance with the Hanseatic League

24 August: Scanian herring market opens, but without Wendish-Saxon League merchants

28 August: King Valdemar and his army depart from Gotland, return to Scania

8 September: Sweden and Hanseatic League conclude an anti-Danish alliance; League makes plans for an armed hostile takeover of the Scanian market

1362 May or early June: Hanseatic League goes to war against Denmark, lays siege to Helsingborg Castle

8 July: King Valdemar in a surprise naval attack wins a decisive victory over the League fleet off Helsingborg

21 August: King Valdemar for the first time refers to himself as 'King of the Danes, Slavs, and Goths', in effect regards himself as King also of the old Gotland Republic

6 November: Hanseatic League and King Valdemar conclude a truce which effectively ends the war with a Danish victory; League compelled to pay massive war reparations

1363 9 April: Princess Margaret weds King Haakon in the presence of King Valdemar and King Magnus

10 November: Duke Albert of Mecklenburg goes to war against Sweden, intent on seizing the Swedish throne for his son, Duke Albert the Younger

1364 18 February: Duke Albert the Younger formally elected and crowned King of Sweden

26 July: Unable to pay his supporters, King Albert of Sweden awards Count 'Iron Henry' of Holstein-Rendsburg the entire island of Gotland as indemnity for 4,000 marks silver (but Iron Henry never gains control of Gotland)

1365 3 March: King Albert defeats King Magnus and King Haakon in the Battle of Gata, and captures King Magnus (who will remain in captivity until 1371)

3 September: King Valdemar and Hanseatic League finally conclude a peace treaty at Vordingborg Castle, King Valdemar restores the League's Scanian market privileges

1366 1 May: Danish army under Duke Eric of Saxe-Lauenburg advances into Swedish territories presently held by King Albert

28 July: King Albert's father, Duke Albert of Mecklenburg, concludes a phony treaty with King Valdemar, which is disregarded by all parties

1367 17 November: Still unsatisfied with present Scanian market privileges and also annoyed by other trade-related issues, Hanseatic League

	decides to declare war against the Kings of Denmark and Norway, in an alliance known as the Cologne Confederation
1368	19 March: Coalition of Hanseatic League, Duke Albert of Mecklenburg, the Counts of Holstein, and disgruntled Danish nobles declare war on King Valdemar
	6 April: Learning of the imminent war, King Valdemar goes into exile in Germany, bringing the royal treasury with him
	16 April: Coalition fleet assembles at Rügen, and then sails to the Strait
	2 May: Mercantile centre of Copenhagen surrenders
	16 June: Copenhagen Castle surrenders
1370	24 May: Treaty of Stralsund between Hanseatic League and King Valdemar concludes the war, gives the League full control, for 15 years, over the castles at the Scanian market and hence over the lucrative Scanian herring trade
1371	30 October: Duke Albert of Mecklenburg concludes a treaty with King Valdemar, agrees to return the Danish territories which he has conquered
1373	24 January: Peace treaty concluded between King Valdemar and the Counts of Holstein and rebellious Danish nobles, who agree to return all conquered territories to King Valdemar
1374	1 December: King Magnus of Sweden dies in a shipwreck off the Norwegian coast
1375	24 October: King Valdemar of Denmark dies of natural causes
1376	3 May: King Haakon's youthful son Olaf II succeeds as King of Denmark with the boy's mother, Queen Margaret, as regent
	15 August: Gotland and Visby acknowledge Olaf as rightful heir and ruler, the first concrete evidence since 1361 of any outsider's real control or at least influence over the island
1380	29 July: King Olaf inherits the Norwegian throne as well (as Olaf IV), again with Queen Margaret as regent
1387	3 August: King Olaf dies, leaving Queen Margaret the ruler of both Denmark and Norway
1389	24 February: Queen Margaret's army, under Heinrich Parow, defeats and captures King Albert at Åsle near Falköping, terminates his reign; soon after, King Albert's supporters, the pirate confederation known as the Victual Brothers, take over Gotland
1391	Mecklenburg fleet under Duke John of Mecklenburg-Stargard plunders coastal settlements on Gotland
1394	Mecklenburg expedition from Stockholm under Albrecht Peckatel lands on Gotland, Visby surrenders; in response, Queen Margaret sends men under Sven Sture to retake the island, which succeeds (before April 1395) except for Visby, which remains under Mecklenburg control
1395	17 June: Ex-King Albert accepts Queen Margaret's rule but in return demands and receives the right to the city of Visby; Queen Margaret retains rural Gotland

CHRONOLOGY

1396   Summer: Duke Eric of Mecklenburg, Albert's son, lands on Gotland, assumes control of the Baltic pirates who call him their king

1397   17 June: Having had her adopted heir, Eric of Pomerania, elected to the kingship of all three kingdoms, Queen Margaret formally proclaims the three-state Kalmar Union of Denmark, Norway, and Sweden and their respective overseas possessions

27 July: Having contracted the plague, Duke Eric of Mecklenburg dies on Gotland; his young widow Sophie appoints the renegade Danish noble Sven Sture governor and, through him, offers all pirates the freedom of the island, as long as they give her and Sven half of their plunder; henceforth, Sophie and Sven function as the effective queen and king of Baltic pirates

1398   17 March: Konrad von Jungingen, Grand Master of the Teutonic Order, sends a fleet and army under Johann von Pfirt from Danzig to Gotland to dislodge the pirates from the island

21 March: Teutonic Order army lands on Gotland

5 April: Teutonic Order takes control over Gotland, Sophie, Sven, and their pirates disperse and leave

25 April: Teutonic Order army returns to Danzig

1399   25 May: Albert of Mecklenburg agrees to give Gotland as indemnity to the Teutonic Order in exchange for a huge payment

1403   12 December: Queen Margaret's army, under Abraham Brodersson, lands on Gotland, hoping to recover it for the Union

1404   January: Queen Margaret's army lays siege to Visby

7 May: Ulrich von Jungingen brings Teutonic Order reinforcements to Visby

1 July: Having failed to dislodge the Teutonic Order, Queen Margaret's army agrees to leave Gotland

1408   27 September: Queen Margaret purchases Gotland from the Teutonic Order, whose garrison leaves

1411   August: King Eric of Pomerania arrives in Visby, builds a strong castle, Visborg, next to the city, which must promise to support the King in his wars

1412   Aiming to reduce the status of Gotland's rural population, King Eric raises taxes, introduces forced labour, and represses the Gotlanders

1426   King Eric introduces the Sound Toll as a means to disrupt League trade and as an alternative income to the Scanian herring market, which shows signs of weakening due to overfishing and changes in spawning patterns: war between Hanseatic League and Kalmar Union

1434   Engelbrekt Engelbrektsson, a wealthy mining entrepreneur, makes himself the leader of a major revolt against Union rule in Sweden

1435   15–17 July: Treaty of Vordingborg Castle concludes the war between Hanseatic League and Kalmar Union

1436   King Eric takes refuge on Gotland; in the coming years he gradually loses his three crowns, and instead supports himself by sponsoring piracy

1447   Visby participates in a Hanseatic Diet meeting for the last time

FALL OF THE MERCHANT-FARMER REPUBLIC

1448   28 July: Swedish army, under Magnus Gren, sent by newly elected Swedish King Charles VIII lands on Gotland

4 December: King Charles's men take Visby, which must swear fealty to the Swedish Crown

1449   4 January: Rural Gotlanders swear fealty to King Charles, renewing their ancient oath to the Swedish Crown at the Gutnalting

April: Danish fleet under Oluf Axelsen Thott reaches Visby; Eric of Pomerania hands over Visborg Castle to the Danes and departs

28 July: Newly elected Danish King Christian I arrives with reinforcements; Swedish army withdraws from Gotland, which henceforth is a Danish possession

1476   Visby loses its status as member of the Hanseatic League

1552   Formal control of the Novgorod trade factory, the last vestige of the Gotland merchant-farmer republic, finally passes from the Gotland national lawspeaker to the Danish governor of Gotland

1557   Danish governor of Gotland receives last rent payment from the Novgorod factory

1645   23 August: Sweden regains Gotland in the Treaty of Brömsebro

Scandinavia and the Baltic Region

xv

Prologue

Two Kingdoms, a Republic, and a Hanseatic Free City

Valdemar IV Atterdag, King of Denmark

Valdemar Atterdag (c. 1321–1375; r. 1340–1375) was the third son of King Christopher II of Denmark and Euphemia of Pomerania. He belonged to a family which had provided rulers to Denmark since the mid-eleventh century and counted the semi-mythical St. Olaf 'the Stout' Haraldsson, King of Norway, among his ancestors.

In the previous century, Denmark had controlled major parts of the southern and eastern Baltic. However, the country had declined significantly since then. Most of the southern and eastern Baltic coast had been lost to one or another German ruler. The Scanian provinces of Scania, Blekinge, and Halland north of the Strait between the Baltic Sea and the North Sea had formed part of the Viking-Age Danish kingdom, but by the time when King Valdemar began his reign, they had already been sold to Sweden.[1] Virtually all remaining Danish territory was in the hands of German nobles from Holstein who had received these lands as security for loans. Denmark had been mortgaged out in parcels as a means to cover what in all but name was state bankruptcy.

Previous kings had tried to keep the Danish realm together and afloat. Early in the century, King Valdemar's uncle King Eric Menved entertained high ambitions of recovering the lost Danish territories.[2] Unfortunately for the Danish Crown, he displayed little understanding of financial affairs. King Eric fought wars in northern Germany and in 1311 organised what some

---

1   The total population of early fourteenth-century Denmark is estimated as possibly one million, of whom as many as between a quarter and a third lived in the Scanias. Michael Nordberg, *I kung Magnus tid: Norden under Magnus Eriksson, 1317–1374* (Stockholm: Norstedt, rev. edn 1997), 31.

2   King Erik VI Eriksen (1274–1319; r. 1286–1319), as the name is spelled in Denmark, carried the nickname Menved. Despite several hypotheses, the meaning of the nickname remains obscure.

FALL OF THE MERCHANT-FARMER REPUBLIC

(surely mistakenly) claim was the first knightly tournament in Denmark.[3] Yet, games and wars were financially so costly that King Eric found no other recourse than giving away most of his territories as surety for loans taken to reconquer the lost lands. In the period 1313 to 1317, he relinquished most remaining royal lands to his creditors, ending up with less than with which he had begun.[4]

King Eric Menved was succeeded by his younger brother King Christopher II, who soon showed even less ability and foresight than his late brother.[5] He is commonly regarded as the ineptest Danish king of all times. King Christopher continued his brother's failed policies, handing out any remaining territories primarily to Holstein nobles.

King Christopher was driven out of the country in 1326. He fled to Germany with Queen Euphemia, their child son Valdemar, and whatever remained of the empty royal treasury. The traditional interpretation is that he travelled to the Imperial court in Bavaria of Holy Roman Emperor Louis IV, known as Louis the Bavarian.[6] More likely, they took up with the Emperor's son and namesake Margrave Louis of Brandenburg.[7] Brandenburg was geographically nearer and, in addition, Margrave Louis was King Christopher's son-in-law.[8] While Brandenburg was the more likely point of refuge, it would not be surprising if King Christopher and young Valdemar at least visited the Imperial Court. In 1329, King Christopher was finally allowed to return to Denmark, but then as King of Zealand and Scania only.

When King Christopher died in 1332, no royal lands remained in Denmark. Hence, no new king was crowned. For all practical purposes, the Kingdom of Denmark had ceased to exist except as a memory of what once had been. Instead, power was wielded by a German, the powerful Count Gerhard of Holstein-Rendsburg, who functioned as regent, kingmaker, and effective ruler of Denmark.[9]

For eight years, there was no king of Denmark. Then Count Gerhard was murdered. It was a sordid affair, because the Count was ill, and the murder

---

3 There is every reason to believe that tournaments had taken place much earlier. Knightly tournaments were held in France, Germany, and England in the twelfth century. In Norway, tournaments were common already in the early thirteenth century. Dick Harrison, *Jarlens sekel: En berättelse om 1200-talets Sverige* (Stockholm: Ordfront, 2002), 266.
4 King Eric Menved already in 1295 relinquished his North Halland territory to the Norwegian Crown, since it hitherto had been held by enemies in exile. In 1310, the Norwegian Crown in turn handed over North Halland to Duke Eric Magnusson of Södermanland, a son of King Magnus Ladulås of Sweden. The Swedish Crown took over North Halland in 1326.
5 King Christopher II Eriksen (1276–1332; r. 1320–1326, 1329–1332).
6 Holy Roman Emperor Louis IV (1282 or 1286–1347; r. 1328–1347), known as Ludwig der Bayer in German and Ludovicus Bavarus in Latin, the language of diplomacy at the time.
7 Sven Tägil, *Valdemar Atterdag och Europa* (Lund: CWK Gleerup, Bibliotheca historica Lundensis 9, 1962), 22.
8 Margrave Louis V (1315–1361) of Brandenburg, commonly known as Louis the Brandenburger, had in 1324 married Margaret of Denmark (1305 or 1308–1340), the eldest daughter of King Christopher.
9 Count Gerhard III of Holstein-Rendsburg (c. 1293–1340) had in 1326, when King Christopher fled into exile, put his own child nephew on the throne as King Valdemar III (c. 1314–1364; r. 1326–1329). In 1329, Count Gerhard just as easily deposed his nephew to allow for the return of King Christopher.

resulted in a brief civil war. Then, on 24 June 1340 (St. John the Baptist's Day, or St. Hans as he was known in Denmark), the 19-year-old Valdemar was elected King of Denmark. Not because of his power, which he had none, but because the influential nobles who held real power regarded him as the less dangerous candidate. But he had the support of the powerful mercantile cities of the Hanseatic League. Irritated by the unrest and piracy of the previous years, they, already a month before the election, transferred their support to young Valdemar in exchange for his confirming their traditional privileges in Denmark, toll-free status, and most importantly, their future rights in the important Scanian herring market – which the Danish Crown no longer held.[10] The League support probably played a key role for Valdemar's election. Clearly, the League wanted to employ King Valdemar as a convenient tool against the Swedish possession of the Scanias – the provinces of Scania, Blekinge, and South Halland.

However, King Valdemar's initial position was weak, with only control of parts of Jutland. He resolved to amend the situation and return his Kingdom to its rightful place among European powers. King Valdemar soon negotiated an advantageous marriage, which brought a dowry of 24,000 marks silver that enabled the repossession of some territories (for an overview of north European currencies, see Appendix 2).[11] King Valdemar then (in 1341) negotiated the release from a Holstein prison of his surviving elder brother, the mentally unstable Otto. In return, Otto relinquished his claim to the throne, and a few years later moved to the east where he took ascetic vows and joined the Teutonic Order. To gain additional revenues, King Valdemar introduced significant tax increases, in particular for the hard-pressed Jutland peasants who were under his personal control.

Even so, King Valdemar lacked the funds to repurchase all lost royal lands. He realised that he had to relinquish such territories that remained beyond his power. In 1346, King Valdemar sold the remaining Danish territories in Estonia to the Teutonic Order for 19,000 marks silver – possibly part of the deal made at this time to persuade the Order to take in his elder brother.[12] It was also a smart move, since Estonia was in rebellion, and the Danes there too few to defend the territory against either the Swedes in Finland or the Teutonic Order in Livonia. King Valdemar used the money thus received gradually to purchase back most of Zealand, the rest of Jutland, and the Danish isles. But he also used the money to hire soldiers and equip armies that could conquer such fortified locations that he could not purchase. In the process, King Valdemar became something of a military entrepreneur. Money bought loyalty and experienced fighting men. Neither commodity could be taken for granted without ready cash.

The money also lasted to enable King Valdemar to go on what essentially was a vacation – but one accompanied by the raising of support abroad. In 1347, accompanied by several noble companions of similar age, King

---

10   Peter Lundbye, *Valdemar Atterdag: Danmarks riges genopretter* (Copenhagen: Ejnar Munksgaard, 1939), 30.
11   Lundbye, *Valdemar Atterdag*, 26.
12   Lundbye, *Valdemar Atterdag*, 53; Tägil, *Valdemar Atterdag*, 113, 130–132.

Valdemar first rode to Lübeck, where he met up with his cousin, Duke Eric of Saxe-Lauenburg (1318 or 1320–1368), a life-long friend.[13] Duke Eric was only one or two years older than the King, and the two came from a similar social background. King Valdemar and Duke Eric then continued to Marienburg in Prussia in the hope to join the Teutonic Order's crusade against the Lithuanians. But the Order was currently at peace with the Lithuanians, so King Valdemar and Duke Eric instead decided to continue the tour with a pilgrimage to Jerusalem. He did not bother to get Papal permission. King Valdemar probably followed the lead of his benefactor Emperor Louis, who frequently was at odds and at war with the Pope. In Emperor Louis's Germany, it was commonly argued that God protected the monarch, and that royal power surpassed the tiresome demands and claims of mere popes and bishops. Having reached Jerusalem, Duke Eric formally dubbed the young King a knight. Having achieved the two goals of reaching the Holy Land and knighthood, King Valdemar then, in turn, dubbed several of his companions knights.

The journey again put King Valdemar in touch with events on the Continent. There was rivalry over the Imperial throne. Hitherto, the House of Wittelsbach, led by Emperor Louis, had held the upper hand. However, their rival, the House of Luxembourg, coveted the Imperial throne and the famous Iron Crown, which in the sixth century was worn by Theoderic the Great, the Ostrogothic ruler of Italy, in the ninth century hallowed the coronation of Charlemagne, the founder of the Holy Roman Empire, and ultimately consecrated many later Holy Roman Emperors.[14]

Sure enough, when Emperor Louis died from a stroke suffered during a bear hunt in 1347, the House of Luxembourg secured the Imperial throne with the election of their candidate, Charles of Bohemia, who already was King of Germany and Bohemia.[15] Crowned Emperor Charles IV, the ascension of a Luxembourg ruler put King Valdemar's brother-in-law and ally Margrave Louis of Brandenburg, the son of the late Emperor, in a dangerous position. Soon, a pretender rose against Margrave Louis. To assist his brother-in-law against the pretender, King Valdemar intervened in Germany from the summer of 1349 until spring 1350, leading an army into Mecklenburg, Brandenburg, and ultimately (when the fighting was over) all the way to Prague. Again, Duke Eric of Saxe-Lauenburg accompanied King Valdemar. The resulting victory over the pretender and the successful diplomatic negotiations that followed safeguarded Margrave Louis's position, much thanks to King Valdemar's support. In 10 years, King Valdemar had

---

13 King Valdemar's mother Euphemia of Pomerania and Duke Eric's mother Elisabeth of Pomerania were sisters.
14 The Iron Crown (*Corona ferrea*) was manufactured out of the gems of a Roman Imperial diadem and, perhaps, an iron band associated with Emperor Constantine I and said to have been beaten out of a nail used at the crucifixion of Christ. The Iron Crown remained one of the most powerful symbols of Imperial rule and in the nineteenth century hallowed the coronations of Napoleon Bonaparte and Emperor Ferdinand I of Austria. It is presently preserved in the Cathedral of Monza, Italy.
15 Emperor Charles IV of Bohemia (1316–1378; r. 1355–1378).

gone from a teenage prince in exile to a major power in European affairs. It was an impressive achievement.

But revenues remained insufficient. King Valdemar accordingly raised the idea of hiring out his services and soldiers as a mercenary. In 1353, he negotiated with King John of France about a contract to invade, or at least raid, England (*pour le pays conquerre ou destruire*) with 12,000 men for a payment of 600,000 gold florins (the equivalent of about 109,100 marks silver), a large amount but one which corresponded to the expense of putting such a huge army into the field. The deal was complicated and entailed the betrothal of King Valdemar's son Christopher to a French princess with a dowry of 100,000 Rhenish gulden, a gold coin minted in Hanseatic cities of essentially the same value as the florin (which made it the equivalent of about 18,200 marks silver). French envoys to Denmark reported back home that King Valdemar had the military resources he claimed.[16] Although the contract was never fulfilled (because King John was captured in the Battle of Poitiers in 1356 and brought to England), the agreement shows that King Valdemar by then regarded himself as a professional mercenary captain, in effect as a man of the same kind as the first German condottieri who already had made a name for themselves in Italy and elsewhere. Possibly, he was again influenced by the political culture in which he grew up in Germany.

King Valdemar was, by all accounts, a ruthless ruler. Several of his political opponents were assassinated. Some had once been the King's close friends. One of them, murdered in late 1358, was the knight Niels Bugge, who seems to have been one of the King's companions to Jerusalem.[17] When suspicions arose that the King was involved, King Valdemar swore a formal oath that he indeed was innocent. While nobody could trace the killers back to the King, certainly nobody prosecuted them for their deeds, which suggests that they enjoyed a certain level of protection. Meanwhile, Danish peasants had to endure a succession of new and significantly higher taxes. Peasant rebellions broke out, but the King had the revolts suppressed, and those who participated lost their farmsteads. There were rumours that King Valdemar associated with witches. Based on persistent legends and folk tales, some gave the King the nickname 'Valdemar the Evil' (Danish: *Valdemar den onde*).[18]

On the other hand, there is little doubt that King Valdemar could display considerable charm when he so desired. He was highly eloquent, successful in diplomacy, and repeatedly managed to bring men over to his point of view. The fierce St. Bridget of Sweden, who never lacked words to criticise those around her, in an attempt to prepare Sweden's King Magnus Ericsson for King Valdemar's silver tongue, described the Danish King as 'this flatterer, this bird-catcher, who plays his flute to entice the birds'.[19]

16　Lundbye, *Valdemar Atterdag*, 75; Tägil, *Valdemar Atterdag*, 225–226, with references.
17　Zealand Chronicle, in Ellen Jørgensen (ed.), *Annales Danici Medii Ævi* (Copenhagen: Selskabet for utgivelse af kilder till Dansk Historie, 1920), 163–188, on 185; S. H. Klavsen, *Ved Lillebelt, eller Middelfartsunds Historie* (Middelfart. Claudius Madsen, 1867), 14–16.
18　Klavsen, *Ved Lillebelt*, 16.
19　Cited in Lundbye, *Valdemar Atterdag, 243*.

King Valdemar spoke Low German as his principal language. King Valdemar's nickname, Atterdag, is believed to derive from Low German *Tertaghe* ('What days!'), an expression which King Valdemar reportedly used in his old age time and time again when attempting to deal with his troubles and hence stuck to him as a nickname. The name Atterdag is only known from later sources and was never used on formal occasions or in contemporary official written sources. Yet, the nickname seems to have been in common use at the end of the King's life. There is no reason to believe that King Valdemar was known as Atterdag before the late 1360s.

In 1341, King Valdemar married Helvig (c. 1320–1374), daughter of Duke Erik of Slesvig and sister of a former king of Denmark.[20] The couple had six known children, but the only one who survived them was a daughter, Margaret (1353–1412), who eventually would rule as Queen Margaret I.

King Valdemar Atterdag as depicted in a contemporary fresco in St. Peter's Church, Næstved, c. 1375.

King Valdemar was unusually tall. When archaeologists opened his grave in 1935 and measured the skeleton, they found that he had been 1.92 m tall. The King was no doubt an imposing man. Numerous legends about King Valdemar describe his frequent romantic liaisons and attraction to the opposite sex. Although none of the legends appears credible, they attest to a popular belief that the tall and handsome (and possibly evil) king had more than his share of liaisons. Queen Helvig already in 1355, when the couple was in their 30s, moved into Esrum nunnery as a lay sister. She stayed there until her death in 1374.

Having restored the core of the old Danish kingdom under his own rule, King Valdemar looked north of the Strait, hoping to regain the Scanias as well. Since Sweden's King Magnus Ericsson was unwilling to sell these provinces, King Valdemar resolved to take them by military force.

The National Lawspeaker of Gotland

Rural Gotland was a semi-autonomous republic under Swedish suzerainty. The chief officer of the rural Gotlanders was the national lawspeaker (medieval Latin: *terre iudex*; old Swedish: *landzdomere*; *landsdomare*). He was an elected official of a type once common in Norse society. The exact procedure for how the election took place is unknown, but he surely was a prosperous merchant-farmer and local chief. The medieval title translates as judge, but while a lawspeaker was familiar with traditional law and the guarantor of legal procedure, his function was more that of a mediator than all-powerful judge.

The rural population of Gotland spoke not Swedish but their own distinct East Germanic language. Today known as Old Gutnish, it was the variant of Old Norse which displays most similarities to ancient Gothic. In their

---

20   Duke Erik II of Slesvig (c. 1288–1325) was the father also of the aforementioned child-king Valdemar III, who briefly occupied the throne during King Christopher's exile in Germany.

native speech, they called themselves *Gutar*, a tribal name of the same origin as that of the ancient Goths. Old Gutnish and ancient Gothic display more similarities than either shows with any other Nordic language.[21] The Old Gutnish-speaking population will here be referred to as Gotlanders.

Once upon a time, the ancestors of the Gotlanders were most probably ruled by men referred to as kings. There is reason to believe that the island which ancient legend referred to as the 'royal' island of the Goths likely was Gotland.[22] However, a millennium later the names of kings in days of yore were probably long-since forgotten on the island.[23] By 1361, Gotland had for centuries been a republic, governed by a traditional Scandinavian assembly of free men, a Thing (Old Norse: *þing*). On Gotland, the assembly was known as the All Gotlanders' Thing (Gutnalting, from probably original *Gutna alþingi*). Dominated by prosperous merchant-farmers, it met in the centre of the island, near modern-day Roma, where in 1163 or, more likely, 1164 was also built a Cistercian monastery, appropriately named Guthnalia. The national lawspeaker presided over the proceedings at the assembly, represented the people as a whole, and when required also functioned as judge. The Gutnalting handled major matters and national policy. If any Gotlander formulated policy at the time of the Danish invasion, it was the national lawspeaker. Everyday disputes were instead decided in local assemblies, which met at regular intervals in customary locations throughout the island, headed by a local lawspeaker (*domare*).

The name of the national lawspeaker at the time of King Valdemar's invasion is lost to history. So are those of his predecessors. The reason may well have been that most assembly proceedings were oral only, as in past times, and never documented in writing. The first national lawspeaker whose name survived into the present was Gervid Lauk, from Lauks farmstead in Lokrume. Gervid Lauk was buried in Lokrume Church in 1380, so certainly lived through the Danish invasion. While it would be tempting to assign his name to the time of King Valdemar's invasion, we will see that the outcome of the campaign makes this highly unlikely. Possibly, Gervid Lauk was then the senior lawspeaker of the North Third (*Norder Treding*; more on which

---

21 Elias Wessén, 'Nordiska folkstammar och folknamn: En översikt', *Fornvännen* 64:1 (1969), 14–36, on 27–28. Wessén, a renowned philologist, argues that the linguistic relationship suggests that the ancestors of the medieval Gotlanders (Old Gutnish: *Gutar*) and the ancient Vistula Goths (Gothic: **Gutans*) originally were the same people, initially shared a language (a variety of Proto-Norse, *Urnordisch*), and that both during the first centuries AD still spoke essentially the same language, which later, in the Pontic region, became classical Gothic as we know it from Ulfila's fourth-century Bible. Incidentally, the institution of 'judge' (latin: *iudex*) existed among the Pontic Goths, too, unless this was a translation error for the Pontic Gothic title of national emperor or king (Gothic: *thiudans*), which to Roman ears may have sounded like *iudex*.

22 Xenophon of Lampsacus and other ancient geographers mentioned an island of enormous size in the Baltic Sea which they called Balcia (by some amended to Baltia) or Basileia, the latter of which would signify 'royal land'. The geographical location of the island corresponds to Gotland. Gaius Plinius Secundus (Pliny the Elder), *Naturalis historia* 4.95.

23 Intriguingly, such names may be preserved by the sixth-century Gothic historian Jordanes, *Getica* 3, 26. Michael Fredholm von Essen, *The Goths 1: From Berig to the Battle of Adrianople* (Wonersh: Society of Ancients, 2021), 7.

below), and promoted to the higher office afterwards, when a replacement national lawspeaker was needed.

At some point, possibly already in the mid-sixth and certainly no later than the end of the ninth century, the Gotland Republic accepted a tributary relationship with the Swedish king.[24] From this time onwards, the Gotlanders paid a small tribute when so was required but otherwise ruled themselves.[25] We do not know how stable the relationship was over time. Few literary sources have survived from these centuries, while archaeological remains suggest major but difficult-to-interpret political developments on Gotland. In short, much could have happened that we presently know nothing about.

Moreover, this was before Christianity was introduced to Gotland in the eleventh and early twelfth centuries. The Christian faith arrived in a largely unknown process that seems to have involved parallel Catholic and Orthodox influences because of the Gotlanders' far-ranging trading relationships.[26] Yet, the tributary relationship in one form or another endured. When the Swedish kingdom finally accepted the Christian faith, in its Catholic form, and with it the new forms of royal organisation that gradually transformed Sweden into what can be described as a European medieval kingdom, the relationship between Gotland and the Swedish mainland grew stronger. Although again few details are known, this development took place no earlier than the late twelfth or early thirteenth century.[27]

The relationship was finally formalised in the mid- to late thirteenth century with an agreement according to which the Gotlanders would provide seven ship to the *ledung* (Old Norse: *leiðangr*) fleet at the disposal of the Swedish King if he called for a crusade.[28] The agreement obligated the Gotlanders to support the crusade, but actual participation was voluntary. If the Gotlanders did not wish to provide ships and men, for instance if the crusade was aimed at their eastern trading partners, they could instead choose to pay a tax in lieu of military service in the *ledung* fleet.

Even so, the relationship with the Swedish king was one of tribute only. While the Church owned lands and had a powerful presence on Gotland, which belonged to the diocese of Linköping in Sweden, the Swedish king

---

24 Sixth century: Michael Fredholm von Essen, *The Goths 2: From Alaric to Theoderic the Great and Beyond* (Wonersh: Society of Ancients, 2022), 127 n. 214; ninth century: the travel notes of the late ninth-century trader Wulfstan, included in the Old English Orosius 1.1.20, published as Joseph Bosworth (ed.), *King Alfred's Anglo-Saxon Version of the Compendious History of the World by Orosius* (London: Longman, Brown, Green, and Longmans, 1859), 22; no date given: Guta Saga, in Åke Holmbäck and Elias Wessén, *Svenska landskapslagar: Skånelagen och Gutalagen* (Stockholm: AWE/Geber, 1979), 290-95, on 292-3.

25 The Torsätra 1 rune stone in Västra Ryd, Uppland, dated to the 1060s or 1070s, notes that Swedes raised tax or tribute (Old Norse: *giald*; runic spelling: kialt) on Gotland. See also Hugo Yrwing, *Gotlands medeltid* (Visby: Gotlandskonst, 1978), 20.

26 Erland Lagerlöf, *Gotland och Bysans: Bysantinskt inflytande på den gotländska kyrkokonsten under medeltiden* (Visby: Ödin, 1999), 26–37, with English summary on 192–205.

27 Yrwing, *Gotlands medeltid*, 21.

28 The old tradition (known as *ledung* in Swedish, *leidang* in Norwegian, and *leding* in Danish) that coastal regions, and eventually some towns, provided men and ships to the King's fleet if called to war for defensive purposes or offensive expeditions abroad had already grown obsolete. Since the late thirteenth century, at the latest, the Crown preferred that the subjects instead paid a tax to cover the King's naval and military expenses.

owned no property or lands on the island. There were no royal officials on Gotland. The Gotlanders did not participate in the election of kings in Sweden, nor did the new king visit the island on his inauguration tour through the realm.

By tradition, Gotland merchant-farmers traded furs, wax, iron, and weapons. While Gotland had few natural resources, the location of the island in the centre of the Baltic Sea enabled them to play a dominant role in the Baltic trade. Trade relations were of long standing. The ancient link between Gotlanders and continental Goths has already been mentioned. Cemeteries in modern-day Grobina, Latvia, generally dated to the period between 650 and 800 AD show that a settlement of both male and female Gotlanders existed there at the time, on territory claimed by the Curonians, a tribe living on the Baltic shore in what is now the western part of Latvia and Lithuania. During the subsequent Viking Age, Gotland remained the undisputed centre for Scandinavia's trade with the East. This is evident from the many Arabic and Byzantine silver coins found on Gotland, dated to the period 800–1140.[29] Indeed, most of the 85,000 Arabic coins found in Swedish archaeological sites derive from Gotland. From the eleventh century onwards, the Gotlanders expanded their trading relationships westwards. As a result, German and English coins grew significantly in number on Gotland in the period 1000–1140. So far, about 92,000 German and English coins have been found on the island.[30]

The Eastern trade followed the route from the Baltic through Novgorod, which emerged as a Scandinavian ninth-century settlement on the chief trade route between the Baltic Sea region and the Byzantine Empire, and Kiev. A runic inscription on the Pilgårds rune stone in Boge, from the end of the tenth century, mentions the Gotlander Ravn, who together with his brothers came to Aifur, the most dangerous of the Dnieper rapids on the trade route to Constantinople. Novgorod ultimately grew into a great city but remained a centre for Gotland's trade, and the foundation for Gotland's wealth. A runic inscription from the 1070s mentions St. Olaf's Church in Novgorod, which was linked to the Gotland Republic's trade factory there, the old Gutagård (German: *Gutenhof*; Russian: *Gotskiy dvor*).[31]

By the twelfth century, the Gotlanders remained northern Europe's leading merchants. They brought furs and wax from Novgorod and the East to Germany, Flanders, England, and elsewhere in the west. Furs were an important luxury product, while wax was of extraordinary importance since all churches for religious reasons needed constant supplies of wax candles. In return, the Gotlanders exported weapons and other goods to the east. They also traded in iron, copper, fish, timber, whale oil, and other necessities for European lands. England, for instance, imported both wooden staves for longbows and essentials for shipbuilding such as tar, pitch, hemp, flax, and especially timber from the Baltic region. Names of Gotlanders appear

---

29 Majvor Östergren, 'Silverskatternas fyndplatser: Farmännens gårdar', Ingmar Jansson (ed.), *Gutar och vikingar* (Stockholm: SHM, 1983), 34–48.
30 Gun Westholm, *Visby 1361: Invasionen* (Stockholm: Prisma, 2007), 55.
31 Yrwing, *Gotlands medeltid*, 131–132.

in written English sources from 1226, when they sold furs and wax to the English court and received trade privileges. In 1248, the English court paid as much as 856 pounds sterling silver for furs and wax carried by Gotland merchants. This payment roughly corresponded to 1,300 marks silver. In comparison, the total annual tax which Gotland owed to the Swedish King by then was no more than 60 marks silver. The Gotland merchant-farmers brought substantial wealth back to the island, as they had done for centuries. Gotland names continue to appear in English records throughout the century, until 1294.[32] All preserved sales notices are dated in winter and spring, which suggests that many merchant-farmers traded abroad during the winter season and then returned home to tend to their farmsteads.[33] Of course, if there were several brothers in a family, they likely divided trading activities and farming among themselves, according to ability and inclination.

The Gotlanders seldom let the subsequent expansion and crusades towards the eastern shores of the Baltic Sea and into the Gulf of Finland interfere with trade. As noted, Greek Orthodox influences had reached the island early and still lingered, despite its subordination to the Catholic Swedish diocese of Linköping. By the 1170s, Gotlanders still traded with Curonians, Finns, Ingrians, and Karelians, including those who refused to accept, or repeatedly lapsed from, the Catholic faith. This did not please the Church. In 1171 or 1172, Pope Alexander III issued the bull *Gravis admodum*, which complained about the ongoing situation. The bull may have been used by the Church to support the authority of the Bishop of Linköping against the wealthy Gotland merchant-farmers who preferred not to let faith interfere with business.[34]

In 1207, the Archbishop of Lund, Andreas Sunesen, visited Gotland on his way back from a crusade in Livonia. As papal legate to Scandinavia, the Archbishop had considerable authority. In a letter perhaps written soon afterwards but which in 1220 or thereabouts became associated with the recently appointed Bishop Bengt Magnusson of Linköping, the Archbishop (who since 1219 again was crusading, this time in Estonia) pointed out that it was preferable that the law was written down instead of being committed to memory by lawspeakers as in the past. Times were changing, and the Gotland code was by tradition somewhat different from the codes on the mainland. Guta Law was indeed written down, on his recommendation and probably around 1220, in Old Gutnish. At the same time, the Guta Saga or Saga of the Gotlanders, which constituted the oral tradition of their history, was written down, too, and included in an appendix.[35]

Meanwhile, the trade route through Novgorod to Constantinople still flourished. The route went by way of the Crimea. Numerous sources, well-known to scholars, attest to the survival of the Gothic language, and a state

---

32 Yrwing, *Gotlands medeltid*, 138–140; Westholm, *Visby 1361*, 60–62, 75.
33 Westholm, *Visby 1361*, 70.
34 Lena Huldén, *På vakt i öster* 1: *Medeltiden* (np: Schildts, 2004), 26–27.
35 Holmbäck and Wessén, *Svenska landskapslagar: Skånelagen och Gutalagen*, lxxi–lxxii. The now extant oldest copy of Guta Law and Guta Saga derives from c. 1350.

known as Gothia, in the Crimea.[36] In addition, there is yet another source, which is particularly intriguing since it not only attests to the survival of Crimean Gothic but also attests to the survival of trade between Gotlanders and Goths. In the Guta Saga, we find the remark that the descendants of Gotlanders who centuries ago had migrated out of Gotland still remained in 'Greece' (the customary Scandinavian name for the Byzantine Empire). Moreover, the descendants even at this late time in their speech 'still have something of our language' (Old Gutnish: *enn hafa þair sumt af waru mali*). As noted, Old Gutnish was the variant of Old Norse which displays most similarities to Gothic. The comment in Guta Saga strongly suggests that Gotland traders retained links with the Crimean Goths well into the Middle Ages. Interestingly, the Guta Saga was written down around 1220, that is, before Continental European merchants re-discovered the Crimea after the Mongol conquests later in the century. In 1229, Pope Gregory IX repeated the Church's protests over the Gotlanders' continuing Eastern trade. This time, the Church complained that the Gotlanders sold weapons, horses, ships, food supplies, and other goods to Russians whose successes subsequently made Finnish population groups lapse from the Catholic faith.[37]

While the trading activities of the Gotland merchant-farmers ranged far and wide, from the British Isles and Germany in the west to the Crimea and Constantinople in the southeast, time was not on their side. By the fourteenth century, trade conditions had changed, and the Hanseatic League had taken over most of the Baltic trade. We do not know exactly when the decline set in, since few surviving documents mention the Gotland merchant-farmers – even though archaeological finds suggest that they amassed considerable wealth over many centuries. The introduction in the early thirteenth-century maritime trade of cogs, larger ships with a greater capacity and hence draught than the traditional Scandinavian merchant vessels, proved a boon for merchants but also meant that the centuries-old, shallow coastal ports of Gotland had to be abandoned for the new, deep-water port in the island's only urban settlement, Visby. The Gotland Republic's trade factory in Novgorod was in 1299 for a while taken over by Hanseatic merchants from Lübeck. Later, Gotland merchants recovered the factory, but henceforth, it served both Gotland merchant-farmers and Hanseatic Visby burghers. In the mid-fourteenth century, German merchants assumed full control of the factory, even though they still paid rent to the Gotland Republic.

The Gotlanders also had to accept a closer relationship with the Swedish Crown. In 1285, Sweden's King Magnus Ladulås pushed through a new tax regime.[38] Henceforth, Gotland would have to pay a more formalised annual tribute and tax in lieu of occasional military service in the ledung fleet. The Gotlanders also had to accept Swedish royal jurisdiction with regard

---

36 Fredholm von Essen, *Goths 2, 113–115*.
37 Yrwing, *Gotlands medeltid*, 69.
38 King Magnus Birgersson (c. 1220-1290; r. 1275-1290) at some point, possibly posthumously, acquired the nickname Ladulås ('barn-lock'). The nickname is commonly believed to derive from legislation introduced by King Magnus to protect the population from extortion and unlawful demands by travelling strongmen and their retinues.

FALL OF THE MERCHANT-FARMER REPUBLIC

to certain crimes such as high treason. However, the Gotlanders would raise the tax by themselves, and the King must send his bailiffs to the island to receive the money which then was to be transported to the mainland at the King's expense and risk. Clearly, the Gotland Republic was not yet ready fully to submit to royal rule. Perhaps for this reason, there is a hint that King Magnus Ladulås at the time favoured German merchants and possibly relied on them for the introduction of the new tax regime for Gotland.[39] Sure enough, we will see that within a few years the German merchants of Visby extended their influence on the island.

By 1361, the Gotland Republic had lost both market share and some political power to Visby. Even so, the merchant-farmers were not yet ready to give up either their autonomy or remaining trade interests.

At a time when stone houses were still rare in Sweden, the rural Gotland merchant-farmers regularly built large stone buildings, including this one at Stora Hästnäs, north of Visby. The ground floor was used as residence, the second floor as a hall, and the third floor served as warehouse. The house was never intended as an isolated tower. The present attached one-storey building is of later date, but there was an attached, smaller building in the fourteenth century as well, when the entire building was covered in white plaster. (Photo: Bene Riobó)

Female servant carrying a well-filled basket and a large wax candle of the type used in Gotland churches, and the prosperous lady of a merchant-farmer house, mid-fourteenth-century, Martebo Church. Part of a series of sculptures with Biblical motifs that still show traces of the original paint which once was used to embellish them. The servant's dress was originally painted green. (Swedish National Heritage Board; photo: Erik Olsson)

Hermann Munter, Mayor of Visby

The city of Visby was governed by a mayor. The name of the mayor at the time of King Valdemar's invasion is strictly speaking unknown. It may have been Hermann Munter (d. 1375), the Visby burgher who witnessed King Valdemar's Letter of Privilege to Visby. Munter was certainly a prominent burgher, and the fact that he witnessed the letter together with the Prior of the Dominican Convent and the Custos ('guardian', the equivalent of a prior)

---

39 Yrwing, *Gotlands medeltid*, 25.

of the Franciscan Convent suggests that he indeed was the mayor of the city at the time. Years later, Munter was described as a mayor of Visby in his funeral record, but the record does not say when he was so appointed.[40] The mayor of Visby at the time of the invasion will for these reasons henceforth be referred to as Hermann Munter for convenience.

We know virtually nothing of Munter's background or family. He was very likely the Hanseatic merchant Hermann Munter who traded in England in 1351–1352.[41] He was likely a relative of Heinrich ('Hinricus') Munter who represented Visby and the Livonian cities at the Hanseatic Diet meeting in 1356.[42] He was possibly related to the Hanseatic merchant Willebrand Munter from Danzig, whose son Johann fought and was captured in the League's war against King Valdemar in the year after the Danish invasion (more on which below).[43]

The central role long played by Gotland merchant-farmers in the Baltic and Eastern trade soon attracted German merchants, who in large numbers moved to the island. The Artlenburg Privilege of 1161 between Duke Henry the Lion of Saxony and the city of Lübeck on the one side and the Gotland Republic on the other, restored to the Gotlanders (Latin: *Gutenses*) their traditional, but temporarily lapsed, trade privileges and exemption from tolls in the cities of northern Germany and the formerly Wendish lands.[44] However, the treaty also, through its request for reciprocity, paved the way for the trading settlement at Visby becoming a free port in which German merchants (Latin: *Teuthonicos*) were permitted to establish trade offices. In 1191 or 1192, the rural merchant-farmers and German merchants on the 'Gotland Coast' (Russian: *Gotskiy bereg*) jointly concluded an agreement with Prince Yaroslav Vladimirovich of the Novgorod Republic.[45] This opened the Novgorod market also to the German merchants, who after 1225 formed a league or association and began to refer to themselves as 'the Germans who frequent Gotland' (Latin: *Theutonici Gotlandiam frequentantes*), or in modern terminology, the Society of Gotland Voyagers. Expanding Visby into the island's first major population centre, the Gotlander and German merchants of the city gradually assumed the leading mercantile role at the expense of the rural Gotlanders. The Gotlanders and Visby merchants gained

---

40   Eva Odelman and Evert Melefors (eds), 'Visbyfranciskanernas bok: Handskriften B 99 i Kungliga biblioteket - Latinsk text med översättning, inledning och register', *Arkiv på Gotland* 5 (Visby: Landsarkivet i Visby/Gotlands kommunarkiv, 2008), 48.

41   *Hanserecesse: Die Recesse und andere Akten der Hansetage von 1256–1430* (Vol. 1) (Leipzig: Duncker & Humblot, 1870), 88, 89.

42   *Hanserecesse: Die Recesse und andere Akten der Hansetage von 1256–1430*, 128–129.

43   *Hanserecesse: Die Recesse und andere Akten der Hansetage von 1256–1430*, 227.

44   Wends was the historical name for the early medieval peoples of north-eastern Germany who at first spoke Slavic languages but over time mostly assimilated with the existing German-speaking population and subsequent German-speaking settlers. Holstein and particularly Mecklenburg were once Wendish lands claimed by Danish kings and German emperors alike. Most of the north German merchant cities were established on former Wendish lands as part of the resettlement and consolidation of yet more German-speaking settlers. The city of Lübeck, which subsequently became the head of the Hanseatic League, was one of them, founded in 1143 on an existing Slavic site, destroyed in 1147, and re-founded by Duke Henry in 1159.

45   S. N. Valk (ed.), *Gramoty Velikogo Novgoroda i Pskova* (Moscow: Izdatel'stvo Akademii Nauk SSSR, 1949), 55–56 (No. 28).

FALL OF THE MERCHANT-FARMER REPUBLIC

a joint Letter of Privilege from King Henry III of England in 1237.[46] In about 1240, the Visby merchants referred to themselves as 'Merchants and Skippers to Visby' (Low German: *Kooplüds en de Schiffers to Visby*). Soon afterwards, they began to enter into treaties on their own terms. In 1280, the German merchants in Visby entered into an alliance with Lübeck which made the city on Gotland a leading member of the group of mercantile centres that was developing into the Hanseatic League.

In 1288, the mercantile rivalry between the Visby merchants and the rural merchant-farmers escalated into open warfare. The direct cause may have been the construction of a city wall, which literally set the German merchants apart from the rural merchant-farmers and possibly was intended for the collection of customs duties. It may also have been Visby's apparent willingness to accept the annual tribute, in effect a higher rate of taxation, for the island in 1285 demanded by Sweden's King Magnus Ladulås in return for protection.

Since Visby in this conflict enjoyed the support of the nascent Hanseatic League, the rural Gotlanders called for support from the east. They enjoyed amicable links of old with the Livonian Brothers of the Sword (Latin: *Fratres militiæ Christi Livoniae*, German: *Schwertbrüderorden*), a knightly order absorbed by the Teutonic Order in 1237 as a mostly autonomous branch subsequently known as the Livonian Order. Some settlements in Estonia and Livonia may even have been in a vassal relationship to Gotland. Possibly, the contacts were mediated by the Cistercians at the monastery Guthnalia in Roma, where the Gotland National Assembly met. Guthnalia owed lands in Livonia as well as on the island of Öland. For this reason, a number of Livonian knights and soldiers joined the Gotland Republic against Visby.[47]

The ensuing war resulted in two indecisive battles between rural and city militias, before King Magnus Ladulås intervened. He gave Visby a free status directly subordinated the Crown, that is, a position similar to the free cities in the Holy Roman Empire and allowed the construction of the city wall.[48] The Swedish King's mediation and goodwill to Visby did not come free of charge. The city, unlike the rural Gotlanders, had to collect and also send the King's taxes to Kalmar on the mainland at the city's own risk and cost. Clearly, the city must yield considerable sovereignty to the King – but in return its status as a centre of trade grew, as did its power and influence on the rest of Gotland. The King's intervention, naturally, also reinforced Swedish royal power over the entire island, which hitherto had been mostly autonomous.

The closer link to Sweden was not welcomed by the Gotland merchant-farmers. In 1313, King Birger Magnusson (the late King Magnus Ladulås's

---

46   Hugo Yrwing, *Visby: Hansestad på Gotland* (Stockholm: Gidlund, 1986), 56. By 1409, if not before, the Visby merchants' office in London was known as Easterlings Halle, from the name Eastern (Baltic) Sea.
47   Strelow, *Cronica Guthilandorum*, 144, which uses the term vassal for supporters in Estonia and Curonia (Courland).
48   Strelow noted that the city wall was completed in 1299. Strelow, *Cronica Guthilandorum*, 147. However, minor improvements were added in the fourteenth century.

son and successor) demanded higher taxes from the island.[49] The Gotlanders refused, after which King Birger led an army to Gotland to force acceptance. The military details of the expedition are unknowable from existing sources. The contemporary Eric Chronicle (*Erikskrönikan*), a rhyme chronicle from the 1320s, named two prominent Swedes who died in the battle and claimed a decisive victory for the Gotlanders.[50] However, this chronicle is very biased, and we know from later documents (specifically, Olaus Petri's Swedish chronicle, written in the sixteenth century but based on older, presently lost documents[51]), that the ensuing negotiations resulted in a truce in which the Gotlanders must accept a total annual tax of 200 marks silver in exchange for continued free trade along the River Neva and onwards to Novgorod and other parts of Russia. Moreover, an extant letter from 1320 in the name of the succeeding king, Magnus Ericsson, proves the tax increase since it orders it abolished from this year onwards.

Although Visby became known as a mostly German city, its origin was a Gotland trading settlement. Numerous townsmen were Gotlanders. It took until 1344 before the two groups of townsmen, Gotlanders and Germans, had coalesced to the point that they henceforth formed a unified city administration. Before this year, there had been a Gotlander city administration and a German city administration, each with a separate formal seal and each likely with one official who served as joint mayor. The two groups to some extent had different interests, although there is nothing to suggest that either by then felt particular communal affinity to the rural merchant-farmers. From 1344 onwards, the city had only one formal seal, hence a unified city administration.[52]

While the ultimate origin of the Hanseatic League lay in the trade co-operations of the German free cities of the twelfth century, it took a significant period of time before the League acquired a formal identity and organisation. This took place only during the Second Hanseatic Diet meeting in 1358. The League had then already operated informally for a long time. Interestingly, the First Hanseatic Diet meeting, held in Lübeck in 1356, was assembled by one Jacob Pleskow, until his move to Lübeck a leading Visby merchant and based on his name likely the descendant of a family that originated in Pskov, an important centre of trade located southwest of Novgorod, which was known as Pleskow in medieval German. The Pleskows had lived for several generations in Visby, where they were well-established already by 1317.[53] This shows the cosmopolitan character of Visby, and indeed Gotland as a whole, at the time.

The Hanseatic League was formally established as a business concern divided into three subsidiaries, each known as a *Drittel* ('Third'). These were the Wendish-Saxon *Drittel*, under Lübeck; the Gotland-Livonian *Drittel*,

---

49 King Birger Magnusson (1280–1321; r. 1290–1318) was the uncle and predecessor of King Magnus IV Ericsson, whom we will meet again.
50 Sven-Bertil Jansson (ed.), *Erikskrönikan* (Stockholm: Tiden, 1987), 144.
51 G. E. Klemming (ed.), *Olai Petri Svenska krönika* (Stockholm: H. Klemming, 1860), 117.
52 Yrwing, *Gotlands medeltid*, 42.
53 Gustaf Lindström, *Anteckningar om Gotlands medeltid* 1 (Visby: Hanse-Production, 1978), 96.

under Visby; and the Westphalian-Prussian *Drittel*, under Dortmund. The Gotland-Livonian subsidiary, headed by Visby, included important merchant towns such as Reval, Pernau, and Riga. The League worked closely with the Teutonic Order in Prussia and Livonia. The Order was indeed the protector of the League. By 1361, the Visby mayor and burghers enjoyed the same power and influence as their counterparts in Lübeck and other major Hanseatic cities in Germany and elsewhere.

The Eastern trade remained the mother trade of the Hanseatic League. Prospects remained good, but on Gotland, there were concerns for the future. The Visby burghers could see that with better and larger ships; the time would come when Gotland no longer was needed as a transit point in the Baltic Eastern trade.

Moreover, the Hanseatic League as a whole had other business interests as well. A key business of the Hanseatic League was the Scanian herring market (more on which below). We will see that the League would go to great lengths to control and monopolise this market which brought huge revenues.

The building presently known as the Old Pharmacy is one of the best-preserved medieval merchant buildings in Visby. Built around 1290 (according to dendrochronological analysis), it has five floors, including warehouse floors, and a basement with a total height of 22 m. In the fourteenth century, a second warehouse of similar size stood next to this one. Goods were hoisted up from the street straight to one of the four upper-floor warehouse doors. The owner and his family lived in an annex behind the warehouse buildings. While the Old Pharmacy is one of the best-preserved Visby buildings, it is not the largest. The presently largest is the Liljehorn family house, built around 1265 (according to dendrochronological analysis), with seven floors, including warehouse floors, and an attic, and a total height of 28 m. The wealth and influence of the leading merchants of Visby was considerable. (Photo: Arkland)

Hanseatic trader of the Riga association, 1360-1370. The relief, which depicts the merchant (centre) negotiating the price of furs with a fully bearded, presumably Russian huntsman from Pskov in a tall hat outside a gate guarded by a knight, captures the appearance of Baltic merchants at the time of the Danish invasion. The merchant wears a green gown and reddish hose. (Painted oakwood carving, St. Nikolai's Church, Stralsund)

Magnus IV Ericsson, King of Sweden

Magnus Ericsson (1316–1374, r. 1319–1355 as King Magnus VII of Norway, r. 1319–1364 as King Magnus IV of Sweden) was the son of Duke Eric Magnusson of the province of Södermanland (a son of Sweden's King Magnus Ladulås) and Princess Ingeborg Haakonsdatter of Norway.[54] In 1319, at the tender age of three, he succeeded his maternal grandfather King Haakon V, who lacked a son of his own, as elected King of Norway.[55] Two months later, he was also elected the successor of his uncle King Birger Magnusson as King of Sweden. This initiated a union between the Swedish and Norwegian Crowns which technically lasted until 1343, but in reality, until 1355.[56]

King Magnus was the suzerain of Gotland and the Danish King's chief rival in the Baltic region. While King Magnus does not appear in person in the history of King Valdemar's conquest of Gotland, the rivalry between the Danish King and him formed the background to the Gotland campaign. King Magnus and King Valdemar were related by a series of marriages, so to some extent the war was a family affair.

King Magnus belonged to an old family of strongmen which had produced a line of powerful Swedish monarchs. King Magnus's family had taken power in Sweden in 1250. The historian Johannes Messenius in 1616 traced the clan's semi-mythical origin to the probably eleventh-century strongman Folke Filbyter (Folke the Horse Gelder) and, around 1100, the strongman's grandson and namesake, the historically verified Folke 'the Fat' (Latin: *Fulco grossus*) Ingevaldsson (c. 1078–1149). Messenius introduced the name Folkung for this powerful clan, hence calling it the Folkung dynasty. This was not a dynastic or family name ever used by King Magnus and his immediate predecessors, so modern historians instead tend to refer to the dynasty as the Bjälbo family, after one of its chief strongholds.

Sweden expanded during the reigns of King Magnus and his immediate predecessors, but progress came slowly. Sweden only developed into a modern, medieval kingdom of the Danish and German type in the mid- to late thirteenth century under the rule of Duke Birger Magnusson (in Swedish known as Birger jarl) and his sons, Valdemar Birgersson and the aforementioned Magnus Ladulås. It was forced modernisation, since the existing chiefs cared little for Continental manners. In the years 1247 to 1251, Duke Birger and his family crushed the rival strongmen. They then ruthlessly reorganised the country and reformed, to their advantage, the system and means for raising tax revenues, which gave added income that enabled them

---

54 King Magnus Eriksson, as the name is spelled in Sweden, was the fourth Swedish king of this name, but Swedish kings were enumerated only from the sixteenth century onwards and then there was some uncertainty about a number of early monarchs. Hence, some historians refer to him as Magnus III of Sweden.
55 King Haakon V 'the Tall' Magnusson (1270–1319; r. 1299–1319).
56 The total population of early fourteenth-century Sweden and Finland, which formed one kingdom, is estimated as between 650,000 and 750,000. The corresponding estimate for Norway is between 300,000 and 400,000, and for Iceland, which formed part of Norway, around 80,000. Nordberg, *I kung Magnus tid*, 31.

to raise soldiers, build castles, and establish towns. The remaining old-style rural strongmen and their retinues were turned into nobles and knights of the Continental style. Stockholm was founded in the early 1250s and within decades developed into a major city. Outlying territories and regions that in previous times had ruled themselves, even if they occasionally and tenuously accepted Swedish overlordship, were henceforth integrated into the kingdom. Royal power grew rapidly.

The young King Magnus came of age in 1332, just in time to face a major crisis and opportunity. King Christopher of Denmark (Valdemar Atterdag's father) had just died. No successor was appointed, since all Danish royal lands by then had been mortgaged to German lords. In response to the unexpected lack of a king, the Scanians took the opportunity to rise against the rule of Count John 'the Mild' of Holstein-Plön, who controlled the Scanias.[57] Count John may possibly have been mild, but he was a German and demanded taxes, neither of which pleased the Scanians. A Scanian delegation, headed by Archbishop Karl Eriksen of Lund, turned to King Magnus, requesting him to take over the province. In response, the young King Magnus ordered a Swedish army into Scania. Following negotiations with Duke Valdemar of Slesvig and Count John, a solution was soon found.[58] King Magnus in 1332 received the provinces of Scania and Blekinge as surety for the loan to the Danish Crown of the astonishing amount of 34,000 marks silver (the equivalent of 7,160 kg of silver), to be paid in instalments.[59] While a huge amount of money, King Magnus was neither naïve nor a fool. The Scanias were wealthy territories, the Scanian herring market produced a substantial annual income in customs fees alone, and King Magnus had every reason to believe that the investment would turn a handsome long-term profit. As a result, the Scanian territories in this year joined into a union with the Swedish Crown.

Eight years later, the newly-crowned King Valdemar of Denmark was so weak that he on 3 January 1341 must renounce in writing his right to Scania and also must sell South Halland province to Sweden for 8,000 marks silver.[60] The Danish King soon renounced the deal, which already in 1342 led to war between Denmark and Sweden. The war went badly for King Valdemar. In the Treaty of Varberg on 18 November 1343, the Danish King acknowledged King Magnus as the rightful suzerain of all the Scanias, in exchange for the total payment of 49,000 marks silver, the previous payments included (as part of the deal, King Magnus returned Copenhagen Castle which for the

---

57   Count John III 'the Mild' of Holstein-Plön (c. 1297–1359).
58   Duke Valdemar V of Slesvig (c. 1314–1364) was the young man who in the period 1326–1329 had been the child-King Valdemar III of Denmark. It will be remembered that the powerful Count Gerhard of Holstein-Rendsburg in 1326, when King Christopher fled into exile, put his own child nephew on the throne as King Valdemar III, and then, in 1329, just as easily deposed his nephew to allow for the return of King Christopher. As Duke of Slesvig, young Valdemar had no formal authority to negotiate the surrender of territory to the Swedish King, but neither did anybody else in Denmark.
59   Nordberg, *I kung Magnus tid*, 44.
60   Lundbye, *Valdemar Atterdag*, 34; Tägil, *Valdemar Atterdag*, 52-53.

calculation was assessed as the equivalent of 7,000 marks silver).[61] The two kings also concluded a treaty of friendship. Henceforth, King Magnus styled himself 'King of Sweden, Norway, and the land of Scania' (Latin: *rex Sveciae, Norvegiae et terrae Scaniae*). As a symbol for this, he adopted three golden crowns on a blue field as a coat of arms for his dynasty.

The purchases had been expensive. Although King Magnus's business instincts were correct, like most kings he lacked the ready cash to pay for his purchases. As a result, King Magnus, too, must borrow money from various secular and clerical notables and give out lands as surety.[62]

King Magnus needed additional revenues to finance essential reforms of state and society. In 1335, he formally abolished slavery in his lands, regulated the upkeep of roads and inns throughout the realm, and, to curb prevalent abuses, limited the number of horses that bishops and knights might bring in their retinues during travel.[63] At around the same time, King Magnus organised large-scale developments in northern Sweden and Finland. In the 1340s or soon thereafter, the King introduced a new national legal code, which consisted of two parts, one for the rural areas and one for the towns. He may also have been the originator of, or at least put on a more formal basis, what can be labelled an early form of parliamentary system based on the four estates (the nobility, clergy, burghers, and peasants). Such assemblies were called on several occasions, notably in 1332 when Scania was included in the Swedish realm, in Uppsala in 1344, and in Söderköping in 1359. One problem that King Magnus could not solve, and which would continue to cause difficulties for Swedish kings for centuries, was state poverty. Sweden had few sources of income. In comparison to the states in Continental Europe, Sweden was a poor country. King Magnus did what he could, establishing major mining works in 1340, 1347, and 1354. This brought some revenues, but not enough to repay all loans.

As King of Norway, King Magnus also worked to develop his possessions on Greenland and in North America. These lands formed the home of thousands of permanent settlers and were a source of valuable goods such as furs and walrus ivory which, not least, paid the money owed to the Church which bishops collected. The first Scandinavian settlements in North America were founded in the early eleventh century. The contemporary French traveller, soldier, and crusader Philippe de Mézières, whom we will meet again, in his description of the world noted that the immense territory of Norway included

> a region opposite the North Star, where it is so cold that all is covered in ice. This region is far away from all other inhabited lands. The aforesaid country, lying under the North Star, is called Godlant ... [It is subject to] the King of Norway,

---

61   Lundbye, *Valdemar Atterdag*, 40–42; Nordberg, *I kung Magnus tid*, 63.
62   Ultimately, King Magnus even had to extort or embezzle ('borrow') the money collected by the bishops in Sweden on behalf of the Pope. When it ultimately became obvious that the Swedish King could not repay the missing funds, the Pope in 1358 had him excommunicated. The Papal act had little impact in distant Sweden.
63   Nordberg, *I kung Magnus tid*, 110–115; Harrison, *Jarlens sekel*, 345.

whose realm is an island. And the King's rule extends so far that he has certain ships, which he sends through the Ocean towards the north to collect the tribute from his subjects in a country opposite Godlant, so far to the north that these royal ships spend three years before they can return to Norway.[64]

The Icelandic Annals mention a ship from Markland (modern-day Labrador) as late as in 1347.[65] By the mid-fourteenth century, however, deteriorating climate conditions made trade more difficult. The caretaker and acting bishop of Greenland, Ívar Bárdarson of the Eastern Settlement, around this time found the Western Settlement on Greenland abandoned, except for wild horses, cattle, goats, and sheep.[66] Since none of the inhabitants had passed through the Eastern Settlement, six days away by sea, only two conclusions were possible. Either all people had suddenly and inexplicably died, or they had migrated a similar distance in the opposite direction, bringing with them as many animals as their ships could carry, to the more temperate lands in North America which for centuries were well-known to them as a source of fruit and timber.[67] In 1355, King Magnus sent a fact-finding mission to Greenland under Paul Knutsson, the lawspeaker of Gula Thing in western Norway, but either the expedition was lost or the King for other reasons, possibly the wars described in this book, never received its report.[68]

King Magnus married Countess Blanche of Namur (in modern-day Belgium) in 1335. The two had met in the previous year when King Magnus visited Namur. In Sweden, Blanche became known as Queen Blanka. The couple had two sons (Eric and Haakon) and three or four daughters, whose

---

64 In original French … *une region devers la tresmontaigne, la ou il faisoit si froit que tout estoit plain de glace. Ladicte region est moult loingtaine de toutes autres terres habitees. Ledit pais est dessoubz l'estoile tresmontaigne, et a nom Godlant … le roy de Norovegue, lequel royaume est une isle de mer. Et dure si loing sa seigneurie qu'il a certaines nefz, lesquelles il mande par la mer Ocean devers septentrion, pour recueillir les truages de ses subgiez en un pais qui est devers Godlant, si loing devers la tresmontaigne que les dictes nefz du roy mectent troys ans avant qu'elles puissant retourner en Norovegue.* Philippe de Mézières, *Le Songe du Viel Pelerin* (Cambridge: Cambridge University Press, 2 vols, 1969), 247–248; Philippe de Mézières, *Songe du Viel Pelerin: Édition critique* (Geneva: Librairie Droz, 2 vols, 2015), 225–227. We will return to what Mézières meant by the direction north. Godlant is usually understood as Greenland, but more likely derived from Old Norse *Vínland hit Góða,* that is, the North American east coast.

65 Gustav Storm (ed.), *Islandske Annaler indtil 1578* (Christiania: Det norske historiske Kildeskriftfond, 1888), 213, 403. Incidentally, the Annals mention the arrival of the Black Death immediately after the Markland ship, which suggests that the plague spread faster along shipping lines than overland.

66 Ívarr Bárðarson, in Finnur Jónsson (ed.), *Det gamle Grønlands Beskrivelse* (Copenhagen: Levin & Munksgaard, 1930), 29–30; *Grönlands historiske Mindesmærker* 3 (Copenhagen: Det kongelige nordiske oldskrift-selskab, 1845), 248–264. Ívarr Bárðarson was acting bishop from 1341 to 1366. His voyage to the Western Settlement, which likely took place in 1342, was still remembered in the 1630s when Bishop Gísli Oddsson noted that the missing inhabitants had moved to North America and abandoned the Christian faith. Ibid., 459–460.

67 As mentioned, out of context, by Ívarr Bárðarson, in Jónsson, *Det gamle Grønlands Beskrivelse,* 32. For a list of valuable goods from North America regularly exported to European markets and hence of great interest to Archbishop Erik Walkendorff of Trondheim, see *Grönlands historiske Mindesmærker* 3, 492–493. The list of goods, believed ultimately to derive from Ívarr Bárðarson, include North American furs from sable, stoat, beaver, wolverine, lynx, moose, and brown bear, as well as goods available at Greenland such as polar bear furs and walrus and narwhal ivory.

68 *Grönlands historiske Mindesmærker* 3, 120–223.

names are lost to history. The petulant St. Bridget of Sweden, who before sainthood served the royal couple as principal lady-in-waiting at court in the late 1330s and taught Queen Blanche Swedish, constantly criticised both of them, ultimately accusing Queen Blanche of everything from lack of piety to poison murders. As for King Magnus, St. Bridget complained that he was 'childish' and dressed sloppily. Meanwhile, King Magnus's sister Euphemia in 1336 married the powerful Albert II 'the Great' of Mecklenburg (c. 1318-1379), who earlier in the same year had come of age and assumed personal rule of this north German duchy.[69] The marriage potentially created a powerful alliance between Sweden and northern Germany.

In 1348, prospects looked good for King Magnus and his kingdom. He sent an army towards the east, declared war against the Novgorod Republic, and occupied territories around the River Neva, including the location of modern-day St. Petersburg. He fully expected to extend his territories in the east as much as he had already done in the south. But then struck one of those disasters that nobody could have predicted. Exactly at the moment when King Magnus prepared the campaign, the Black Death, a bubonic plague pandemic, reached Europe. The plague first struck a Crimean trading station operated by Genoese merchants in late 1347. When the Genoese returned to Italy, they carried the plague with them. When King Magnus's army embarked for the eastern front, the plague had reached central France. When the Swedish and Novgorod armies engaged in battle in 1349, the plague devastated England, Germany, and Hungary. The plague reached Sweden in 1350, while fighting in the east still was ongoing. It soon killed off between a third and a half of the population. Individual losses were horrifying, and for the kingdom, the losses in tax-paying population resulted in a catastrophic economic crisis. That the plague also struck Novgorod and Pskov in 1352 was no consolation to King Magnus. By then, he had already been forced to abandon the war. The Swedish King had no more men, and precious little revenue from either taxation or trade.

And more problems were on the way. The union of the Swedish and Norwegian Crowns of 1319 was technically dissolved in 1343, when King Magnus had his younger son Haakon (1340–1380; r. 1355–1380) elected King of Norway as Haakon VI. To complete the dynastic scheme, King Magnus in 1344 had his elder son Eric (1339–1359; r. 1357–1359) elected successor to the Swedish and Scanian throne. Both boys were very young at the time and lacked lands of their own. But the years passed, and King Magnus remained in power. When young Haakon came of age in 1355 and assumed personal rule over Norway, Eric was already tired of waiting for his kingdom. Having married Beatrix of Bavaria, he in October 1356 rose against his father from the important stronghold of Kalmar.[70] A number of

---

69 Mecklenburg's power increased further when future Emperor Charles IV on 16 October 1347 promoted Albert and his younger brother John of Mecklenburg to Princes of the Holy Roman Empire (Latin: *princeps imperii*; German: *Reichsfürst*), that is, immediate vassals of the Emperor. On 8 July 1348, the two princes were also elevated to dukes.
70 Beatrix of Bavaria (c. 1340–1359) is generally believed to have been the daughter of the aforementioned Margrave Louis of Brandenburg and his first wife, Princess Margaret of Denmark, the eldest daughter of King Christopher of Denmark. This made Beatrix Emperor

FALL OF THE MERCHANT-FARMER REPUBLIC

rebellious strongmen and bishops joined Eric against King Magnus. So did foreign notables, such as Count Adolph of Holstein-Plön.[71] Another, more important, ally became Duke Albert of Mecklenburg who joined the rebels in exchange for the hugely important Skanör and Falsterbo castles which guarded the Scanian herring market. Young King Eric gave away parts of the Scanias to the Duke of Mecklenburg's sons Henry III (c. 1337–1383), who in time would make a name for himself as Henry 'the Hangman', and Albert III (c. 1338–1412). We will soon encounter both young men again.

The civil war ended with a negotiated settlement in April 1357, which formally divided Sweden. Eric received the Scanias, large areas in the west (Götaland), and Finland. Soon, he also received Stockholm Castle and major parts of the Swedish eastern core territories (Svealand). King Magnus retained the rest, in reality the smaller and less revenue-rich parts of the kingdom. Father and son shared royal power. Eric was recognised as King of Scania.

Unfortunately, this solution satisfied neither party, so the civil war soon resumed. In early 1359, King Magnus and Queen Blanche visited King Valdemar. It was in the interest of the Danish King that both Kings Magnus and Eric remained weak, without any one party growing too strong. King Magnus also brought his younger son, King Haakon of Norway. During the meeting, King Valdemar betrothed his six-year-old daughter Margaret to the 18-year-old King Haakon. In addition, King Magnus promised King Valdemar Helsingborg Castle, possibly the strongest in Scania, if he provided assistance against the Swedish King's wayward son.

Effigy believed to depict King Magnus, Trondheim Cathedral, 1330s. (Unknown photographer)

In spring 1359, King Valdemar led his army into Scania, where he confronted King Eric's men. The Danes then returned home. However, in June 1359, Eric and his wife Beatrix suddenly died, presumably from the Black Death. Having reconciled his differences with his various domestic enemies, King Magnus was in November 1359 again sole ruler of Sweden. Perhaps overestimating the security of his position, King Magnus broke the betrothal between King Haakon and Margaret and resumed contact with Eric's previous allies in Mecklenburg and Holstein, entering into an alliance with Duke Albert in August 1359.

The German notables were King Valdemar's competitors, so these initiatives again turned King Magnus's former ally, King Valdemar, into his enemy. Moreover, the Swedish civil war had shown King Valdemar how weak King Magnus had become, and in particular, how weak his rule was over the Scanias.

Louis IV's granddaughter and King Valdemar's niece. Others have argued that she instead was a daughter of Emperor Louis. Considering that the wedding of Eric and Beatrix took place in Brandenburg, the traditional explanation seems far more likely.

71 Count Adolph VII/IX of Holstein-Plön (c. 1327–1390) was the only son of the aforementioned Count John the Mild of Holstein-Plön who had lost the Scanias.

1
The Scanian Herring Market

While Gotland was the Baltic centre for the Eastern trade, Scania was the economic hub of the entire Baltic region. It was no wonder that King Valdemar coveted the Scanias. Mercantile life in the Baltic region orbited not around kings and bishops, but fish – and one fish in particular, the Scanian herring.

From around 1200 onwards, the world's most important fish market for herring and hence, one of the most important markets for any kind of goods in the Baltic region, was the Scanian herring market. It was held annually from 24 August (St. Bartholomew's Day) to 9 October (St. Dionysius the Areopagite's Day) on the shore between the two small Scanian castle towns of Skanör and Falsterbo. Goods could be brought in already from 15 August (Assumption of Mary), when bailiffs were ready to levy customs duties. For the rest of the year, this was a barren coast of little interest. But when the herring market approached, fishermen would arrive from near and afar to erect huts, trading booths, and temporary shops close to the area where the herring was spawning. When this seasonal event took place, it was said that herring was so abundant that one could scoop up the fish with one's hands. There is evidence that commercial fishing of herring in the region took place already around the year AD 800.

The demand for fish was huge in western and central Europe. Following the very nearly universal acceptance there of Catholic Christianity, the Church was able strictly to forbid the eating of meat on Fridays and during Lent, the 40-day fast from Ash Wednesday to Easter. But fish was permitted

Presently known as the Atlantic herring (*Clupea harengus*), the autumn-spawning herring in the waters between Denmark and Scania constituted the commercially most easily exploited of the four key Baltic herring stocks. Autumn spawners were bigger than spring spawners, hence were most heavily exploited. As a result, autumn spawners are presently too few for commercial fishing. Modern-day commercial catches in the Baltic Sea are 90 per cent spring spawners. (Artwork: Gervais et Boulart, 1877)

nourishment, and none was more easily available than Baltic herring. Herring had a high fat content, which also made it an inexpensive source of protein during winter. Moreover, merchants had found that it was possible to conserve fish by salting. The addition of sufficient quantities of common salt to fish can indeed drastically reduce or even prevent bacterial action. This discovery, apparently made in the twelfth century, enabled the export of herring in barrels as far afield as to France, Spain, and Italy.

The aforementioned French soldier and crusader Philippe de Mézières visited the Scanian market in the mid-1350s, and later described it:

> And God has so ordered his handmaid Nature that for two months a year, and no more, that is to say in September and October, the herring makes its passage from one sea to the other through the Strait, in such vast numbers that it is a great wonder. So many pass through the Strait in these two months, that in several places in this 15-league Strait one can cut them down even with a dagger. Now comes the other wonder: by old custom, every year in these two months boats and ships from all over Germany and Prussia assemble in the aforementioned Strait to fish the herring. The common assumption is that 40,000 boats do nothing else during these two months but fish herring, and in each boat, there are at least six men and in many there are seven, eight, or ten. Besides these 40,000 boats, there are 500 ships of big or medium size, which do nothing else but collect and salt in barrels the herring taken by the 40,000 boats. And it is customary that the crew from all these vessels during these two months live on the coast in huts of wood and boughs or reeds stretched out along the 15 leagues opposite the kingdom of Norway. They load the large ships with herring in barrels. And after two months and eight days or so, you cannot find a single boat or herring in the whole Strait.
>
> This is a great army of people to catch such a small fish, because if you count them, you will find that during these two months more than 300,000 people do nothing else but fish. And since I, old and weak pilgrim, when I formerly voyaged by sea to Prussia, in a great ship, passed along the aforementioned Strait in beautiful weather and during the fishing season, and saw the aforementioned rowing boats, boats, and large ships, and on the way partook of the herring which the fishermen gave us; who together with many other locals assured me about the two wonders, I decided to describe them for two reasons: first, so that we can acknowledge the grace, which God has granted Christians with this abundance of herring, with which all Germany, France, England, and many other countries are fed during Lent, since poor people can afford a herring but not a great fish; and second, when I call to mind the 40,000 boats, the 500 large ships, and the 300,000 Christians assembled together in these two months, they would be enough to conquer not only the Holy Land and Jerusalem, but Damascus and the whole of Syria …[1]

---

1 Mézières, *Le Songe du Viel Pelerin*, 248-250; Mézières, *Songe du Viel Pelerin: Édition critique*, 228–229. Most historians believe that Mézières's visit to the Scanian market took place in 1364, but if so, he would probably not have referred to Scania as part of Norway, and he would have noticed the uncertain truce between King Valdemar and the League. For this reason, an autumn in the period 1354–1356 appears far more likely, before Eric was crowned King of Scania.

While the old crusader possibly exaggerated the number of boats, ships, and people engaged in the Scanian herring market when he years later reminisced about the event, he was not far off the mark. Except for the skipper, a fishing boat crew did not consist of professionals. Numerous peasants and townsmen from the entire Baltic region joined the fishing venture at market times as seasonal workers.

The volumes of trade were huge. We have reliable data in the form of accounts and receipts for customs duties from, in particular, the city of Lübeck. These records show that in 1368, at least 182 cargo ships sailed from Lübeck to Scania with another 9 going directly to Malmö, Scania's rapidly developing permanent mercantile centre. In 1369, the same records show as many as 212 ships sailing from Lübeck to Scania with another 10 bound for Malmö.[2]

The merchant ships from Lübeck bound for Scania were described as consisting of two categories. Largest was the cargo transport (*navis*), by which was meant a cog. The smaller category of ship was simply called ship (*schuta*). This signified a smaller cargo vessel. Some of the latter may essentially have been fishing boats, although they were certainly capable of carrying cargo, and a large *schuta* may well be equal in cargo capacity to a small *navis*.[3] Perhaps the two categories simply corresponded to what Philippe de Mézières referred to as 'ships of big or medium size'.

Tonnage was measured in a Low German volume unit called *last* (pl. *leste*) which simply meant 'cargo' and corresponded to about two tons. The origin of the term was an Old Norse volume unit called *lest* (Danish: *læst*).

With regard to herring, a *last* equalled 12 full barrels. It follows that the average weight of six herring barrels was one ton. The majority of large cargo ships (*naves*) carried a cargo of from 15 to 25 *leste*. A cargo ship with this capacity accordingly carried from 180 to 300 herring barrels, the equivalent of about 30 to 50 tons of cargo.[4] A few cargo ships had a greater cargo capacity, while some smaller ones, as noted, had no greater capacity than the largest fishing vessels.

---

2   Curt Weibull, *Lübeck och Skånemarknaden: Studier i Lübecks pundtullsböcker och pundtullskvitton 1368–1369 och 1398–1400* (Lund: CWK Gleerup/Fahlbeckska Stiftelsen 2, 1922), 12, 18, 43.

3   Weibull, *Lübeck och Skånemarknaden*, 32.

4   Weibull, *Lübeck och Skånemarknaden*, 33.

FALL OF THE MERCHANT-FARMER REPUBLIC

Year	Imports	Value	Value	Imports	Exports	Turnover
	Herring (barrels)	*Herring*	*Other goods*	*Total*		
1368	38,440 barrels	-	-	-	31,037.75	unknown
1369	34,375 barrels	-	-	-	54,225.5	unknown
1398	66,557.75 barrels	99.836.5	7,383.75	107,220.25	47,549.5	154,769.75
1399	71,042.75 barrels	106.563.25	5,985.75	112,549	40,534.25	153,083.25
1400	66,876.75 barrels	66.876.75	8,411.75	75,288.5	40,465.75	115,754.25
Bergen trade (1399)		n/a	16,665	n/a	8,608	25,273
Stockholm trade (1400)		n/a	-	-	-	25,000 (ca.)
Rock salt from Lüneburg (annually) corresponding to: 95,000 –119,000 barrels						

Table 1. Overview of known trade data for Lübeck in the Scanian herring market, and comparative data for Lübeck's Bergen and Stockholm trade. All figures in marks silver, except where barrels are indicated. (source: Weibull, *Lübeck och Skånemarknaden*, 12, 17, 26–27, 37–38, 44–45)

On average, Lübeck alone imported at least 36,400 barrels of herring per year in the 1360s (Table 1).[5] At the same time, Rostock, Wismar, Stralsund, Greifswald, Stettin, Kolberg, and the Prussian towns imported another 62,100 barrels. This meant that only the Baltic Hanseatic towns imported at least 98,500 barrels of herring per year, or more than 16,400 tons.[6] The figures cited derive from surviving accounts. Since we cannot be certain that all accounts survived into the present, actual volumes may well have been significantly larger. The conclusion must be that the Baltic Hanseatic towns certainly imported no less than 100,000 barrels of herring per year. Huge volumes were imported by the North Sea towns as well, although figures are unknown. The export records for rock salt from Lüneburg shows that by this time no less than 95,000 and quite likely up to 119,000 barrels of herring were salted in the Scanian market with Lüneburg salt alone. Or more, since some salt exports may have been included in unspecified records and in any case, not all salt export records may have been preserved.[7]

Later in the century, the herring exports grew even larger. In 1398, a total of 399 ships from Lübeck sailed to Scania (where Malmö by then had assumed the role of primary market). In 1399, the number rose to 476, and in 1400, to 519.[8] This, of course, was the very figure cited by Philippe de Mézières earlier in the century.

---

5 Weibull, *Lübeck och Skånemarknaden*, 17.
6 Weibull, *Lübeck och Skånemarknaden*, 19–20.
7 Weibull, *Lübeck och Skånemarknaden*, 36.
8 Weibull, *Lübeck och Skånemarknaden*, 24–25, 28, 43.

In the years 1398–1400, Lübeck alone imported on average 68,200 barrels of herring (Table 1).[9] The monetary value of the imported herring was, in Lübeck, in most years assessed as around 100,000 marks silver (Table 1).[10]

Based on a similar volume calculation as for the years 1368 and 1369, it follows that the Baltic Hanseatic towns alone at the turn of the century imported more than 200,000 barrels of herring per year, or more than 34,000 tons.

Based on such data, total catches of herring in the waters between Denmark and Sweden have been estimated at up to 50,000 tons per annum. Evidence suggests that the herring was overfished already in the thirteenth century.[11] Yet, the herring production, despite some fluctuation, seems to have remained mostly stable throughout the Middle Ages.

But the Scanian herring market was important for other reasons as well. While herring was the most important goods that was sold at the herring market, it was not the only one. Merchants arrived from Lübeck and other Hanseatic towns, England, Scotland, Flanders, and Normandy to buy and sell herring, but also to trade in other goods supplied by Scandinavian merchants, nobles, and peasants. Traders arrived from Denmark, eastern Norway, and Sweden, as well as the rest of the Baltic, with a wide variety of goods. The goods included furs from Russia, iron from Sweden, horses, butter, tar, grain, and other goods from Scandinavia, Prussia, and Livonia. The Continental merchants, in turn, brought cloth from Flanders, sea salt from the Biscay coast of Spain and France, wine from France, and other luxury goods.

Hanseatic merchants benefited from both exports and imports. In 1368, exports to Scania from Lübeck alone were worth 30,872.25 marks, with exports to Malmö valued at another 165.5 marks. In 1369, Lübeck's exports to Scania had risen to 52,704.5 marks, with exports to Malmö valued at another 1,521 marks (Table 1).[12]

The import of other goods from the Scanian market to Lübeck was smaller, but still significant. Their average annual value for imports to Lübeck was estimated as 7,300 marks. Most consisted of cloth (Table 1).[13]

Moreover, the herring market engaged far more trades than seasonal fishermen and traders. To preserve the herring necessitated huge volumes of salt and an enormous number of barrels for conservation. These were mostly provided by the Hanseatic League, with salt from Lüneburg and barrels mainly from Lübeck. But workers were needed as well. Lübeck provided an additional, seasonal, and mostly female work force in the form of so-called 'gilling-women' (*ghelleconen*) who removed the gill bones, gutted, and cleaned the fish, and 'packing-women' (*leggheconen*) who swiftly salted and laid the cleaned fish in barrels.

---

9   Weibull, *Lübeck och Skånemarknaden*, 26–27, 37.
10 Weibull, *Lübeck och Skånemarknaden*, 44.
11 Lane M. Atmore, Lourdes Martínez-García, Daniel Makowiecki, Carl André, Lembi Lõugas, James H. Barrett, and Bastiaan Star, 'Population Dynamics of Baltic Herring since the Viking Age Revealed by Ancient DNA and Genomics', *PNAS* 2022, 119: 45 (https://doi.org/10.1073/pnas.2208703119).
12 Weibull, *Lübeck och Skånemarknaden*, 12.
13 Weibull, *Lübeck och Skånemarknaden*, 26–27, 38.

Herring and other goods exchanged hands also elsewhere along the Scanian coast, in particular in Malmö, which soon contributed to the herring market with a share comparable to that of Skanör and Falsterbo and ultimately exceeded it.

The financial importance of the Scanian herring market was huge (Table 1).[14] For Lübeck alone, total turnover at the Scanian herring market easily exceeded 150,000 marks silver. For the Baltic League cities as a whole, total turnover probably exceeded 450,000 marks, and this does not include the turnover produced by Dutch, English, and other merchants.

These turnover figures should be compared to those of Lübeck's trade with other partners. In Scandinavia, two of Lübeck's most important trading partners were Bergen, in Norway, and Stockholm, in Sweden. Total turnover was around 25,000 marks silver in both centres of trade (Table 1).[15] The Scanian market trade dwarfed the Swedish and Norwegian markets. From an economics perspective, Scania was from about 1200 onwards the financially absolutely most important region of Scandinavia.

The Scanian herring market retained its importance over time. In the 1520s, the number of boats that fished herring in the Strait still reached 7,515, each with a five-man crew, which equals more than 37,500 men.[16] In 1494, a total of 174 gilling-women still worked in Falsterbo and Skanör.[17] Their work produced a total of about 50,000 barrels (4,200 *leste*), or about 8,400 tons of herring.[18] The same volume, about 50,000 barrels, was noted as late as in 1882.[19]

And then there was the entertainment. Those who made profits, great or small, celebrated their gains in the thousands of temporary drinking booths and brothels raised on the coast. When darkness fell, so that customs inspectors no longer could assess the catch, the bailiffs formally closed the sea for further fishing until the next morning. The merchants and fishermen then had to find other things to do, and for many that meant unsavoury entertainment. The wearing of a cuirass or the carrying of a crossbow, or indeed any weapon, was strongly prohibited in the marketplace. Yet, brawls, drunken or otherwise, were commonplace in the evenings.

The frantic fishing, gutting, packing, trading, and merrymaking continued until 9 October, when the market officially closed and all ships and boats immediately departed.

The Scanian herring market was a cornerstone of the Hanseatic League's revenues, but it also yielded a substantial income to whatever king controlled it. Both the coast and the two castles, Skanör and Falsterbo, were royal lands. Hence, the Crown controlled the market through bailiffs who charged fees and customs duties for essentially everything that took place in the market.

---

14 Weibull, *Lübeck och Skånemarknaden*, 44–45.
15 Weibull, *Lübeck och Skånemarknaden*, 44–45.
16 Dietrich Schäfer, *Das Buch des lübeckischen Vogts auf Schonen* (Lübeck: Hansischer Geschichtsverein, 2nd edn 1927), xliii.
17 Schäfer, *Das Buch des lübeckischen Vogts*, lxiii.
18 Schäfer, *Das Buch des lübeckischen Vogts*, xliii. Here, Schäfer accidentally confuses tons and barrels, but the meaning is clear.
19 Weibull, *Lübeck och Skånemarknaden*, 14.

The fishermen had to pay fees for their boat and space on the beach. Traders had to pay a market fee. The drivers of carts and wagons had to pay a fee for each cart. The women who sold beer and mead from booths in the market had to pay fees, too, based on every barrel that was opened. Even the gilling-women were liable to pay fees for carrying out their work. When there was a brawl, each participant was fined. It was free to bring goods into the market, but all goods brought out were liable to a customs duty. The customs fees for taking goods out of the market was about one percent of their value, or usually somewhat less for herring. Unsold goods were charged half customs fees, that is, at a rate of about 0.5 percent.[20] The revenues from the Scanian herring market soon grew into the biggest recurring post within the Danish Crown's budget. With an annual export of possibly up to 300,000 barrels of herring, plus other goods, and a total market turnover probably well in excess of 450,000 marks, the Crown's revenues which derived from the Scanian herring market were significant.

In the late fourteenth century, the royal revenue totalled about 6,000 Cologne marks silver, or about 1.4 tons of silver – a revenue stream that suggests a total market turnover not of 450,000 marks but close to 600,000 marks.[21] This was a substantial amount of revenue for a king. Yet, even under normal business conditions, the Hanseatic League could raise far more income from trading than the Crown could ever extract as customs duties. Moreover, the League wanted a monopoly on the Scanian market. Although exact figures remain unknown, it is not far-fetched to estimate that a monopolistic League might expect to be able to extract about half of the market value for goods brought in and sold in the Scanian market, as opposed to the one percent gained by royal customs officers. If so, annual revenue might well reach 300,000 marks silver or thereabouts. Or, in bulk, about 70 tons of silver per year. Even with deductions for wages and incidental expenses, this was a truly astonishing amount of money, far more than any Scandinavian king could dream of raising in a lifetime.

We will see that the Hanseatic League was willing to pay King Valdemar hard cash for their trading privileges in the Scanian market. In June 1360, a League delegation went to see King Valdemar to ask for a renewal of their trading privileges in the Scanian market in exchange for a payment of 1,000 marks. They were indeed prepared to offer the King 1,200 marks.[22] Interestingly, the Scanias then belonged to the Swedish Crown. King Valdemar wanted, but had not yet regained, the Scanias, so the League clearly regarded the payment as an investment into the future. Yet, King Valdemar knew the value of what the League asked for, and ultimately, in May 1361, we will see that the League, after some initial irritation, had to pay as much as 4,000 marks silver in exchange for the Crown guaranteeing their trading privileges in Denmark, and the Scanian market.

---

20 Lundbye, *Valdemar Atterdag*, 131.
21 Lundbye, *Valdemar Atterdag*, 131.
22 *Hanserecesse: Die Recesse und andere Akten der Hansetage von 1256–1430*, 163–165; Dietrich Schäfer, *Die Hansestädte und König Waldemar von Dänemark: Hansische Geschichte bis 1376* (Jena: Gustav Fischer, 1879), 259–260; Schäfer, *Das Buch des lübeckischen Vogts*, xxxv.

Fisherman at the Scanian herring market, as depicted in print from 1555. His work garments are representative also of those in the late fourteenth century. The sea teemed with fish. It was said that if you stood a halberd in the shallow water, it would remain upright because of the huge amounts of herring that pushed against it from all sides. (Olaus Magnus, Historia de gentibus septentrionalibus 20)

Twentieth-century aerial photograph of the area along the shore known as Hovbacken, the site of the Skanör section of the herring market. The neat rows of dugouts are the remains of huts used during the market. In the middle ages, they were located directly on the shore. Later, the shoreline moved outwards, all the way to the twentieth-century beach huts visible at the present water edge (lower centre). However, the shoreline is now receding, so in the early twenty-first century most of the beach huts were swallowed up by the sea. (Photo: Esaias (Esse) Ericsson, The IK Workshop Society at www.ikfoundation.org)

2

The Conquest of the Scanias

By the late 1350s, tensions and rivalry had grown for some time between King Valdemar of Denmark, King Magnus of Sweden, and the powerful Duke Albert of Mecklenburg. Any rivalry between these notables by necessity also involved the counts of Holstein. Among them was the aforementioned Count Adolph of Holstein-Plön. Another was the larger-than-life Count Heinrich 'Iron Henry' of Holstein-Rendsburg.[1] In July 1359, Duke Albert and the Counts of Holstein set out with a fleet to raid King Valdemar's lands. They landed on and occupied the island of Fehmarn.

Of the three assailants, it was Iron Henry (Latin: *Ferreus Henricus*; Low German: *Isern Hinrik*) who had the most extensive military experience. In 1344–1345, Iron Henry had joined a crusade into Prussia with King John 'the Blind' of Bohemia and King Louis I of Hungary and Croatia.[2] In 1346, he probably fought in the battle of Crécy on the side of King Edward III of England against France, incidentally the first major battle in Europe in which gunpowder weapons were used. Iron Henry certainly participated in the conquest of Calais in 1347. In 1348, he joined King Magnus in Sweden's war against the Novgorod Republic. In 1350, he was back in English service in Calais. Over the years, Iron Henry fought King Valdemar's Danes on several occasions. At times, he also operated warships on pirating ventures.

In August 1359, King Magnus of Sweden joined the coalition against King Valdemar. Despite the presence of well-known warriors such as Iron Henry in the anti-Danish coalition, King Magnus probably overestimated his own strength and underestimated the resources available to King Valdemar when he joined the coalition. King Valdemar had increased his power significantly since he was elected

The redoubtable Iron Henry, as depicted on his seal. Iron Henry's armour and helmet are characteristic of those of German knights at the time. Elaborate, crested helmets of the horned type remained very popular in the Empire. (Author's collection)

---

1 Count Heinrich 'Iron Henry' II of Holstein-Rendsburg (c. 1317–c. 1384/1385) was the eldest son of the aforementioned Count Gerhard III of Holstein-Rendsburg who had been the kingmaker and de facto ruler of Denmark.
2 King John the Blind of Bohemia (1296–1346; r. 1310–1346) allied with King Philip VI of France and, although blind, fought and fell in the Battle of Crécy in 1346. He was considered the personification of chivalry. King Louis I of Hungary and Croatia (1326–1382; r. 1342–1382) was known as King Louis the Great and Louis the Hungarian, and ultimately also became King of Poland.

King of Denmark two decades earlier. At this point, King Valdemar had plans of his own. Besides, he knew that he could handle his German rivals by other means than warfare.

On 24 May 1360, King Valdemar convened a national assembly in which he, through a display of strength as well as his renowned eloquence, acquired the consent of the Danish nobility to attempt the conquest of the Scanias. This was no time to sit on the fence. Holstein and Mecklenburg were already at war with Denmark, and Sweden's King Magnus had joined the Germans. The time was ripe to take back the realm's most prosperous province, and all the riches therein.

Apparently immediately after the national assembly, in late May or early June, King Valdemar informed Lübeck that war with Sweden was imminent, and that he could not guarantee the security of Hanseatic League personnel or goods if they remained in the Scanias. In response, League representatives, as noted, asked King Valdemar for a renewal, in exchange for a cash contribution, of their trading privileges in the Scanian market – which they of course knew for the last two decades belonged to Sweden.[3] Perhaps King Valdemar had expected this response, and their support. Or, perhaps the opportunism of the League was a happy surprise that played in King Valdemar's hands. So much is clear, that the League showed its willingness to support, or at least not oppose, King Valdemar's war in the Scanias, as long as they could count on beneficial terms after the fighting was over.

Danish forces landed in Scania in probably late June. The exact date is unrecorded, but when Hanseatic envoys arrived in Copenhagen on 26 June, King Valdemar was already in Scania. The King personally led the army, assisted by his son Christopher and his life-long friend Duke Eric of Saxe-Lauenburg. On 4 July, he seized Malmö. While detached Danish units rapidly took control over the rest of the Scanias (except North Halland), the main force in early July moved against Helsingborg Castle, the key fortress on the Scanian side of the Strait. On 7 July, King Valdemar gained control of the town outside Helsingborg Castle. On 10 July, he laid siege to Helsingborg Castle itself.

King Magnus was taken by surprise. Clearly, he had not anticipated that the Danes would go on the offensive. He was also out of funds, so lacked the means to raise fresh soldiers. Neither was the Swedish nobility very interested in fighting for the Scanias. Although a Swedish army under Duke Erengisle (Swedish: Erengisle jarl) and Carl Ulfsson assembled at Lake Ring (Swedish: Ringsjön) in central Scania, it remained fairly passive in the face of the rapid Danish operations. Because Scania, although under Swedish suzerainty, technically was regarded as a separate country, the Swedish nobility possibly

---

3   *Hanserecesse: Die Recesse und andere Akten der Hansetage von 1256–1430*, 160–167; Schäfer, *Die Hansestädte und König Waldemar*, 259–260. Schäfer later changed his interpretation, instead arguing that the documents in question, which are undated, fit the situation 'infinitely better at the end of 1363'. Schäfer, *Das Buch des lübeckischen Vogts*, xxxv, n. 1. However, in light of the League's keen interest in the Scanian market in 1360, there is no reason to assume that the traditional dating is wrong.

argued that they were not obliged to serve in foreign wars. Their presence, while it lasted, did nothing to slow down the Danish offensive.

Out of funds and soldiers, King Magnus retreated to the north. He handed over Helsingborg Castle to his ally, Duke Albert of Mecklenburg. What King Magnus did not know was that the Duke already had negotiated a secret deal to switch to King Valdemar's side at an opportune moment. Negotiations then began in earnest. Duke Albert somehow contrived to give King Valdemar Helsingborg Castle, over which he assumed control at some point after 20 September (likely in early October).[4] This gave King Valdemar the freedom to continue the conquest of the Scanian provinces. With the fall of Helsingborg Castle, the entire Scanias – Scania, Blekinge, and South Halland – fell to King Valdemar.

The only Swedish commander who refused to yield to King Valdemar was the commandant of Lindholm Castle in southern Scania, which with its 3.5 metres-thick brick walls was the second strongest castle in the Scanias. However, the Zealand Chronicle informs us that a combination of 'threats and great monetary payment' (*partim minis et partim magna pecuniarum summa*) ultimately persuaded him to surrender.[5]

King Valdemar could now control the Scanian herring market. And this brought the Hanseatic League into the picture. King Valdemar clearly hoped to gain the support of the growing power of the League against his enemies. This was an astute move, since the League desperately wanted to regain their old Scanian market privileges. The League traded with everybody, but League members had resented King Magnus's attempts to blockade the Gulf of Finland while he was at war with the Novgorod Republic. They also resented, possibly even more, the increased customs duties and fees that King Magnus had imposed on the Scanian herring market. Danish kings had imposed fees, too, but King Magnus's bailiffs were apparently more demanding and thorough in their insistence on payment. This greatly facilitated King Valdemar's negotiations with the Hanseatic League. Already on 17 July 1360, King Valdemar promised the League to protect their trade, 'after God has helped Us recover Our inheritance, that is, Scania'.[6] Naturally, the League must pay King Valdemar suitable compensation for protection, of an amount still to be determined, but this was a customary business condition that Hanseatic merchants were accustomed to.

To reassure the League further, on 6 March 1361 King Valdemar's ally, Duke Eric of Saxe-Lauenburg, concluded a non-aggression treaty with Lübeck which specifically referenced the Duke's service for the Danish King.[7]

---

4   In response, King Magnus gave Kalmar County as surety to King Valdemar's declared enemy, Iron Henry of Holstein-Rendsburg.
5   Ellen Jørgensen (ed.), *Annales Danici Medii Ævi* (Copenhagen: Selskabet for utgivelse af kilder till Dansk Historie, 1920), 187. The name of the commandant of Lindholm Castle is lost to history. King Magnus had in 1343 appointed his knight Jens Hasenberg commandant of the castle but is unknown whether he remained there after 17 years.
6   Franz Blatt (ed.), *Danmarks riges breve* 3:5: *1357–1360* (Copenhagen: Det danske sprog- og litteraturselskab/Munksgaard, 1967), 347.
7   Franz Blatt (ed.), *Danmarks riges breve* 3:6: *1361–1363* (Copenhagen: Det danske sprog- og litteraturselskab/Munksgaard, 1969), 11–12.

FALL OF THE MERCHANT-FARMER REPUBLIC

On 19 May, representatives of the League cities of Lübeck, Wismar, Rostock, Stralsund, and Stettin met to agree on how to divide the payment of 4,000 marks that King Valdemar had demanded in exchange for the Letter of Privilege that would confirm their trading privileges in Scania and all of Denmark. That they would agree went without saying; the lucrative Scanian herring market was worth so much more than this and certainly justified a monetary contribution in exchange for a Letter of Privilege. On 25 May, the League representatives from Greifswald joined the others in the decision.[8] This was essentially the Wendish-Saxon *Drittel* of the Hanseatic League, which was headed by Lübeck. Having resolved the issue of King Valdemar's payment, the Hanseatic League was now on friendly terms with King Valdemar. The League did not feel that it had anything to fear from the Danish King or his allies, and King Valdemar may also have aimed to reassure the League that he had no designs on its cities and accordingly wished his southern border to remain at peace while he conducted the war against Sweden.

Yet, we will see that in reality, not everybody in the League was convinced that the deal with King Valdemar was a good one. There were men in the League who were just as opportunistic as King Valdemar. For now, though, both League cities and King Valdemar maintained a friendly façade.

---

8   *Hanserecesse: Die Recesse und andere Akten der Hansetage von 1256–1430*, 181–183; Schäfer, *Das Buch des lübeckischen Vogts*, xxxv.

3

King Valdemar's Strategic Goals

After King Valdemar's conquest in 1360 of the Scanian territories previously lost to Sweden, he may have felt the time ripe to move against other Swedish territories, which would seem the natural continuation of his Scanian campaign.

There are no surviving documents that describe King Valdemar's strategic goals. In similarity to most of his rivals, the Danish King was an opportunist. He may never have written down his strategic goals but instead kept a number of objectives to himself and possibly his closest associates, changing them from time to time as opportunities arose. Nonetheless, it seems very likely that in 1361, King Valdemar's immediate strategic goal was to prevent King Magnus from reconquering the Scanias. The narrow Kalmar Strait formed the customary – and safest – sea line of communication between Sweden and the Scanias. In comparison, the overland route was a logistics nightmare, with dense forests, difficult terrain, and undeveloped roads. The Kalmar Strait was secured by the important port and castle of Kalmar on the mainland side and Borgholm Castle, located opposite Kalmar Castle, on the Öland side. King Valdemar knew that King Magnus could use Kalmar as a staging post for an offensive with the aim to reconquer the Scanias. Kalmar Castle was strongly fortified. Yet, this port and castle depended on the island of Öland, which served as the primary source of food supplies for Kalmar.

If King Valdemar could seize Öland, he could deny the Swedes the necessary supplies for launching a campaign into the Scanias out of Kalmar. Besides, Öland and its resources were easier to seize than the strongly fortified Kalmar. It is by no means certain that King Valdemar had the necessary number of men and siege equipment successfully to lay siege to a stronghold the size of Kalmar, which was protected by a strong castle and a town with a population of around 3,000 people within a curtain wall.[1] On the Swedish mainland, it was only Stockholm, with an estimated 5,000 to 6,000

---

1   Harrison, *Jarlens sekel*, 488.

inhabitants, which was larger and more strongly fortified.[2] In fact, Kalmar and Stockholm were the only Swedish mainland population centres that were protected by curtain walls.[3]

However, assuming that Öland was King Valdemar's first objective, and Kalmar his second, if an opportunity arose, what were the Danish King's plans for Gotland, which furthermore was situated at a longer distance from the mainland?

Gotland, the prosperous centre of the Baltic Eastern trade, was only loosely attached to the Swedish Crown. It paid minimal taxes, so King Magnus had not invested much, if anything, in its defences. Because of the current, post-Black Death state of the Swedish economy, it was unlikely that King Magnus would be able, or willing, to send an army to the remote island. In short, Gotland was an important centre of trade but of no great immediate utility to the Swedish King. This opened an opportunity. However, the island was also of no great utility to King Valdemar. If he conquered Gotland, this would cause minimal harm to King Magnus and only yield a remote territory of little immediate value, like Estonia which he had sold to provide funds for more urgent expenses.

King Valdemar may have considered the chance to plunder rural Gotland as a viable reason for a campaign there. There are numerous legends about King Valdemar and Gotland. Some are more credible than others. One tells about a Gotland exile, Nils Guldsmed ('Goldsmith'), whose daughter had been mocked in Visby because of her beautiful and expensive clothes. When things did not go well on the island for Nils Guldsmed and his daughter, the story goes that they instead sought out King Valdemar. Nils Guldsmed then told King Valdemar that the Gotlanders had more gold than they could carry, that their pigs dined from troughs made of silver, and that their wives span with distaffs made of gold.[4] In short, there was good plunder to be had on Gotland.

In another, far less credible legend, the seventeenth-century Visby historian Hans Nielssøn Strelow relates how King Valdemar in 1360 made a clandestine trip to Gotland in the guise of a merchant in order to spy out the land. The disguised King then, to gain more information, seduced a local maiden, the daughter of a wealthy farmer named Unghanse from Öja on southern Gotland (where there indeed was a prosperous farmstead named Unghanse). Having got what he came for and wanted, King Valdemar later abandoned the girl. The story, concocted centuries later, goes that the angry

---

2   The absence of even rudimentary data means that the population of fourteenth-century Stockholm is hard to estimate. Estimates for later centuries include, in the 1460s, at least 6,000; in the 1530s, some 6,000 to 7,000; and in the 1580s, some 8,000 to 9,000. Stig Hadenius (ed.), *Historia kring Stockholm* (Stockholm: Wahlström & Widstrand, 1967), 81, 141, 191.
3   Kalmar and Stockholm would remain unique defensive sites until Viborg formally was founded in 1403 on the eastern border with Russia. And Viborg most likely received its walls only in the 1470s.
4   Strelow, *Cronica Guthilandorum*, 173–174.

KING VALDEMAR'S STRATEGIC GOALS

Visby burghers ultimately threw the unfortunate maiden into a tower, bricked up the entrance, and left her to die.[5]

Yet another legend tells that King Valdemar was discovered during the escapade and had to flee from pursuers. At Vännes in Sundre in southern Gotland, he then found another girl, a goat shepherd, who allowed the handsome (and, we should remember, two-metre tall) stranger to hide under her skirts.[6]

Unfortunately, there is no evidence that King Valdemar ever visited Gotland before the invasion. Nor does it seem likely. Yet, the story of Nils Guldsmed suggests that King Valdemar had heard stories about the wealth on Gotland. It would indeed be surprising had he not, considering the central role the island played in the Baltic Eastern trade. And for sure, Detmar's near-contemporary Lübeck Chronicle remarks that King Valdemar told his men about Gotland pigs dining from troughs made of silver before they embarked on their ships.[7] While the legend of Nils Guldsmed cannot be corroborated by other information, it rings true in so far as disgruntled exiles tend to tell their new patron whatever he wants to hear in order to ingratiate themselves. King Valdemar may well have been tempted by the riches that many said existed on the island.

Until now, there have been two primary, and conflicting, hypotheses on King Valdemar's further strategy and the reason for his designs on Gotland.

The Swedish historian Gun Westholm has suggested that King Valdemar invaded Gotland on behalf of Mecklenburg. If so, the reasons were complex. Although Duke Albert of Mecklenburg already in 1336 married King Magnus's sister Euphemia, he was an accomplished opportunist who for decades attempted to gain power in both Sweden and Denmark. King Magnus gave major parts of Scania to Duke Albert as surety for loans. In the 1350s, the Duke also gained influence in Halland. In addition, he controlled the revenue from the Kopparberg ('Copper Mountain') mine and three districts of Uppland Province (Fjädrundaland) in central Sweden. Meanwhile, Duke Albert skilfully played both sides. He made King Valdemar in 1350 betroth his three-year-old daughter Princess Ingeborg to Duke Albert's 13-year-old son

The wealth and interconnectedness of Gotland within the northern world was considerable. This king from a chess set, dated to the fourteenth century, was made of walrus ivory from western Greenland. (Gotland Museum, Visby; photo: Raymond Hejdström)

---

5 To the delight of tour guides, the tower remains and is still known as the Maiden's Tower. Unfortunately, this particular tower was only built in the fifteenth century, many decades after the alleged event. Besides, the reference to a maiden (Swedish: *jungfru*) more likely relates to its size, being the smallest tower in the city wall. Alternatively, the name derives from the volume measure of the same name, which corresponds to 0.08 l, and indeed was the smallest such measure. Richard Steffen, 'Valdemarssägnerna och Jungfrutornets gåta', *Gotländskt Arkiv* 16 (1944), 49–70.

6 Alfred Theodor Snöbohm, *Gotlands land och folk: Hufvuddragen till en teckning af Gotland och dess öden från äldre till nuvarande tider* (Örebro: Abraham Bohlin, 1871), 147–148. Snöbohm based his book on folk tales collected no later than 1843 by Pehr Arvid Säve, who collected them in his manuscript *Gotländska Samlingar* 1 (No. 259, p. 99–100).

7 Karl Koppmann (ed.), *Die Chroniken der niedersächsischen Städte* 1: *Lübeck* (Leipzig: S. Hirzel, Die Chroniken der deutschen Städte 19, 1884), 529.

Henry as part of a complex deal in which King Valdemar also promised the Duke a dowry of 10,000 marks silver but only in exchange for Helsingborg Castle, which Duke Albert apparently promised to extract from King Magnus and give to King Valdemar. However, nothing came out of this scheme, and the betrothal was seemingly broken, together with the Mecklenburg-Danish alliance, in 1354, when Duke Albert again returned to the side of King Magnus.

We have seen that Duke Albert again switched side, this time to re-join King Valdemar when the Danes conquered the Scanias in 1360. As a reward, King Valdemar again acknowledged the betrothal of Princess Ingeborg with the Duke's son Henry (the couple finally married in 1362).

Westholm's hypothesis is that King Valdemar agreed to conquer Gotland on behalf of Duke Albert as part of the reinvented alliance and, possibly, in lieu of monetary payment of Princess Ingeborg's dowry. Or the deal was to hand over Gotland in exchange for Duke Albert not contesting King Valdemar's planned conquest of the Scanias, in which Mecklenburg had important interests. Either way, Hanseatic support was easily available from the important League cities of Lübeck, Rostock, and Wismar, which because of their geographical locations were under the formal protection of Duke Albert of Mecklenburg. Circumstantial evidence in the form of Duke Albert's and his family's apparent post-invasion belief that he had a claim on Gotland or at least Visby might support the hypothesis.[8] If so, King Valdemar would in effect have set out to conquer the island on a mercenary contract, of the kind he in 1353 had negotiated with King John of France.

King Valdemar had, indeed, occasionally intervened militarily in support of his allies. When Louis of Brandenburg found himself under threat from the new Emperor, Charles IV, and other German enemies, the Danish King had marched south, inspired both by the desire to support his ally and brother-in-law and by the profit this might entail, if it turned into a mercenary venture. Yet, this campaign is attested to by contemporary sources. No surviving documents conclusively prove the hypothesis that King Valdemar set out to conquer Gotland on behalf of Duke Albert. Besides, we have seen that the Hanseatic interest in the venture rather lay in gaining control over the lucrative Scanian herring trade than appeasing Mecklenburg in exchange for protection.

Instead, the Swedish historian Dick Harrison suggests that King Valdemar from the outset planned for an initial attack on Öland followed by an attack on Gotland. For the reasons already mentioned, Öland was the prioritised objective. But if the Öland venture succeeded, Gotland would be comparatively easy to conquer. The chance that King Magnus would send men to defend the island was slim. The only strong fortification on the island was the city wall around Visby. King Valdemar probably regarded the Visby burghers as amenable to a negotiated settlement. In short, King Valdemar sailed to Gotland because the opportunity arose, the island was easy to take, a conquest would bring some profit, and if he then could hold on to the

---

8   Westholm, *Visby 1361*, 192, 218–227.

island, this might complicate the strategic picture for King Magnus whenever he attempted to go on the offensive against Denmark.[9]

While Harrison's hypothesis to some extent can be described as following up on traditional views of the Gotland invasion, the circumstances that he postulated are correct. Unfortunately, we have no surviving documents to prove, or disprove, this hypothesis either. Moreover, the hypothesis that King Valdemar sailed to Gotland with his army for no other reason than because he could, remains unsatisfying. Every Scandinavian king knew that sending a fleet and army overseas was a risky undertaking. The weather conditions of the Baltic Sea were unpredictable, and it happened more than once that entire fleets were lost. The Danish possession of Gotland would not prevent King Magnus from sailing south along the coast towards Kalmar, and then onwards to the Scanias. Gotland's position was based on its central location in the Baltic Eastern trade. From a military perspective, the island had little strategic value.

Harrison's hypothesis becomes more credible if we add the strategic picture of King Valdemar's alliance with the Hanseatic League. His mercenaries were expensive. So were the Danish knights (for reasons which will be explained). King Valdemar's finances were hardly better than those of his adversary, King Magnus. Öland was at the time primarily an agricultural territory. Its conquest would be a good strategic move but would likely not result in the ready cash required to pay King Valdemar's men. In comparison, Gotland was a centre of trade. There, he could expect to find gold and silver, either as a contribution from the Visby burghers or, better, by looting the unfortified and isolated farmsteads of the island's wealthy merchant-farmers.

For these reasons, we suggest that King Valdemar's recent mercantile alliance with the Hanseatic League was the key to his interest in Gotland. King Valdemar was, as usual, short of cash. The island was indeed wealthy and ripe for plunder, assuming that the Hanseatic Visby burghers did not interfere. And they had no reason to, since King Valdemar's and Duke Eric of Saxe-Lauenburg's recent agreements with the League would assure that Visby stayed neutral, in case of a Danish attack on rural Gotland.

If King Valdemar assumed that the Visby burghers would stay neutral, he may also have assumed that the rural population of Gotland would not fight, or at least not be able to provide effective resistance. What could mere peasants possibly do to his professional soldiers? At the bottom of the feudal system, peasants commonly lacked both leadership, organisation, and proper weapons. King Valdemar had encountered peasants in Germany and Denmark, and they had seldom proven to be a major problem.

---

9   Dick Harrison, *Visby brandskattning* (Lund: Historiska Media, 2020), 98.

German mercenary infantryman

A professional soldier from the German Baltic coast, he wears armour that is almost as complete and just as functional as that of a knight. He wears a broad-brimmed kettle hat over a chainmail coif, and a sturdy coat-of-plates cuirass over a chainmail hauberk, which in turn is worn over a padded quilted *gambeson*. Armoured cuisses protect the thighs, with iron *poleyns* strapped over the knees, iron greaves over the lower legs, and iron *sabatons* which cover the top of the feet. In addition, the soldier wears gauntlets made of numerous small iron plates riveted to leather gloves. His primary weapon is a guisarme, which most likely was a crescent-shaped double socketed axe on a long shaft, used similarly to a halberd. In addition, this soldier carries a broadsword as sidearm. (Illustration by Giorgio Albertini)

Gotland rural militia soldier
This Gotland rural militia soldier wears a broad-brimmed kettle hat over a chainmail coif with the rectangular lower edge that was typical for Gotland, and plate shoulder armour pieces of a type found in the Visby mass graves. He wears a sturdy coat-of-plates cuirass over a chainmail hauberk, which in turn is worn over a padded quilted *gambeson*. This militia soldier is armed with a traditional pole-axe, a long dagger, and a knife, and carries a buckler slung over his back. (Illustration by Giorgio Albertini)

4

King Valdemar's Invasion Army

The Danish military establishment differed little from its counterparts on the Continent. Because of the mutual border and frequent personal and mercantile contacts, the Danish feudal system mostly kept pace with developments in Germany. We have seen that King Valdemar, although born a Dane, habitually spoke Low German. He also employed numerous low-ranking German nobles as commanders and advisors.

There is no known record of the size of King Valdemar's army. Based on the size of similar, better-known armies engaged in Baltic overseas expeditions, most historians estimate that King Valdemar brought about 50 ships (a combination of cogs and smaller vessels) with some 2,500 soldiers and between 150 and 200 horses.[1] However, in 1364 the Hanseatic League estimated one Danish fleet to carry 3,000 soldiers.[2] It accordingly seems likely that King Valdemar brought approximately 3,000 men. Although there is no way to prove this estimate, it is at least unlikely that he brought more. The number which reached Gotland was likely lower still, since we will see that King Valdemar first campaigned on Öland and left a garrison there.

The King was accompanied by several prominent Danish and German strongmen. Among them were the Danish knights, Valdemar Sappi, Claus Limbek, and Henning Podebusk and among the Germans, naturally Duke Eric of Saxe-Lauenburg whom we have already met. All had proven themselves in King Valdemar's service, and most had been loyal for years.

---

1   Nils V. Söderberg, 'Hur gick det till?', *Gotländskt Arkiv* 33 (1961), 21–26. Comparisons are commonly made with the army that the Hanseatic League raised to attack Helsingborg Castle in 1362 (62 ships with 2,730 soldiers), and with the army that the Teutonic Order sent to invade Gotland in 1398 (84 ships with 4,000 soldiers and 400 horses). Note that the League army was intended to operate together with Swedish and Norwegian allies, while the Teutonic Order army was on its own and expected a hard fight against veteran mercenaries from Mecklenburg and numerous combat-proven pirates, who then had made Gotland their base.

2   City Council of Stralsund to counterpart in Rostock, 6 May 1364. Lundby, *Valdemar Atterdag*, 157; Tägil, *Valdemar Atterdag*, 318. King Valdemar's vassals then had a fleet with 3,000 soldiers in Grønsund Strait between the islands of Falster and Møn, ready to attack Stralsund or Rostock.

KING VALDEMAR'S INVASION ARMY

Duke Eric of Saxe-Lauenburg, it will be recalled, was King Valdemar's cousin and life-long friend, and had even dubbed King Valdemar a knight on the pilgrimage to Jerusalem. He likely flew a standard with a golden (yellow) crowned eagle on a blue field.

Valdemar Eriksen Sappi (fl. 1351–1367) was the bastard brother of Queen Helvig and the aforementioned Duke Valdemar of Slesvig, and therefore King Valdemar's bastard brother-in-law. In 1359, Sappi led an army into North Frisia on behalf of King Valdemar to suppress the de facto peasant republic there.[3] Sappi, knighted in or around 1360, was an experienced soldier. He flew a standard with eight red water-lily leaves ('water-leaves') or, possibly, hearts on a golden (yellow) field, which same suggest indicated his kinship to the royal family.

Nicolaus or, more commonly, Claus Limbek (c. 1312 – c. 1372), had decades ago switched allegiance from Holstein to King Valdemar, supported the King in the 1343 Treaty of Varberg, and was one of the King's senior men on Jutland. His name was occasionally written Lembeck, after the name of the village which was the family's presumed origin. Since 1343 or 1344, Limbek also served as Lord High Justiciar (Latin: *dapifer*; Danish: *drost*[4]), effectively the King's deputy – except for the period 1351–1353 when he instead joined a Jutland noble revolt against the King. Limbek also joined the King's enemies in the revolt of 1357–1360. While he was not averse to switching allegiance again, at this point in time, King Valdemar was his first choice. King Valdemar knew that Limbek's loyalty was conditional. Stories tell of the former, late in life, regretting that he did not kill his vassal when he could, while other stories say that the latter only mumbled his oath of allegiance to the King, changing some words so that it was invalid. Claus Limbek flew a standard with two blue slanted beams on a silver (white) field. The fact that Limbek joined the campaign to conquer Öland and Gotland is interesting; at least later in the century the Lord High Justiciar was the one who ruled the country when the King was abroad. Possibly, King Valdemar did not trust Limbek enough to leave him behind.[5]

Henning Podebusk (1310–1388), a knight of a noble family of Slavic strongmen related to the princes of the island of Rügen, was one of King

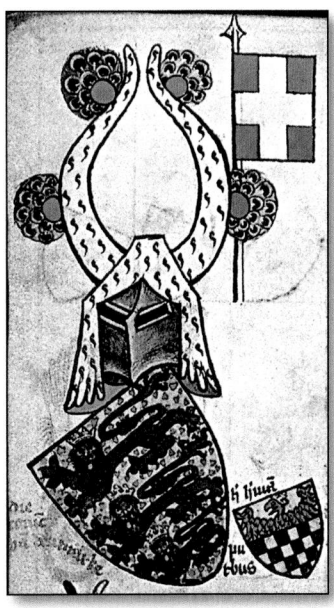

The Danish royal coat of arms, which derives from King Valdemar's time, and the already traditional Danish flag, a white cross on a red field.

---

3   The coast and islands of North Frisia technically formed part of the Duchy of Slesvig (also known as Southern Jutland). In reality, North Frisia functioned as a semi-autonomous peasant republic which regularly found itself invaded by Danish armies in search of taxes and other tangible signs of loyalty to the Crown. Weak kings failed to enforce loyalty, but King Valdemar repeatedly had his men move in to suppress the North Frisians, in 1344, 1354, and 1359. North Frisia was not the only semi-autonomous peasant republic in the region. Just to the south was Dithmarschen, an area of marshlands inhabited by semi-autonomous peasants who stubbornly guarded their independence against all comers, which by this time often meant the counts of Holstein-Rendsburg.

4   The Latin term *dapifer* originally signified the individual who brought the meat to the table at a feast.

5   In 1368, Limbek for the third time joined an uprising against the King, which meant that he joined every revolt against King Valdemar's rule (1351–1353, 1357–1360, 1368–1372). Limbek died at an unknown time between 6 July 1368 and 24 January 1373. Claus Limbek and his formidable wife Ide Hartvigsdatter Krummedige could be savage to their unfortunate peasants. Later legends inform us that on dark nights, their ghosts can be seen hunting across the sky above their stronghold Tørning Castle, near Haderslev, with their pack of huge, black dogs.

Valdemar's most trusted commanders, and would ultimately be appointed Lord High Justiciar. Podebusk flew a standard with a black eagle on a golden (yellow) field.

It has been suggested that the aforementioned young Duke Henry of Mecklenburg participated in the campaign.[6] No contemporary source mentions Duke Henry, who as noted in time would make a name for himself as Henry the Hangman. Yet, we have seen that he since long was betrothed to King Valdemar's daughter, Princess Ingeborg. Moreover, we have seen that Henry's father, Duke Albert of Mecklenburg, again had switched to King Valdemar's side in 1360. It would accordingly not be surprising to find Duke Henry among King Valdemar's German allies, nobles, and knights. Duke Henry flew a standard with the crowned black bull's head of Mecklenburg on a golden (yellow) field.

We might also have expected the Marshal, Anders Frost (of the family later known as Bildt), to have been present, since he by tradition led the knightly cavalry. However, Frost is not mentioned in any source. This suggests that only few mounted knights joined the expedition.

Other nobles in the army included one or both Roorda brothers from Frisia, over which King Valdemar was suzerain. We do not know if Bavo or Schelto Roorda was in a position of command.

King Valdemar relied significantly on foreign, primarily Holstein, nobles. Out of 70 men whom King Valdemar appointed commandants of royal castles, 23 were of non-Danish, mostly German, origin.[7] Some of them surely joined King Valdemar's army with their men for the Öland and Gotland campaign. Most were of low rank and had little or no land. We do not know their names, but one likely participant was Fikke (Vicko) Moltke, of a minor noble family ultimately from Mecklenburg which had moved to Denmark in the early fourteenth century. With little property of their own, the Moltkes relied on service with the King. In 1362, King Valdemar appointed Fikke Moltke commandant of the important Vordingborg Castle. He is unlikely to have done so, had not Moltke already distinguished himself in royal service. The appointment was a successful one, and henceforth, Moltke commanded a series of royal castles and finally became a member of the Council of the Realm.

It has been estimated that a total of between 300 and 320 knights lived in Denmark between 1340 and 1375. Of these, between 80 and 100 were of foreign, mostly German origin, including 65 knights who served the Danish King on active duty. This means that from one quarter to one third of the knights in Denmark at the time were of German origin. All did not serve at the same time. Some had already lived in Denmark for two or three generations, so it can be argued that they no longer were Germans. Others

---

6   Westholm, *Visby 1361*, 166.
7   Niels Bracke, *Die Regierung Waldemars IV: Eine Untersuchung zum Wandel von Herrschaftsstrukturen im spätmittelalterlichen Dänemark* (Frankfurt am Main: Peter Lang, Kieler Werkstücke, Reihe A: Beiträge zur schleswig-holsteinischen und skandinavischen Geschichte 21, 1999), 109.

were first-generation immigrants, including the ultimately most influential of them all, Henning Podebusk from Rügen.

Moreover, at least 20 of the 65 foreign knights who served King Valdemar were at some point referred to as formal councillors of the king. Yet, the informal number was higher, if we take into account those who merely appeared as signatories of the King. The Germans were roughly equal in number to the native Danish members of the Council of the Realm.[8]

There must have been Danish nobles in King Valdemar's army, too, because we know that Danish soldiers fought on Gotland (more on which below). The Danish army already included a significant number of knights armed in the modern manner. There was, so far, little difference in armament and training between those men who carried the title knight (Latin: *miles*) and those who had not yet been elevated to this rank and henceforth had the title squire (Latin: *armiger*). King Valdemar was interested in chivalric customs and frequently held knightly tournaments on Zealand as a means of keeping his men fit for combat.[9] He probably also participated himself. In war, he would dub some of his men knights before every battle would commence so as to infuse a high level of confidence within his units.

While we can assume that some knightly cavalry accompanied King Valdemar, their number was probably limited, in light of the difficulties in transporting horses overseas. As noted, the apparent absence of the Marshal suggests the same conclusion. The King himself and his closest retainers would certainly have fought on horseback. So would the other senior nobles in his entourage. However, the majority of King Valdemar's invasion army accordingly fought on foot.

Knights in the kind of armour commonly used by German and Danish knights, with coat-of-plates cuirasses over long-sleeved chainmail hauberks for added protection. Some knights wear closed helmets of the so-called great helm type, others open bascinets. Fresco dated to c. 1370. St. Mauritius's Church, Söll, Austria. (Author's collection)

---

8   Juha Heinänen, 'On German Knights in Denmark during the Reign of Valdemar Atterdag 1340–1375', *Ennen ja nyt* 4, 2004 (http://www.ennenjanyt.net/4-04/heinanen.pdf).
9   Bracke, *Die Regierung Waldemars IV*, 115.

FALL OF THE MERCHANT-FARMER REPUBLIC

The knight Heinrich von Platen, as depicted in a stained-glass window at Døllefjelde Church, Lolland, to which he perhaps contributed. Heinrich von Platen and his family were likely of Brandenburgian origin. Dated to the period 1350–1400, the painting shows a Danish knight who wears a great helm with a crest consisting of leaves arranged as a panache spreading outwards. The torso is protected by what looks like lamellar armour with shoulder plates but may be the artist's rendition of a coat-of-plates cuirass over a chainmail cuirass. The knight wears a steel gauntlet and carries a sword typical of the time. Thighs and legs are protected by splinted armour. The flat-top shield displays his coat of arms: two uprooted trees on a golden field. (National Museum, Copenhagen)

The arms and armour of a well-heeled Danish knight, 1363. The bascinet comes with a turnbuckle above the forehead to secure a visor. But he also carries a traditional great helm with a horned crest of the type that remained popular in Germany. The knight wears a tight, sleeveless surcoat of very modern style, under which an unseen plate cuirass provides added protection. Plate cuirasses were just becoming common in Germany but had not yet made an impact in Scandinavia. Three iron chains from the cuirass secure his broadsword, ballock dagger, and the great helm or shield. (Effigy of King Valdemar's son Christopher, from his tomb, Roskilde Cathedral)

KING VALDEMAR'S INVASION ARMY

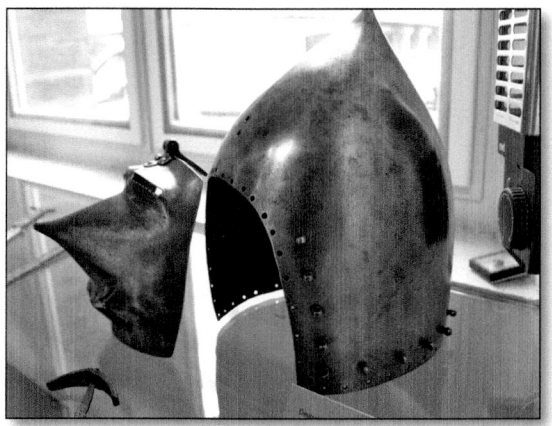

Visored bascinet (Hundsgugel), fourteenth century. The small, pierced rivets that extend out from the surface around the lower edge of the helmet, known as vervelles, were used to attach an aventail. A leather cord was strung through the vervelles to secure the leather edge of the aventail. (Cologne Municipal Museum; photo: Andreas Franzkowiak)

Front and rear view of knight carved on the Levitic pew in Verden Cathedral, dated to the period 1360–1370. The two sides of the coat-of-plates cuirass were buckled together on the back, which also attached the solid, epaulette-type shoulder pieces, several of which were found in the Visby mass graves. Note also, the gauntlets of numerous small plates (attached to the outer fabric or leather), the splinted arm armour with elbow plates, and the great helm that was only worn when the situation so warranted. (Author's collection)

Armoured gauntlet found in a Visby mass grave, of the same type as depicted in the Levitic pew in Verden Cathedral. (History Museum, Stockholm; photo: Katarina Nimmervoll)

Soldiers

In the early years, King Valdemar mostly had no choice but to enlist German mercenaries, since Danish soldiers simply were unavailable to him. However, over the years he increasingly often found himself forced to forgo expensive but reliable German mercenaries in favour of Danish feudal units. The persistent lack of funds meant that King Valdemar had to find ways to mobilise native forces. The Danish Crown had two types of native units at its disposal. First, the Danish nobility and feudal units. Second, the men under the command of castle commandants, dependent on and accordingly, loyal to King Valdemar. The King could order such men to join him on foreign military adventures, such as the 1349–1350 campaign in Germany and the invasions of Öland and Gotland. The commandants would then bring some of the castle garrison as a field force.

While we do not know how King Valdemar raised men specifically for the campaign against Öland and Gotland, it was probably in a similar manner to when he in January 1356 raised an army for a march into Jutland. The King then ordered all his retainers in Zealand to mobilise under Bo Falk and meet him in Ribe on 12 January. He also ordered each of his bailiffs to send him one crossbowman to assemble in Kolding on 2 February.[10]

For domestic military campaigns, King Valdemar could also call up burgher militia and peasant levies. Much debate has concerned the extent to which King Valdemar could levy peasants. The old system (Danish: *leding*) of calling up free peasants with ships had gradually ceased to function in Denmark. However, the *leding* institution still existed, and the King retained the right to call up the peasant levy, in particular for defensive purposes. On one occasion in 1355, the Zealand Chronicle reports that King Valdemar

---

10 Lundbye, *Valdemar Atterdag*, 86.

ordered both the nobility and peasant levies armed with crossbows (*militares quam rustici cum balistis*) to follow him on a campaign to the island of Langeland.[11] In 1358, the King ordered the nobility, burghers, and peasants of Zealand to muster in the town Slagelse. Then, King Valdemar and the newly mobilised men crossed the sea to Nyborg Castle, held by a commandant loyal to him on the island of Fyn, and there simply incorporated its garrison in the royal field army. Instead, he inserted burgher militia and peasant crossbowmen (Latin: *sagittarios*, 'shooters') from Zealand as a replacement garrison.[12] Since almost every year within King Valdemar's reign saw some military action, we can assume that the system of levying peasants remained in operation.

The peasants, when called up for *leding* duty, had to muster men who brought their own weapons. They would also bring crossbows that were normally stored in and possibly belonged to, the churches.

Nonetheless, many modern historians assume that most of King Valdemar's soldiers were mercenaries enlisted in Germany. Certainly, any men brought by Duke Eric would have been German professionals. As for the rest, we should probably instead envisage a combination of German mercenaries and Danish soldiers under the command of nobles and castle commandants. While King Valdemar technically could call up the Danish nobility, each of whom was supposed to join the campaign with his personal fighting men, they under most circumstances did not serve for free. For extended campaigns, and in particular for service abroad, the King was expected to remunerate each knight for his service, and that of the fighting men he brought in his retinue. At around this time, a knight expected 20 marks silver for six months of service. A squire expected 15 marks silver for the same period. While these rates were lower than the cost of enlisting mercenary cavalry (which cost one mark per week), the Crown might easily face additional expenses when relying on its knights and squires. If the knight lost his warhorse in battle, the King was expected to remunerate him for the cost of a replacement. Likewise, if the knight ended up in captivity with the enemy, the King was expected to pay his ransom.[13] The cost for either might be substantial. A trained warhorse stallion cost 140 marks at the time. In comparison, the average riding horse cost 17 marks.[14]

Arms and Armour

Danish knights wore full armour of the up-to-date style, then produced in Germany. This typically meant a coat-of-plates cuirass worn over a long-sleeved chainmail hauberk for added protection.

---

11 Zealand Chronicle, in Jørgensen, *Annales Danici Medii Ævi*, 180; Bracke, *Die Regierung Waldemars IV*, 115.
12 Zealand Chronicle, in Jørgensen, *Annales Danici Medii Ævi*, 183; Bracke, *Die Regierung Waldemars IV*, 113–114.
13 Lundbye, *Valdemar Atterdag*, 16.
14 Lars O. Lagerqvist and Ernst Nathorst-Böös, *Vad kostade det? Priser och löner från medeltid till våra dagar* Stockholm: LT, 4th edn 1997), 46.

Coat-of-plates armour was constructed by riveting iron plates to the inside of a waist-length sleeveless covering or coat made of leather or fabric. The iron plates were usually attached directly to the inside of the covering, but outside riveting occurred too, in particular on the shoulders, which formed the transition to the epaulette-style shoulder pieces. In its fundamentals, coat-of-plates corresponds to the brigandine armour brought to Europe by Mongol invasion armies.

The fashion-conscious knight would wear a tight, sleeveless surcoat. If he had the means, he would wear a modern plate cuirass for added protection under the surcoat. Plate cuirasses were just becoming common in Germany but had not yet made an impact in Scandinavia. Besides better protection, the plate cuirass usually included three iron chains to which the knight could secure his broadsword, dagger, and whatever additional item he wished to keep handy, most likely the great helm or shield.

The armour included iron rerebraces that covered the outsides of the upper arms, to which they are secured by buckled straps. The lower arms were protected by hinged and buckled iron vambraces. Some, but by no means all, knights wore *couters* to provide additional protection to the elbows, which were becoming increasingly common, but not yet universal, in Germany. The knight would also wear iron gauntlets made of numerous small iron plates.

A knight would wear armoured *cuisses* (Old French for 'thighs') to protect the thighs, usually with iron *poleyns* covering the knees and splinted armour greaves consisting of strips of metal attached to a fabric or leather backing to protect the lower legs. He would typically protect his feet with *sabatons* made from small overlapping iron plates. In addition, legs and feet were protected by chainmail chausses (leggings) under greaves and *sabatons*.

Some knights still wore traditional closed helmets of the so-called great helm type. Horned crests remained popular in Germany. Although mostly used for tournament purposes, high-ranking individuals may have used them even on the battlefield. Other knights instead preferred the open bascinet. A bascinet usually had a turnbuckle above the forehead to secure a visor of the up-to-date dog-faced or 'houndskull' (*Hundsgugel*) type. An attached chainmail aventail provided additional protection for the face and neck.

Most knights carried shields of the flat-top type which was intended to be used more actively than the older, larger types of shields.

Knights carried lances, with broadswords or falchions as primary sidearm. The falchion was a heavy straight sword or cleaver with a single cutting edge, which easily cut through fabric or chainmail armour. Some Germans carried war hammers. The war hammer is generally believed to have become common in Scandinavia only from the fifteenth century onwards. While no archaeological remains of war hammers have been found in archaeological contexts related to the Danish invasion on Gotland, the wounds inflicted on some skulls in the Visby mass graves suggest that some men in King Valdemar's invasion army possibly used them.

Senior Danes may have carried a knobbed mace as a sign of command. Several such mace heads, habitually dated to the period from the twelfth to the fifteenth centuries but some quite possibly older, have been found in Danish contexts. The mace head, of cast copper alloy (bronze) and around 8 cm in length, is typically shaped like a flattened ball covered with rows of projecting knobs and sharp points. While similar Eastern maces existed already in ancient times, the type which from the ninth century onwards disseminated throughout eastern, central, and northern Europe is believed to have originated in Kievan Rus' metal foundries and was based on local adaptations of Khazar mace types. This type of mace was particularly popular in the Russian lands in the twelfth and thirteenth centuries, from which the type disseminated into Scandinavia.[15] Specimen have been found as far afield as in the British Isles.

The infantry, too, wore chainmail and coat-of-plates armour. Kettle hats were popular, but bascinets were in use among infantrymen, too. Most other items of armour worn by knights had by this time become commonplace among professional soldiers as well.

Infantrymen usually carried crossbows or polearms. Either category of soldier would have carried a sword as sidearm. Most north German crossbows had bow staves of composite construction. Archaeological finds from a cog sunken at Kalmar include crossbow bolts (also known as quarrels, from Old French) with fletching placed at an angle. This was a type of bolt known as vireton (also from Old French). The special fletching made the bolt spin in flight to achieve a high degree of accuracy. The crossbowman would generally span his crossbow with the belt hook and stirrup method.

However, a find at Mästerby on Gotland has been tentatively identified as part of a crossbow windlass or possibly a cranequin, the latter a tool which because of its slow and complicated spanning procedure was more suitable for hunting than warfare.[16] If correctly identified, this suggests that not all soldiers who fought on Gotland relied on the belt hook and stirrup to span the crossbow.

An infantryman with polearm probably carried either an early halberd of the German or Swiss type, or a guisarme, which is believed to have been a crescent-shaped double socketed axe on a long shaft.

Most men would also carry a dagger. Nobles and knights often carried a roundel dagger, so named after the distinctive round, disc-shaped guard and pommel. Men of all social groups, including King Valdemar, carried a ballock dagger, so named after the distinctive shape of its guard, with two rounded lobes. Particularly pugnacious men of all social groups might instead carry the distinctive baselard dagger, which may have been Swiss in origin and named after the city of Basel. It was characterised by the hilt which is best described as H- or I-shaped.

---

15 Type 3 in Kirpichnikov's typology. Anatoliy Nikolayevich Kirpichnikov, *Drevnerusskoye oruzhiye* 2: *Kop'ya, sulitsy, boyevyye topory, bulavy, kisteny IX-XIII vv.* (Moscow: Nauka, 1966), 47–57, pl. 26–29.

16 Maria Lingström, *Mästerby 1361: 2011 års resultat* (Mästerby: Forskningsgruppen Mästerby 1361, 2012), 6.

FALL OF THE MERCHANT-FARMER REPUBLIC

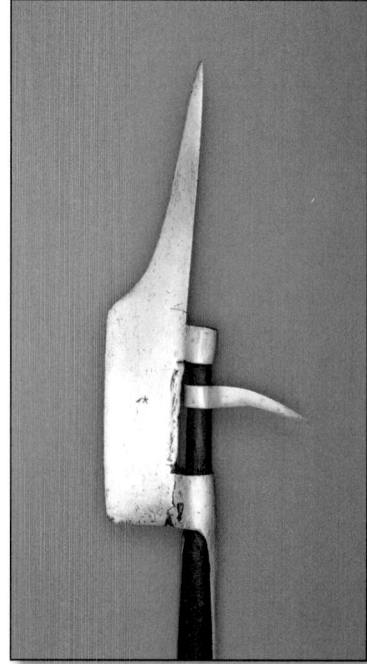
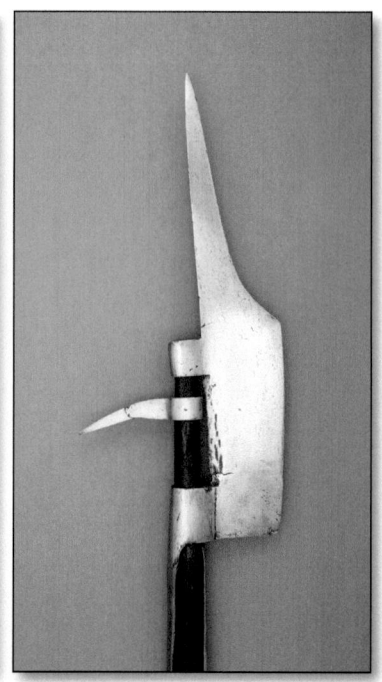

Halberd from Fribourg, dated to the period 1375–1400. This was likely the type also used by German mercenaries and burgher militias in northern Germany and Denmark. Total length 213.9 cm), length of head 45 cm, width 20.6 cm, weight 2.4 kg. (Metropolitan Museum of Art, Object No. 14.25.35)

The guisarme is believed to have been a crescent-shaped double socketed axe on a long shaft, used similarly to a halberd. (As depicted in Gawain and the Green Knight, an illuminated manuscript from the late fourteenth century)

Mace found in Anderslöv, Scania. (Photo: author)

KING VALDEMAR'S INVASION ARMY

Baselard dagger. This type of dagger, very popular in the fourteenth century, may have been Swiss in origin and named after the city of Basel. Commonly known as basler, the type was characterised by the H-shaped (alternatively known as I-shaped) hilt. Commonly carried by pugnacious men of all social groups, this baselard is dated to the fifteenth century but is possibly older. Total length 40 cm, blade length 28.5 cm. (Art Institute of Chicago; Object No. 1982.3473)

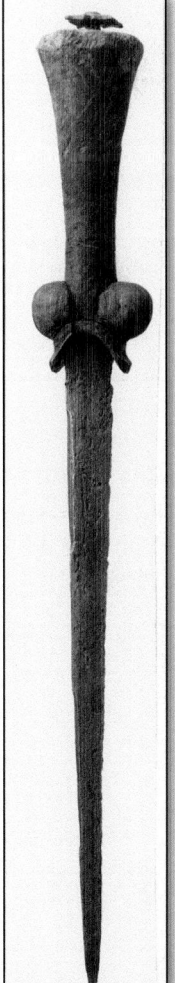 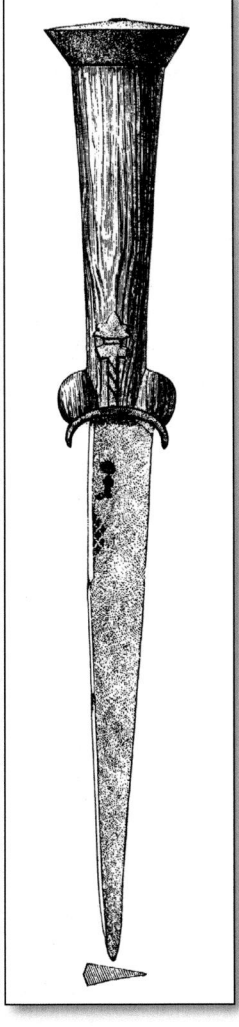 

Ballock daggers of the style common in the fourteenth century. Named after the distinctive shape of its guard, with two rounded lobes. Commonly carried by men of all social groups, including King Valdemar, which we have seen in the contemporary fresco in St. Peter's Church, Næstved. The ballock dagger remained popular throughout the sixteenth century and over time adopted an increasingly suggestive hilt shape. The single-edged blade was commonly triangular for additional strength. A preserved ballock dagger from Scania has a total length 33.3 cm and a blade length of 22.2 cm. (A: Glimmingehus, Scania; photo: Anna-Lisa Myrsten; B: Hans Hildebrand, after an original from Hälsingland Province, Sweden; C: Abbey Museum Ten Duinen, Koksijde; photo: Lokilech)

Roundel dagger. Named after the distinctive round, disc-shaped guard and pommel, the roundel dagger was primarily carried by the gentry and nobility. Length was commonly around 35 cm. This fourteenth-century roundel dagger has a total length of 33 cm and a blade length of 24 cm. Blade width is 1.5 cm, blade thickness 1 cm, and weight 198.4 g. (Metropolitan Museum of Art, Object No. 26.145.31)

Artillery and Firearms

King Valdemar had access to siege engines (*machinas*) of various types. Non-gunpowder artillery was commonplace in Denmark. In 1359, King Valdemar employed breaching machinery such as rams (*arietes*) when he laid siege to the castles of Sønderborg and Randers.[17] Unfortunately, there is no record of which siege engines, if any, he brought on the Gotland campaign.

It seems certain, however, that King Valdemar's army brought one or more hand-carried firearms. This was unsurprising since firearms in the previous three decades had become relatively common in Continental warfare. Gunpowder was made from charcoal, sulphur, and saltpetre. Charcoal was commonplace and sulphur was easily imported from Iceland, so it was only saltpetre which had to be procured by different means. Master gunners probably made their own gunpowder. Quantities may have been small and quality occasionally inexact, but gunpowder was certainly available.

While we do not know which types of guns King Valdemar employed in his army, nor how many, archaeological excavations tell us something of the projectiles which they fired, and the damage they caused. Over a period of several years, Maria Lingström excavated the battlefield at Mästerby. So far, 30 small essentially quadrangular projectiles of mostly lead or iron have been found during the battlefield excavation at Mästerby. Most were from 6 to 12 mm in size, each with a weight of from 1 to 5 g. All were found together with crossbow bolts, which suggests that the two types of weapons were discharged simultaneously against the same targets.[18] It was impossible to estimate the number of firearms, whether several or only one. Similar

---

17 Zealand Chronicle, in Jørgensen, *Annales Danici Medii Ævi*, 187; Jonas Hedberg (ed.), *Kungl. Artilleriet: Medeltid och äldre vasatid* (Stockholm: Militärhistoriska Förlaget, 1975), 23.
18 Maria Lingström, *Mästerby 1361: 2011 års resultat* (Mästerby: Forskningsgruppen Mästerby 1361, 2012), 6; Maria Lingström, *Mästerby, 1361: Battlefield Archaeological Perspectives on the Danish Invasion of Gotland* (Uppsala: Uppsala University, Department of Archaeology, Ancient History and Conservation, dissertation, Aun 56, 2025), 76–80.

firearms and projectiles were probably used also at Visby, but then went unnoticed since early twentieth-century archaeologists did not expect to find any firearm projectiles.

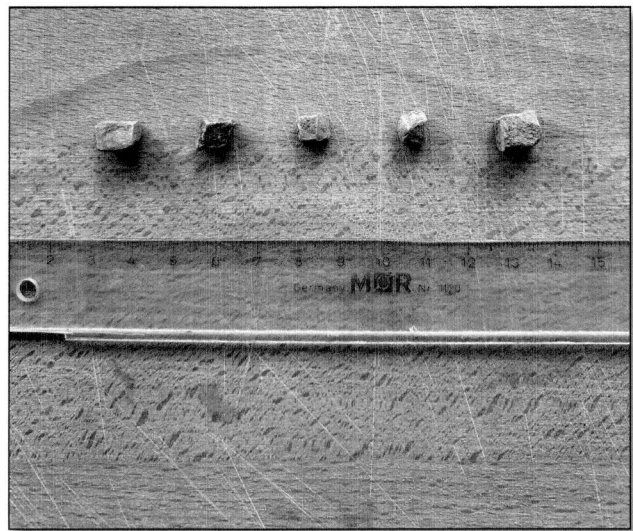

Projectiles of lead and iron excavated at Mästerby. (Photo: Maria Lingström)

Bengt Thordeman, who published the finds from the Visby mass graves, knew that some of the earliest known European handguns had been found in Sweden and found it conceivable that firearms were used in the campaign. However, his chief osteologist Bo E. Ingelmark could not confirm any skeletal damages that could be definitely attributed to bullet wounds. As a result, Thordeman concluded that firearms either were not brought to Gotland, or did not play any significant role in the campaign.[19] Unfortunately, Ingelmark may have been biased in his view that gunpowder weapons were not used. Already Edward Clason, the first osteologist who investigated the Visby mass graves, wondered about the 18 cranial holes which shared the common feature that their inner size, as regards the inner cortical bone, was larger than the outer size, which made them look similar to holes caused by rifle bullets.[20]

The conclusion then seems to be that King Valdemar's soldiers brought one or more handguns. These were probably of the first and apparently earliest type which consisted of a short barrel cast in bronze, with a short conoidal socket for attachment to a much longer wooden stock, or pole, in the manner of a spearhead. While the inside of the barrel was smoothbore, the exterior of the barrel might be round, hexagonal, or octagonal, sometimes with a reinforced muzzle. The touchhole was generally simple, merely a cup-shaped hole with a vent leading down to the charge.

---

19 Bengt Thordeman, *Invasion på Gotland 1361: Dikt och verklighet* (Stockholm: Hugo Geber, 1944), 144.
20 Edward Clason, 'Om i Korsbetningsgraven vid Visby funna skelett', *Kungl. Vitterhets Historie och Antikvitets Akademiens Handlingar* 28: 3 (1925), 257–297, on 296.

Cavalry handguns were cast in one piece. A cavalry handgun generally had an internal calibre of from approximately 6 to 10 mm but was typically loaded with many small projectiles instead of a single, larger one. In 1364, the Commune of Perugia ordered 500 guns of this type, which is illustrated in a drawing attached to the purchase order. Known as a *bombarda*, these guns were made of cast bronze or copper with a length of from 12 to 20 cm and primarily used by cavalry. Another common designation for this kind of handgun was *sclopum* or *sclopetum*, meaning 'bang' or 'banger', or the similar *tonitrum* ('thunder'). The High German name was *Donnerbüchse* ('thunder gun').

Infantry carried similar but apparently slightly heavier handguns. Hand-carried firearms for infantry use were early on fitted with a hook-like projection or lug under the belly which was used for steadying the gun against a battlement or similar structure when firing. Such a weapon accordingly became known as a 'hook gun' or, in northern Europe, simply a 'hook' (Swedish: *hake*, from German: *Hakenbüchse*; Dutch: *haakbus*; Swedish: *hakebössa*, with the final addition coming from Low German *bussa*, which itself derived from Latin *buxa* or *pyxis*, 'box'). In French-speaking regions, this term was confused with the Latin word for bow (*arcus*) and ultimately developed into harquebus and arquebus, respectively. Like the cavalry handgun, the infantry variant was cast in one piece, with a short conoidal socket for attachment to a wooden stock. These guns generally had a length of around 20 cm or more, at times up to 32 cm. Internal calibre was larger, too, approximately 20 mm or more.

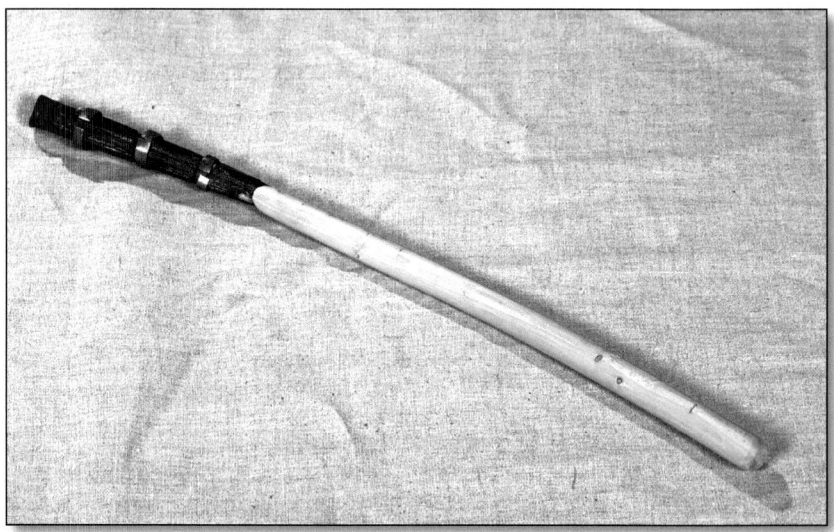

A mid-fourteenth century handgun of bronze, found in Stockholm. The metal section, 12.8 cm in length, is inserted into a wooden stock. The internal calibre is approximately 6–10 mm. The handguns which the Commune of Perugia ordered in 1364 were of similar type. Most of the stock and all copper reinforcements in the photograph are reconstructions. (Medieval Museum, Stockholm)

KING VALDEMAR'S INVASION ARMY

A Swedish late fourteenth-century hand-carried infantry handgun of bronze with a hook-like projection for steadying. Known as the Mörkö gun, this firearm has a length of 19.8 cm (excluding stock), and a weight of 947 g. It bears the effigy of a single bearded man and the inscription MARIA, presumably a religious invocation. The gun is cast in one piece, with a short conoidal socket for attachment to a wooden stock. Its internal calibre is 21 mm. (History Museum, Stockholm; photo: Sven Rosborn)

Early handguns could not be aimed in the modern manner since the sparks from the touchhole might burn the gunner's eyes. Those gunners (probably all) who wore some kind of rigid breastplate almost certainly supported the gun butt against the chest. We do not really know how the cavalry and infantry gunners actually fired their weapons. Possibly, the slow match had already come into use. Or, possibly, a second man ignited the gun. Firing procedures would have been simpler with regard to cannons, which were placed in fixed locations. Then a hot iron could be employed to ignite the gunpowder. However, the use of a hot iron seems impracticable for use on the battlefield.

We do not know if King Valdemar also brought cannons on his expedition. If he did, they did not play any decisive role in the campaign. He would certainly not have fielded them in the fens at Mästerby, where his handgunners clearly operated with some effect. Yet, King Valdemar may have found it prudent to bring artillery as a means to intimidate Visby, which we will see was almost certainly defended by cannons. Besides, his fleet included several cogs, some of which likely carried cannons of some type.

If the Danes brought cannons, they were probably similar to the already-described handguns, but larger. The previous, but already obsolete, generation of cannon had been vase shaped. One surviving bronze example from Loshult, Sweden, confirms that the type was used in Scandinavia. Contemporary illustrations show that this kind of cannon, at times fixed to a table, at least initially was employed to fire large arrows. However, by the 1360s, the new kind of cannon had probably already been introduced, even though we have no archaeological finds in Scandinavia which confirms this. The new type was either cast of bronze or built of iron bars soldered lengthwise into a tube, with iron rings pushed around the barrel for reinforcement. The iron rings tightened into place as they cooled. Barrel length was probably around 30 to 60 cm. The cannon was probably emplaced on the ground, supported by soil or logs, and aimed at stationary, or almost stationary, targets. Projectiles were either small and irregular in shape, like those employed in handguns, or larger and made of iron or lead. The former was employed against formations of soldiers, and the latter against fortifications. However, the effect on stone walls was probably insignificant, until larger cannons were developed which fired cannon balls of stone. Since the earliest known record of a bombard firing cannon balls of stone derive from Italy and date to 1371, it is unlikely that King Valdemar brought such weapons to Gotland.[21]

The Fleet

As noted, the old *leding* system of calling up free peasants with ships had gradually ceased to exist in Denmark and was, with regard to ships, indeed formally abolished by King Eric Menved in 1304. Henceforth, a new organisation was established according to which peasants were divided into groups, each consisting of men who collectively had an income of 10,000 marks. Each group was ordered to supply, equip, and man a cog of 100 tons (50 *leste*). The peasants had to provide supplies for a campaign season of 16 weeks. Although the new organisation mostly remained on paper, and probably never was used, it provided the basis for how to raise a royal fleet. When King Valdemar needed ships, he ordered the towns to provide them. In the past, the towns could instead have chosen to pay a special tax. Now, they must provide ships and presumably also man them.

Reconstruction of a byrding, a traditional clinker-built small merchant vessel excavated in Kalmar ('Kalmar 1'). Introduced in the thirteenth century as an innovation that could take more cargo than earlier vessels, this was a relatively short, broad, clinker-built boat that could take a crew of from 12 to 30 men. Length: 11–12 m. (Photo: Boatbuilder)

---

21   Hedberg, *Kungl. Artilleriet: Medeltid och äldre vasatid*, 33.

KING VALDEMAR'S INVASION ARMY

The Danish fleet had employed cogs since the old *leding* fleet was reorganised in 1304. By the time of King Valdemar's campaign, cogs had become significantly larger, often exceeding 120 tons (60 *leste*).

The King also ordered his *lensmænd* to provide ships as well as men. The *lensmænd* were a small group of royal officials each responsible for a local administrative area known as a *len* ('domain, fief'). The position was not hereditary, so the official depended on the King. Such a man, known as a *lensmand* (pl. *lensmænd*), combined military and civilian functions.

For the Scanian campaign in 1360, King Valdemar ordered not only his towns but also the monasteries to provide ships and armed men.[22] Unfortunately, no records on the number and size of ships have survived.

Depiction of a large byrding, dated to the thirteenth century. Fide Church, Gotland. (Author's collection)

Reconstruction of a cog excavated in Kalmar ('Kalmar 2'), dated to the mid-fourteenth century. The cog, a strongly built ship with flat, clinker-built bottom and caravel-built sides, dominated Baltic trade from the early thirteenth century onwards. Original length c. 20 m, and beam c. 6 m. (Maritime Museum, Stockholm; photo: Anneli Karlsson)

---

22   Lundbye, *Valdemar Atterdag*, 112.

FALL OF THE MERCHANT-FARMER REPUBLIC

Reconstruction of a cog dated to 1380, found in Bremen and presently displayed at the German Maritime Museum in Bremerhaven. Length 23.27 m, beam 7.62 m, and estimated tonnage 90 to 130 tons. (Photo: Wolfgang Fricke)

Traditional clinker-built warships remained in common use in Scandinavian waters. Such a ship is portrayed in a fresco in Skamstrup Church, Denmark, dated to the period 1380–1400. The painting depicts the legend of St. Olaf racing against his brother Harald for the Norwegian Crown. The heathen Harald sails the traditional ship, while St. Olaf (not illustrated here) sails a modern cog. (Photo: author)

5

The Gotland Rural Militia

Whatever King Valdemar and his men may have thought, the rural merchant-farmers of Gotland were not feudal peasants of the type which they had encountered in Germany and suppressed in Jutland. Far from it. The Gotland merchant-farmers valued their ancient freedoms (primarily, their traditional low level of taxation), were comfortably well-off with an ample supply of weapons in their farmsteads, and repeatedly showed that they were willing to fight anybody who wanted to subject them to taxation or otherwise reduce their economic well-being. They fought against the Visby burghers in 1288, against Sweden's King Birger Magnusson and his demand for additional taxes in 1313, and did not hesitate to fight King Valdemar in 1361.

By tradition, the Gotland Republic was divided into three territorial units, known as 'Thirds' (*treding*, pl. *tredingar*; Old Norse: *Þriþiung*; Late Latin: *Terciana*).[1] Each was for judicial purposes centred around a Thing. The Thirds were prosaically named, respectively, the Northern, Middle, and Southern Third (*Norder treding, Middel treding, Suder treding*). The Thirds were for practical purposes divided into six smaller units, known as 'Sixths' (*setting*, pl. *settingar*), each governed through a Sixth Assembly, a Setting Thing. Each Sixth was named after the location of its primary Thing. The total number of Things was about 20, each of which governed several parishes.[2] Gotland had about 96 parishes; the number changed from time to time (Table 2).

---

1 The related English term was *riding*, an administrative third part of a county from Old English *Þriðing*, which itself was a loanword from Old Norse.
2 At least in 1412, when the national lawspeaker, the three Third pastors, and 20 Thing lawspeakers confirmed an agreement with King Eric of Pomerania (more on whom below).

Northern Third
Bro Sixth – four Things – 12 parishes
Rute Sixth – three Things – 16 parishes
Middle Third
Hejde Sixth – three Things – 19 parishes
Kräklinge Sixth – three Things – 19 parishes
Southern Third
Hoburg Sixth – three Things – 16 parishes
Burs Sixth – four Things – 14 parishes

Table 2. Territorial administration of rural Gotland, in Thirds, Sixths, Things, and Parishes

The Setting Thing was under the judicial control of a lawspeaker (in Old Gutnish possibly known as a *settingsdommer*, although the term only appears much later). Rural Gotland had no villages or towns, only dispersed farmsteads.

To the six Sixths was from 1161 added the emerging town and free port of Visby. It seems likely, although we do not know for sure, that in the thirteenth century each Sixth as well as Visby would provide one of the seven ships to the Swedish *ledung* fleet, when the King ordered men for a crusade.

Population

It is difficult to estimate the population of rural Gotland. It is commonly held that the island in the first half of the fourteenth century had some 50,000 inhabitants. However, the arrival of the Black Death in 1350 resulted in a major population loss, by some estimated as up to 75 percent.[3] Even a 50 percent loss, which is equally plausible, would have left the island with a population of no more than 25,000 inhabitants.

The Black Death was a severe blow. According to Strelow, the plague claimed the lives of 8,000 people in Visby alone.[4] Strelow possibly exaggerated, but there is no doubt that the Black Death significantly reduced population numbers. Moreover, the disease recurred regularly in the coming years.

Unfortunately, an estimated pre-Black Death population of 50,000 is difficult to reconcile with the number of farmsteads on the island. The number of farmsteads is also important from a military perspective, since the rural population mobilised based on the farmstead, parish, and Sixth structure. With an estimated average farmstead population of 10 people of all ages, male and female, such a high population would require around

---

3   Harrison, *Visby brandskattning*, 150.
4   Strelow, *Cronica Guthilandorum*, 161, 162.

4,000 farmsteads, with the rest of the population accounted for by Visby. Unfortunately, there is no evidence that Gotland had that many farmsteads even in the early fourteenth century, when trade still brought significant revenues to the rural farmers.

Many historians argue that Gotland, because of the losses from the Black Death, by 1361 had only about 1,500 farmsteads.[5] This figure derives from the fees (technically 'ransom') that were payable by each parish to avoid the episcopal visitation which was due every third year. Each visitation demanded substantial contributions in supplies, money, and labour to support the travelling bishop and his entourage. But the bishop lived in Linköping on the mainland and often preferred a monetary contribution instead of having to take the trouble to travel all the way to Gotland (and even when he visited, he only inspected half the number of parishes). Apparently, the Gotlanders too preferred to avoid episcopal visitations, so the fee payment system was acceptable to both parties. The data appear in the so-called 'taxation list' (*Taxa procurationis*, also known as the taxus list), which is very approximately dated to the thirteenth or fourteenth century. We only know the list from a sixteenth-century copy.[6] While it in some cases includes the number of *decimantes* (farmsteads owing tithes), the data is incomplete, undated, and essentially unverifiable. The estimate of 1,500 farmsteads is nonetheless generally repeated, perhaps primarily because the figure of 1,500 farmsteads also appears in sixteenth- and seventeenth-century records of far better provenance.[7] Moreover, the figure of 1,500 farmsteads was well-known in the seventeenth century and is cited even by contemporary foreign observers.[8]

However, the figure did not even then give the complete picture. At least 91 vicarages should be added, as well as certain other farms. This produces a figure of 1,630, not 1,500, farmsteads.[9] Besides, farmsteads were far from permanent. Nor is there reason to assume that the same families always worked the same, ancestral farmsteads. Rural Gotland was not a static society. Most Viking-Age silver hoards were found in areas which were abandoned and not farmed in later centuries. Both farmstead sites and rural roads changed over time. Many old farmstead foundations were ploughed out,

---

5   Westholm, *Visby 1361*, 133; Harrison, *Visby brandskattning*, 20.
6   Claudius Annerstedt (ed.), *Scriptores rerum Svecicarum medii ævi* 3:2 (Uppsala: Edvard Berling, 1871–1876), 290–293; Richard Steffen, 'Länsarkivets aktpublikationer 4: Handlingar rörande Visby domkyrka, dess jordar och inventarier', *Gotländskt Arkiv* 5 (1933), 45–60, on 55–58. See also Efraim Lundmark, 'Bilefeld, Strelow och de gotländska kyrkornas kronologi', *Fornvännen* 20 (1925), 162–180.
7   Specifically, the House Labour Book (*Husarbetsboken*) of 1557/1560 and the Audit Book (*Revisionsboken*) of 1653. See, e.g., Tryggve Siltberg, 'Gotlands gårdssamhälle 1413–1900 och ödegårdsfrågan 1514–1750', *GUSEM* 2 (Gutilandorum Universitas Scholarium et Magistrorum; Högskolan på Gotlands historiska förening, 2011), 233–277.
8   Notably, in the 1663 edition of a book by Adam Öhlschläger, better known as Olearius, who just had served as secretary to successive embassies sent by the Duke of Holstein to Muscovy and Persia. Adam Olearius, *Ausführliche Beschreibung Der kundbaren Reyse Nach Muscow und Persien* (Schleswig: Johan Holwein, 1663), 69.
9   Tryggve Siltberg, 'Gotlands bebyggelse 1614: Gårdar, människor och organisation', *Gotländskt Arkiv* 62 (1990), 125–152.

so do not remain.[10] The total number of farmsteads must accordingly have been significantly higher than 1,500. There is good reason to believe that Gotland was heavily populated in the first half of the fourteenth century.[11] Archaeological finds from the period AD 200–600 already suggest a total of about 2,000 farmsteads. However, the number and locations of farmsteads fluctuated widely over the centuries, with a peak in the thirteenth century, which saw population numbers most probably unsurpassed until the late eighteenth century.[12] In short, the verifiable sixteenth-century data tell us little of the island's population in the 1360s.

Fortunately, a contemporary figure is available in a tax record from 1413. It states that Gotland by then had about 2,300 farmsteads or households (Swedish: *mantal*) liable to taxation in cash and/or enforced labour.[13] While the exact meaning of this record's terminology has been debated (farmstead, household, labour?), we will see that it was prepared for King Eric as a means to extract, by harsher methods, significantly higher taxes. Hence, the data was certainly regarded as authentic by the King's tax collectors. And for a fifteenth-century rural tax register to be functional, it must be linked to landed property, that is, active farmsteads.

The 1413 tax record thus enables us to estimate the number of farmsteads, which likely was mostly unchanged since 1361. Although population recovery in the sixty years since the Black Death first struck may have led to the emergence of new farmsteads, others would have been lost in the many wars that we will see took place between 1361 and 1413. Assuming that the average farmstead counted 10 people of all ages, male and female, this figure leads to an estimated total rural population in 1361 of some 23,000. It seems likely that the mobilisation potential for defensive purposes was 20 percent, that is, two men per farmstead. Based on this figure, we can estimate the male rural population of military age as around 4,600.[14] However, we need to bear in mind that the number of inhabitants per farmstead may still have been somewhat lower in 1361 than later. Possibly, some farmsteads could only mobilise one male of military age. On the other hand, it is unlikely that all males on the island would be mobilised. In areas far from ongoing military operations, some would have remained at home to protect family, farmsteads, and livestock.

---

10 Majvor Östergren, *Mellan stengrund och stenhus: Gotlands vikingatida silverskatter som boplatsindikation* (Stockholm: Stockholm University, Institute of Archaeology, dissertation, 1989), 201, 208, 242–244.

11 Nils Blomkvist, 'Folk och gårdar på medeltidens Gotland: En nyckelfråga för östersjöforskningen', *Från Gutabygd 2010* (Visby: Gotlands Hembygdsförbund, 2010), 61–126, on 69–73.

12 Gustaf Svedjemo, 'Gårdar byar och social struktur på Gotland under järnåldern och medeltid', *Arkeologi på Gotland* 2 (Visby: Uppsala University & Gotland Museum, 2017), 183–190, on 185; Gustaf Svedjemo, *Landscape Dynamics: Spatial analyses of villages and farms on Gotland AD 200–1700* (Uppsala: Uppsala University, dissertation, 2014), 217–18.

13 Oscar Bjurling (ed.), *Das Steuerbuch König Eriks XIII: Versuch einer Rekonstruktion* (Lund: Ekonomisk-historiska föreningen i Lund 4, 1962), 66–67.

14 Interestingly, this figure is similar to the census of male Gotlanders aged 20–45, capable of bearing arms, in 1810, which was 4,639. The island's population had then increased, but the mobilisation potential of fourteenth-century Gotland was more inclusive, hence larger, with regard to age. Söderberg, 'Hur gick det till?', 21.

THE GOTLAND RURAL MILITIA

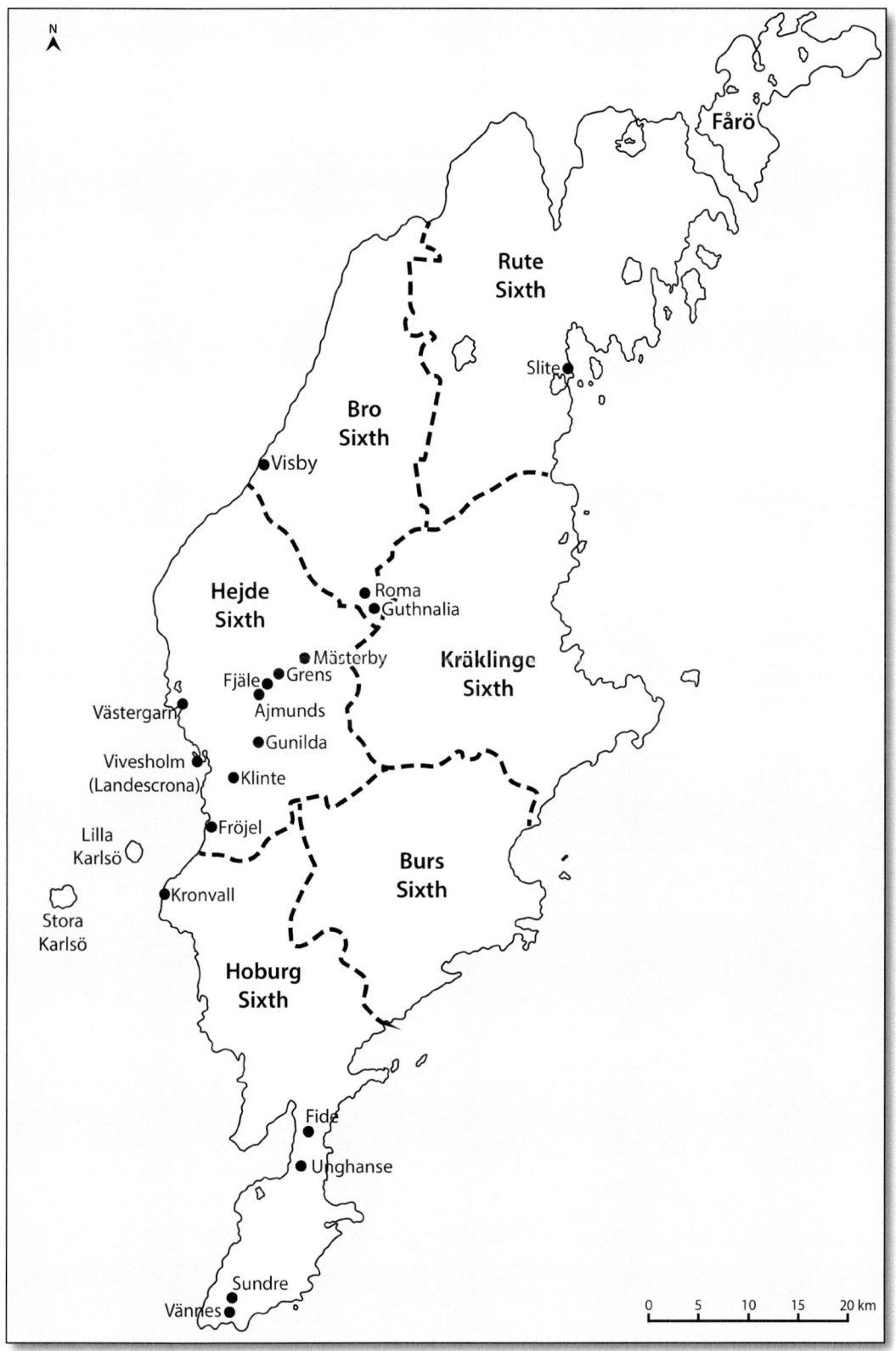

Gotland.

The Rural Militia

Gotland was a merchant-farmer republic of free men, but as in every republic, not everybody was equal. The wealthiest merchant-farmers constituted a rural gentry, with some families possibly reaching the level of powerful magnates within their Sixth. They did not maintain slaves or serfs. Nor did they use Continental-style heraldic coats of arms for recognition. Instead, they used house marks of traditional style. Yet, their wealth assured them positions as lawspeakers and local chiefs. If anything, their social position corresponded to that of a Viking-Age chieftain, and many were likely the descendants of such men.

From a judicial point of view, the rural militia may have been under the authority of the national lawspeaker. Little is known of decision-making within the rural militia as a whole. We do not know whether the national lawspeaker also commanded the fully mobilised rural militia, or more likely, whether this role was assumed by other persons of suitable experience and standing.

It was the Sixth which raised the rural militia. Each Sixth militia was commanded by a Sixth Captain (*settingshövding*). We know this from the fact that in 1288 the full rural militia was commanded by six captains, one for each Sixth.[15] He may, or not, have been the local lawspeaker. Each local assembly would send a contingent of armed men to join the militia, under the command of a prominent member of the community.

The number of farmsteads in each parish varied between four and about 30. The biggest parishes were in the south. It is estimated that the smallest farmsteads would have raised one or two men each, while the larger in times of plenty probably could raise four men each.[16]

Most of what we know about the Gotlanders who formed up in the rural militia derives from osteological analysis of the finds from the mass graves at Visby.

Osteological analysis took place already during the early twentieth-century excavations, and then under the leadership of Edward Clason.[17] However, the sheer volume of finds at the time precluded a detailed examination of each as an individual. The primary osteologist at the time when the data was finally published,

Two soldiers of the rural militia, armed respectively with sword and buckler and spear, and a member of the gentry in what may be a lamellar cuirass with great helm and modern flat-top shield but, curiously, no leg armour. (Källunge Church, Gotland, mid-fourteenth century; photo: Wolfgang Sauber)

---

15   Strelow, *Cronica Guthilandorum*, 145.
16   Westholm, *Visby 1361*, 133; Harrison, *Visby brandskattning*, 103–104.
17   Clason, 'Om i Korsbetningsgraven vid Visby funna skelett', 257–297.

Bo E. Ingelmark, based his age analysis mostly on the progress of the third molar ('wisdom tooth'), a method that he himself regarded as rough and unreliable. Moreover, Ingelmark's notes have since been lost, so we only have the published report.[18] This means that the data acquired, although valuable, need to be used with caution. Ingelmark focused most attention on age groups and disabilities. Moreover, it seems that Ingelmark in his research was influenced by the idea of a massacre of unarmed peasants and accordingly let this assumption guide his analysis. As a result, he concluded that a large share of the rural militia consisted of young boys, old men, and cripples.[19]

Soldiers of the rural militia, armed respectively with sword and buckler, morning star or goedendag, and battle axe. All wear helmets and good armour, except that they lack leg armour. (Källunge Church, Gotland, mid-fourteenth century; photo: Wolfgang Sauber)

These conclusions have not been confirmed by more recent investigations. Notably, the remains of women and small children were found in the mass graves, but none displayed battle wounds. These skeletal remains likely derive from older graves that had nothing to do with the battle, since the mass graves, when dug, intruded into the cemetery of Solberga Abbey (Latin: Mons Solis), a nunnery.

Men on Gotland were regarded as old enough to serve from age 18.[20] Based on research from 2002 led by Ebba During, less than a third of the dead were 20 or younger. However, of those in this age segment, the vast majority were around 18 to 20 years old. The youngest dead who displayed battle wounds, a single individual, was 16.[21] The conclusion must then be that just above three quarters of the dead were of military age.[22] Considering that the Gotlanders were raised as a militia for homeland defence, not an expeditionary force, there is nothing inherently surprising about these figures.

Interestingly, the preliminary results of Clason, Ingelmark's predecessor as chief osteologist, correspond better with current analytical data.[23]

In short, the age range of the dead was unremarkable for conditions of war in any century, including our own. The same goes for physical health and

---

18 Bo E. Ingelmark, 'The Skeletons', Thordeman, *Armour from the Battle of Wisby,* 149–209.
19 Specifically, 22% too young, 14% senile, and only 64% fit for military service. Thordeman, *Armour from the Battle of Wisby,* 159.
20 Guta Law 54, in Holmbäck and Wessén, *Svenska landskapslagar: Skånelagen och Gutalagen,* 238, 242.
21 Westholm, *Visby 1361,* 245–246; Marie Flemström, Jessica Larsson, and Petter Åkeson, 'Hic sepulti: En förnyad analys av skelettmaterial från Korsbetningen', *Gotländskt arkiv 79* (2007), 151–158, on 156.
22 Thomas Neijman, *The Gotlandic Rural Militia: A Study of the Invasion of Gotland 1361 in Response to a Modern Narrative* (Master thesis, Stockholm University Department of History, 2017), 69.
23 Clason, 'Om i Korsbetningsgraven vid Visby funna skelett', 265.

disabilities. On average, the dead were about 173 cm tall.[24] The majority of the men were in good health. A few individuals had disabilities from disease, such as tuberculosis, or hard labour, mostly related to their age, which had resulted in minor skeletal disabilities. However, most disabilities would not have prevented them from functioning normally, and their number was well within the usual range for pre-modern osteological remains.[25] The skeletal materials contained many examples of broken legs and arms that had healed incorrectly. Some skulls showed old and partially healed wounds that suggested that the men had survived and recovered from previous fights or battles.

Arms and Armour

The Gotland rural militia was not an army of Continental knightly cavalry. It had more in common with the traditional Scandinavian armies of the Viking Age and indeed of ancient Germanic society.

However, while the basic organisation and tactics of the rural militia thus differed significantly from King Valdemar's Continental army, there was little difference with regard to arms and armour.

According to Guta Law, all Gotlanders must be ready to serve on coastal guard duty from age 18 onwards. We can assume, although this is nowhere stated, that this duty included manning the lookouts and beacons. Those aged 20 and above must have a full set of weapons at home and be willing to fight when mobilised.[26] To own a full set of weapons was both a right and an obligation for a free man. Unfortunately, the Gotland legal code, unlike several Swedish ones, did not specify exactly what constituted a full set of weapons. Elsewhere in Scandinavia, a full set was at the time usually interpreted as a spear, sword, bow, shield, helmet, and sometimes a cuirass. Many would carry an axe instead of sword, and by the fourteenth century, the crossbow had gone far in overtaking the bow as the rural population's favoured missile weapon. Gotland was a major producer of swords and spearheads until the mid-thirteenth century, so there is no reason to believe that the rural population lacked weapons.[27] Spearheads have been found during battlefield archaeological excavations at Mästerby and Visby.

Other pole arms included battle axes of traditional type, and the spear-axe, which is known from Scandinavian literary sources and is commonly believed to have been an early form of halberd.

In addition, we know from both archaeological finds at Visby and contemporary pictorial evidence that Gotlanders used the combination of a spiked club with a spear that in English is commonly known as a morning star or *goedendag* (Dutch for 'good day'). The morning star was a spiked

---

24 Flemström, Larsson, and Åkeson, 'Hic sepulti', 157.
25 Flemström, Larsson, and Åkeson, 'Hic sepulti', 158.
26 Guta Law 54, in Holmbäck and Wessén, *Svenska landskapslagar: Skånelagen och Gutalagen*, 238, 242.
27 Yrwing, *Gotlands medeltid*, 101.

club which, in similarity to the Flemish *goedendag*, had a sharp metal spike inserted in and extending out of the head, like a short pike. This was a weapon frequently used by militia units, including perhaps most famously, by those of medieval Flanders in the fourteenth century to great effect against French knights. The simplicity of the weapon suggests that it despite the known mercantile links between Flanders and Gotland possibly was a homegrown development in both locations, as well as elsewhere across Europe. Morning stars remained in common use in Scandinavia throughout the seventeenth century, when it was used by groups as diverse as Swedish burgher militias, Danish sailors commandeered to serve on land, and Swedish peasant levies, who indeed used them well into the eighteenth century. In Swedish towns, morning stars were sometimes used by town watchmen into the nineteenth century.

As far as is known, the Flemish met a cavalry charge by setting the *goedendag* in the ground, held with both hands and secured by one's foot. The thick knob under the spear-like spike then served the same purpose as the crossbar on a boar-spear, that is, safeguarding against the horse accidentally impaling itself and then continuing into physical contact. Having halted the charging cavalryman, the *goedendag* was employed as a club.

Butt-spikes of polearms were found during archaeological excavations at Mästerby, which suggests that at least some spears or other polearms had them.

An archaeological find from Mästerby shows that large, single-edged fighting knives were used on Gotland.[28] The best-preserved knife found was 36 cm long, even with the point missing. The type was known as *ryting* in Swedish and were said to be able to cut off a spear shaft.[29]

There is every reason to believe that the Gotlanders also brought bows and crossbows to war. Crossbows had by the fourteenth century become the primary weapon of rural Scandinavians. None from this century survived into modern times, but based on surviving specimens from later centuries, a rural crossbow had a total length of about 1.1 to 1.15 m and a weight of about 3.5 to 4 kg.

The traditional Scandinavian round shield seems to have gradually disappeared. In its stead, a smaller type of flat wooden round shield, known as buckler (Old Norse: *buklari*), emerged no later than the thirteenth century. Based on archaeological finds and pictorial art, the buckler replaced the old infantry shield and was in common use in the mid-fourteenth century, if not before. Commonly from 35 to 40 cm in diameter, the buckler was held at arms-length from the body, like its predecessor the round shield, and was constantly kept in motion. More a parrying weapon than a shield, its small size made the buckler popular also for shipboard use. The buckler had a large, round iron boss which covered the fist-grip bar, and was commonly reinforced with iron, both on the surface and along the edge. The iron reinforcements were often highly decorative, at least in bucklers preserved

---

28   Maria Lingström, 'Fjäle myr 1361: Arkeologiska undersökningar av slagfältet från dagarna före slaget vid Visby ringmur', *Fornvännen* 104 (2009): 33–44, on 38–39.
29   Hildebrand, *Sveriges medeltid* 3, 360–361.

FALL OF THE MERCHANT-FARMER REPUBLIC

into the present. While some have used this as an argument that bucklers were not used by peasants, rural militia soldiers were depicted with bucklers in Gotland churches.[30]

The rural militia had access to modern armour, but Gotlanders had not gone to war for two generations, so older styles probably remained common.

We know much about Gotland armour from the mass graves at Visby. In Sweden, the coat-of-plates cuirass was known as *plata*. A chainmail coif was called *muza* (or *musu*), unless this indeed was the common word

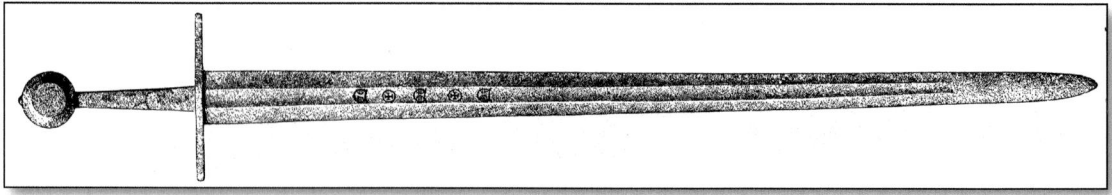

Swedish sword, fourteenth century. (Hans Hildebrand)

Swedish fourteenth-century sword preserved into the present. Although badly corroded, parts of the sword's leather-covered wooden scabbard have survived, together with the chape. Total length 103 cm, width 6 cm, sword guard width 18 cm. (Småland Museum, Object No. M 67628)

Kettle hat, dated to the fourteenth century and found at Hof, Vestfold, Norway. Weight 2.037 kg, length 33.3 cm, width 31.0 cm, and height 17.0 cm. (History Museum, Stockholm: photo: Gabriel Hildebrand)

---

30 Sigurd Grieg, 'Skjoldene i middelalderen', Bengt Thordeman (ed.), *Nordisk kultur 12B: Vapen* (Stockholm: Albert Bonnier, 1943), 67–89, on 69–71. See also Anon., '12 norske middelalderbuklere', *Middelalder, Våpen og rustning og merket skjold*, 4 December 2021 (https://hoveloghage.wordpress.com/2021/12/04/12-norske-middelalderbuklere/; https://hoveloghage.wordpress.com/tag/skjold/).

THE GOTLAND RURAL MILITIA

Contemporary Scandinavian illustrations, including this probably Danish illumination dated to the fourteenth century, sometimes depict what looks like large cheek pieces attached to the kettle hat. While finds from later, better-documented centuries show that cheek pieces do not always survive even if the helmet is preserved, no such fourteenth-century cheek pieces are known from archaeological finds. Possibly, the artists only attempted to depict the chainmail coif or fabric headgear which invariably was worn under the kettle hat. (Codex Hardenbergianus, Copenhagen)

This depiction of the death of St. Olaf was made in Iceland in the last quarter of the fourteenth century. Large poleaxes of the same type and very similar helmets appear also in contemporary effigies in Gotland churches. (Illumination from the Icelandic Flateyjarbók, Reykjavik)

Another Icelandic illumination from the last quarter of the fourteenth century. The same weapons and items of armour were used on Gotland, including the early firearm over which the top pair of soldiers are fighting. (Illumination from the Icelandic Flateyjarbók, Reykjavik)

FALL OF THE MERCHANT-FARMER REPUBLIC

 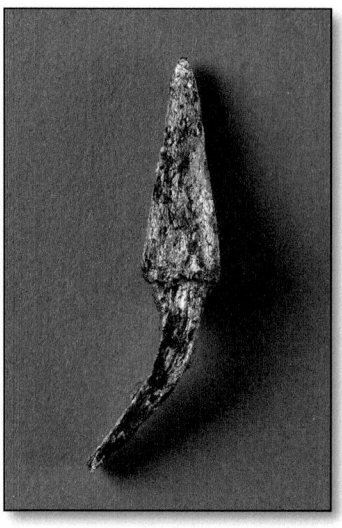 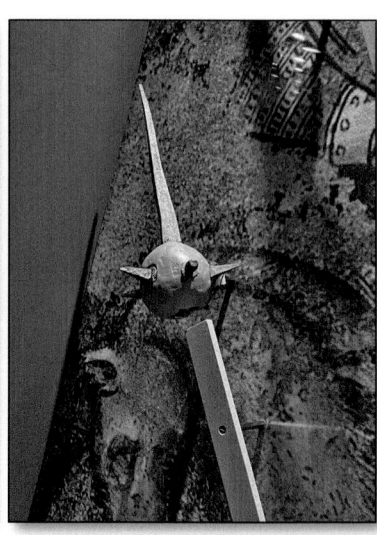

Square points with tangs, originally inserted into a morning star. Length: 5.8 cm. Found in the mass graves at Visby. (History Museum, Stockholm; photos: Gabriel Hildebrand and author)

Hunting knife with a hilt of bone and silver fittings decorated with mythical animals, found in the mass graves at Visby. Length: 29 cm. What may have been a small pommel is missing, with only the rivet remaining. (History Museum, Stockholm; photo: Gabriel Hildebrand)

Unsurprisingly, the Eastern mace was used on Gotland as well as in Denmark. It may have been used as a sign of command. The mace head is knobbed, of cast copper alloy (bronze), is shaped like a flattened ball covered with rows of projecting knobs with a hollow cylindrical shaft which suggests that it was fixed to either a wooden or metal pole. This mace was found in Vallby, Hogräns Parish, on Gotland. (Author's collection)

THE GOTLAND RURAL MILITIA

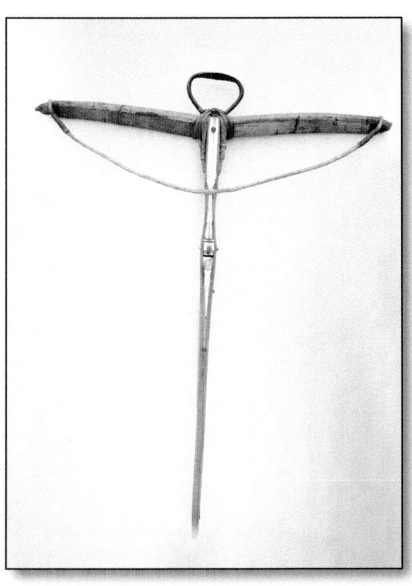

Crossbow with wooden prod arms of undetermined age. The fourteenth-century crossbows used on Gotland may have been of a similar type. Without a bow string, or as here with an improperly strung bow string, the prod arms arch forwards. When strung, the prod is under tension. (Royal Armoury, Stockholm)

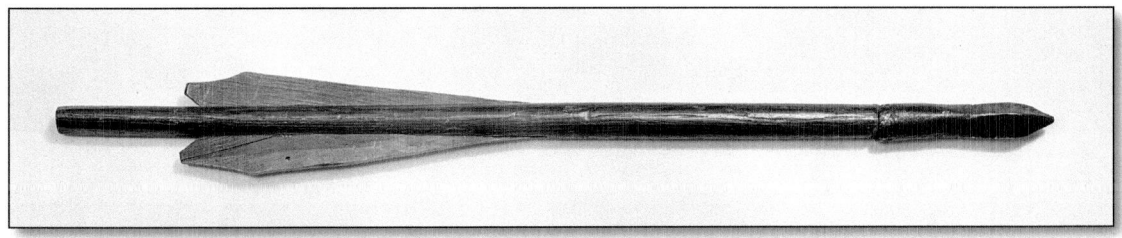

Crossbow bolt with wooden flights, habitually dated to the fourteenth to sixteenth centuries. The same type of arrowheads was found in the archaeological remains of the Battle of Visby. (Royal Armoury, Stockholm)

Buckler from Åmli, Valle, Setesdal, Norway. The decorative rose pattern corresponds to a variety of contemporary items throughout Scandinavia, including a brooch or buckle found in a Visby mass grave. Diameter 36 cm. (Museum of Cultural History (KHM), University of Oslo, C1568; photo: Adnan Icagic/KHM)

Buckler from Matrand, Eidskog, Hedmark, Norway. Dated to the late fourteenth or early fifteenth century. Diameter 35 cm. (Museum of Cultural History (KHM), University of Oslo, C31924; photo: Adnan Icagic/KHM)

FALL OF THE MERCHANT-FARMER REPUBLIC

for any chainmail garment. Both terms were known since the 1280s and 1290s, respectively.[31] The archaeological finds show that both coat-of-plates cuirasses and chainmail were in common use. However, many, perhaps most of the dead at Visby lacked leg armour. While contemporary illustrations, including on Gotland, sometimes depict leg armour, and items such as poleyns covering the knees were found at Visby, such gear was likely not in universal use within the rural militia.

The chainmail coifs found in the mass graves that could be typologically determined were all of the type which lacks ventail (a loose chainmail flap next to mouth which could be laced or hooked up to cover the chin and mouth, or left loose to allow easier breathing, speech, or eating and drinking). Moreover, the lower parts of the chainmail coifs consisted of two square or rectangular flaps of chainmail which protected the upper part of the breast and back respectively. In addition, most or all seem to have had an inner lining of probably linen which provided limited padding and retained the shape of the coif. Fragments of the lining have survived into the present.[32]

The archaeological finds in the Visby mass graves include two individuals (those who wore cuirasses No. 4 and 25) who seem to have worn the chainmail coif collar inside the cuirass, which is contrary to virtually all contemporary pictorial evidence.[33] Whether this was a common practice, a coincidence, or mere individual choice, remains unknown.

The archaeological finds at Visby and Mästerby include cuirasses of two types: coat-of-plates and lamellar armour. Based on the number of finds, coat-of-plates cuirasses were more common. This was also the type worn by most Germans and Danes. However, lamellar cuirasses were apparently in reasonably widespread use, too. The excavated lamellar armour, which mostly consisted of broken pieces, was of traditional Eastern type, commonplace in Eurasia including eastern Scandinavia. One reason why more coat-of-plates cuirasses were found in Visby mass graves may be that they, being riveted, survived the conditions of burial better than lamellar cuirasses, which tended to fall apart when the lacing that held the cuirass together moulded and vanished in the soil.

We have seen that coat-of-plates armour was constructed by attaching iron plates to the inside of a waist-length sleeveless covering or coat which, based on those cases in which fragments remain, was made of leather. It seems quite certain that fabric, also, might be used instead of leather. The iron plates were usually riveted on the inside of the covering, but outside riveting occurred too, in particular on the shoulders. Some plates

Chainmail coif without ventail but (unseen in this reconstruction) with inner lining. (Tommy Hellman)

---

31 Hans Hildebrand, *Sveriges medeltid* 3 (Stockholm: P.A. Norstedt & Söner, 1898), 338.
32 Tommy Hellman, *Ringbrynjehuvor från massgravarna vid Korsbetningen: Några frågor rörande deras konstruktion samt en jämförelse med en i England återfunnen, som äkta betraktad ringbrynjehuva* (Stockholm: Stockholm University, Department of Archaeology, 1995).
33 Thordeman, *Armour from the Battle of Wisby*, 106.

were fastened horizontally, others vertically. A few cuirasses only protected the chest, not the back. The result was a durable, reasonably lightweight, but rigid cuirass in which the iron plates were hidden under a fabric surface. As noted, in its fundamentals coat-of-plates corresponds to the brigandine armour brought to Europe by Mongol invasion armies. Gauntlets were produced in a similar manner.

Lamellar armour was constructed in a manner that already had existed for many centuries and accordingly was widespread throughout Eurasia. A lamellar cuirass was built of numerous lamellae with regular perforations through which thongs were drawn, weaving the lamellae into horizontal rows. These were in turn attached to each other by yet more thongs. Lamellae could be made of almost any rigid material, including hardened leather. However, by this time Gotland and eastern European lamellar armour, as far as is known, exclusively consisted of iron. The result was a tough but lightweight and very flexible cuirass, which provided good protection.

Bengt Thordeman, who documented the excavated armour at Visby, divided the reasonably complete 25 excavated cuirasses into six main types, the first five of which consisted of coat-of-plates armour.[34] It seemed to him that a sequence could be determined, from presumably older cuirasses with many plates to more recent ones with fewer plates. Thordeman, and most later scholars, interpret the reduced number of plates as a chronological development, an interpretation which neither can be proven or disproven. For pictorial examples of the excavated armour, see Appendix 1.

Thordeman noted that the only lamellar cuirass (No. 24) found in a reasonably intact state at Visby in fact had been altered. Probably correctly, he deduced that it had been modernised, that is, given a more up-to-date appearance. In remaking, every row of lamellae had been dealt with as if it had been a single large plate. The remade 'plates' had then been covered by leather or fabric and riveted to the inside of the cover.[35] The modifications almost certainly explain why the cuirass ultimately was found intact, instead of disintegrating as the other known lamellar cuirasses. However, since the modification of the cuirass seems not to have added any additional level of protection, it was most likely carried out for aesthetic purposes. The owner of the cuirass did not wish to look old-fashioned.

The remnants of other lamellar cuirasses show no traces of ever having been riveted to the inside of a fabric or leather cover, so were likely worn uncovered as when originally manufactured.[36] The lamellar cuirasses were probably not newly-acquired, since the Eastern trade had decreased in the fourteenth century, but they need not have been retained for centuries as early archaeologists seem to have assumed.[37] We have seen that Gotland merchants until very recently, and possibly still, retained links to Novgorod and the Russian principalities, the Crimean Goths, and the Byzantine Empire, where this type of armour remained in common use throughout the fourteenth

---

34   Thordeman, *Armour from the Battle of Wisby, 210–244, 345–404.*
35   Thordeman, *Armour from the Battle of Wisby, 225.*
36   Thordeman, *Armour from the Battle of Wisby, 220, 411–413.*
37   Thordeman, *Armour from the Battle of Wisby, 24, 225.*

century and beyond. Interestingly, the lamellae of the reconstructed lamellar cuirass (and possibly the broken ones as well) overlapped upwards, which provides superior protection from below, hence suggests that it originally was intended for use by a cavalryman.

Interestingly, isotope analysis suggests that the modernised lamellar armour No. 24 was not worn by a Gotlander.[38] Was it perhaps worn by somebody from the eastern shore of the Baltic?

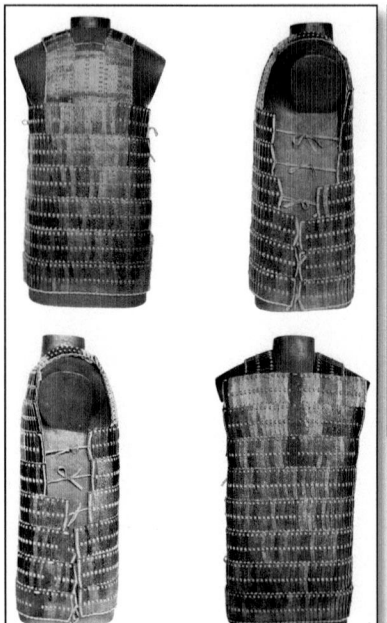
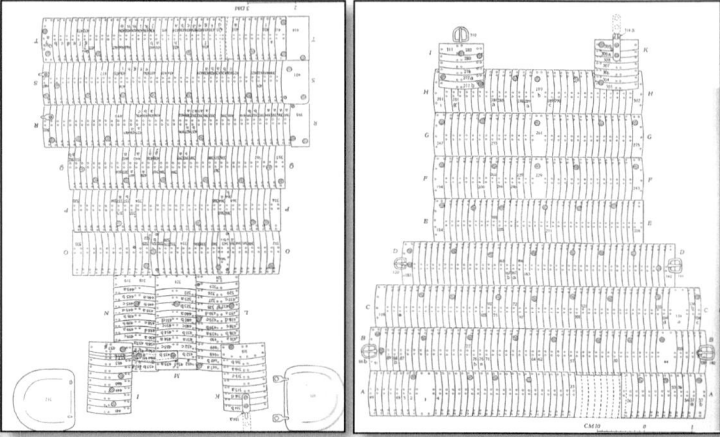

The complete lamellar cuirass found in a Visby mass grave. Thordeman labelled it cuirass No. 25. (Photo and drawing: Bengt Thordeman)

It is often assumed that all the cuirasses found in the Visby mass graves belonged to members of the Gotland rural militia. However, this is not necessarily so. The presumed youngest and most modern cuirass (No. 7) included eight bronze emblems which embellished the outer side of the leather cover on the chest. These included three shaped as fleurs-de-lis, two as shells, and three as knightly escutcheons. The latter three carried heraldic emblems which showed that the owner of the cuirass was linked to the Frisian noble family Roorda. The shell-shaped emblems tell that their owner had made at least one pilgrimage to the grave of St. James in Santiago de Compostela in Spain, where pilgrims bought shell emblems as symbols of the shrine. We do not know if he was a noble or a retainer of the Roorda family. If he was a noble, the dead man may have been one of the brothers Bavo or Schelto Roorda.[39] Either way, as a Danish subject he almost certainly fought in the Danish army, which shows that the mass graves also include many Danish dead.

Isotope analysis confirms the presence of Danes among the dead. We will see that the battle was not entirely one-sided. In fact, preliminary results

---

38   Neijman, *Gotlandic Rural Militia*, 65.
39   Westholm, *Visby 1361*, 250.

THE GOTLAND RURAL MILITIA

from the isotope analysis suggest that only two-thirds of the sampled dead individuals derived from Gotland, while one-third did not.[40] Although, as in previous conflicts, a small number of individuals from the eastern Baltic may have fought alongside the Gotlanders, many of the sampled one-third non-Gotlanders can accordingly be attributed to the Danish army.

We can assume that not all militia was as well-armed as the prosperous merchant-farmers. Farm workers were surely raised, too. Detmar's Lübeck Franciscan Chronicle claims that the peasants were 'unarmed and unused to battle' (Low German: *de bünnen weren ungewapent unde strides unbewonen*).[41] This is the only contemporary chronicle that claims that the Gotlanders were unarmed. Since the chronicle was written in Germany, it may well make assumptions that were based on local, not Gotland, circumstances. The Gotlanders had been at peace for years, so it seems credible that they were unused to battle. Yet, the Visby mass graves prove that many were well-armed.

Heraldic emblems linked to the Roorda family, and shell emblems from the grave of St. James in Santiago de Compostela in Spain. (History Museum, Stockholm; photo: Katarina Nimmervoll)

Most Gotlanders would have worn ordinary civilian, woollen garments when they went into battle. Gotlanders raised a particularly hardy breed of sheep. The coarse fleece of the Gotland sheep was grey, and shed naturally in spring, although by this time, farmers had begun to shear their sheep. The grey wool was made into wadmal, a cloth that had been fulled, or 'waulked' (treated in hot water to cause the fabric to contract and become partially felted), to make it impermeable to wind or rain. The fabric was usually not dyed but retained its original grey colour.

Effigy of a knight in Lye Church, Gotland, dated to c. 1350 and depicting the popular Herod's Massacre of the Innocents motif. The knight wears a long-sleeved chainmail hauberk with integral mittens under an old-style loose surcoat and a dated, flat-topped great helm. There is a hint that he wears a coat-of-plates cuirass over the hauberk. The soldier wears similar armament but no helmet, only a chainmail coif or possibly the padded headgear worn under a helmet. (Author's collection)

---

40   Neijman, *Gotlandic Rural Militia,* 70. Further analysis will take place to clarify this issue.
41   Koppmann, *Die Chroniken der niedersächsischen Städte* 1, 529.

FALL OF THE MERCHANT-FARMER REPUBLIC

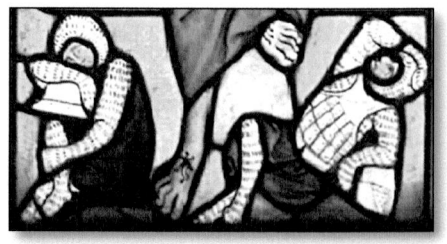

Stained glass window from Lye Church, Gotland, dated to c. 1350 and depicting a sleeping soldier (left) and knight (right). The soldier wears a kettle hat over a chainmail coif and a long-sleeved chainmail hauberk with integral mittens. He possibly wears a coat-of-plates cuirass under an old-style loose surcoat. If not, his armament can only be referred to as dated. The knight, too, wears a chainmail coif and a long-sleeved chainmail hauberk with integral mittens. Legs and feet are protected by chainmail chausses. He wears a coat-of-plates cuirass over the hauberk, and a helmet, which either is a dated (but not flat-topped) great helm with attached face mask, or more likely at this time, an attempt by the artist to depict a visored bascinet. (Author's collection)

Stained glass window from Hablingbo Church, Gotland, dated to c. 1350 and depicting two soldiers and, behind the primary soldier, a knight. The motif is the popular Herod's Massacre of the Innocents. The soldier wears typical arms and equipment of the period, which shows that Gotland was no backwater with regard to military styles. His head is protected by a kettle hat over a chainmail coif. He wears a distinctive cuirass over a long-sleeved chainmail hauberk with separate gauntlets that lacks protective plates. The cuirass is difficult to identify because of artistic conventions of a type also present in Eastern Europe and possibly the Byzantine Empire but is presumably intended as consisting either of lamellar or coat-of-plates armour. The soldier's legs are protected by plated leg armour including iron poleyns, greaves, and on his feet, iron sabatons that only cover the tops of his feet. The knight behind him wears what probably is a visored bascinet. The soldier in the rear may wear a bascinet, or possibly only the padded headgear always worn under a helmet. (Uppsala University Museum)

THE GOTLAND RURAL MILITIA

Another depiction of the popular Herod's Massacre of the Innocents motif, this time in the mid-fourteenth-century Martebo Church. Two soldiers, each depicted in a coat-of-plates cuirass over a long-sleeved chainmail hauberk. The one to the left wears an old-style loose surcoat and a kettle hat over his chainmail coif. (Photo: Bene Riobó)

Sleeping soldiers, as depicted in the mid-fourteenth century Stånga Church, Gotland. Each man wears a long-sleeved chainmail hauberk with integral mittens under an old-style loose surcoat. The flat-topped great helms look dated but may still have been in use among the rural gentry. (Photo: author)

Soldiers portrayed in the popular Herod's Massacre of the Innocents motif, as depicted in the mid-fourteenth century Stånga Church, Gotland. Each man wears a long-sleeved chainmail hauberk with integral mittens under an old-style loose surcoat, with dated, flat-topped great helms. (Photo: author)

FALL OF THE MERCHANT-FARMER REPUBLIC

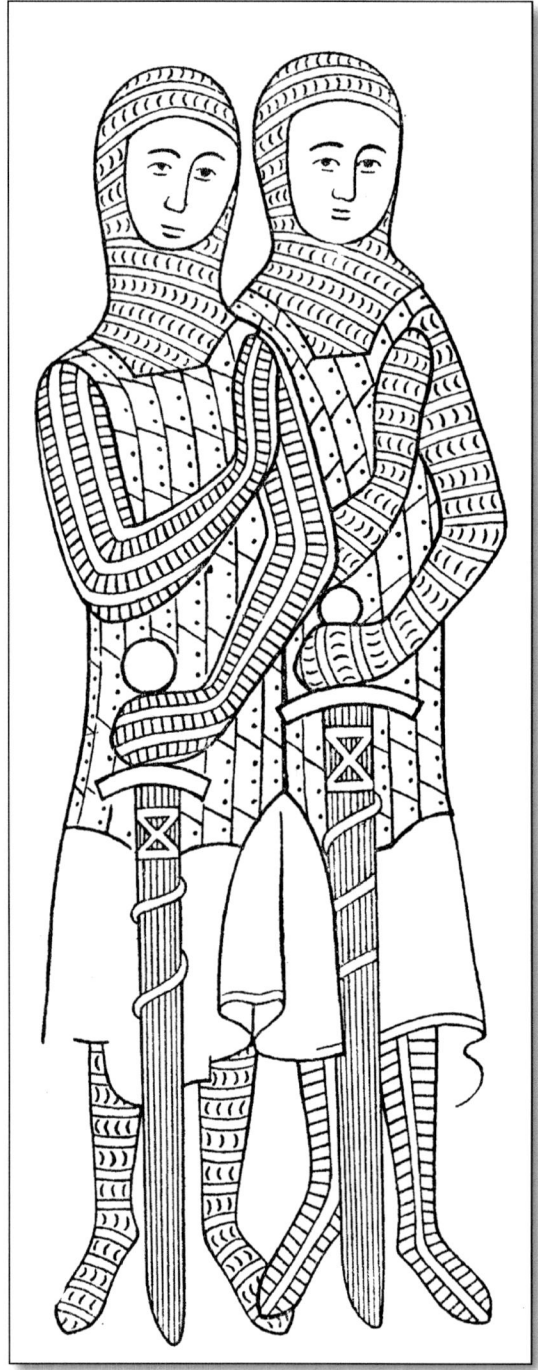

Reconstructed drawing of two Swedish knights depicted in a wall panel painting in Björsäter Church, Linköping diocese, Östergötland province, dated to around 1350 or soon thereafter. Both wear long-sleeved chainmail hauberks, chausses, and coifs, with coat-of-plates or possibly lamellar armour covered with fabric. Both have attached their sword scabbards to their sword belts with laces in the traditional manner. Gotland did not support knights of the Danish or Swedish type, but individual merchant-farmers may have worn similar armour and equipment.

Present condition of the wall panel painting, which because of harsh usage over the centuries suffered damages before it in 1910 was moved for safekeeping to the History Museum, Stockholm.

Cavalry

Several spurs, or parts thereof, of the type used by knightly cavalry were found at the battlefields of Visby and Mästerby. Some Gotlanders were sufficiently wealthy to fight on horseback in the Continental manner. However, Gotland horses were small. The domestic Gotland Pony stands between 115 cm and 130 cm in height, which made it less suitable for knightly cavalry.

Six of the seven horseshoes found in the Visby mass graves were of a size more suitable for small Gotland horses than European warhorses. This means that some of the militia was mounted. We do not know whether they also fought mounted. The horseshoe of Continental size probably, but not necessarily, belonged to one of King Valdemar's knights.

Gotland churches still display mid-fourteenth-century depictions of knights, so it remains plausible that a few merchant-farmers possessed the full panoply of a mounted knight, as well as warhorses of the Continental type.

The Gotland Pony is an old breed of pony or small horse native to Gotland, where it ran feral in the fourteenth century. The Gotland Pony stands between 115 cm and 130 cm, with a coat that most commonly is dun, bay, chestnut, or black. (Photo: Sallis Lindqvist)

Besides, in 1358 the Calendarium in the Visby Franciscan Chronicle noted that the then Mayor, Johannes (Hans) Kosvelt, from a family which also did business in Reval, donated a horse to the convent. He added the condition that it could only be used for the needs of the brothers and Church and 'that this horse should not at all be loaned to anyone for tournaments or other games' (Latin: *ut equus ille nec pro hastiludiis vel aliis lusibus*).[42] This condition suggests that tournaments of some kind took place on Gotland, and that men on the island had the means and equipment to participate. It seems quite likely that some of the merchant-farmer gentry were among them.

---

42 Odelman and Melefors, 'Visbyfranciskanernas bok', 42–43.

FALL OF THE MERCHANT-FARMER REPUBLIC

Knightly tournament as depicted on Gotland. Wooden panel painting, dated to the period 1250–1300. (Väte Church, Gotland, presently in History Museum, Stockholm; photo: author; drawing: Hans Hildebrand)

Knights of Continental style fighting non-knightly cavalry in conical helmets of Slavic style with feathers or plumes arranged as a panache spreading outwards. Traditionally interpreted as a Christian motif which was popular in the Middle Ages (the martyrdom of the Theban Legion in AD 286, the legendary saints of which were occasionally depicted with standards displaying a red cross on a white field), the combat scenes seem far more typical of the turbulent fighting on Gotland involving the Baltic mercenaries and pirates known as Victual Brothers (more on whom below). However, the possibility remains that some cavalrymen provided by the rural gentry of Gotland wore conical helmets of this style, which for centuries had been common in the East where they had many trading partners. Late fourteenth or early fifteenth-century fresco of soldiers in combat in Bunge Church, Gotland. (Photo: Wolfgang Sauber)

  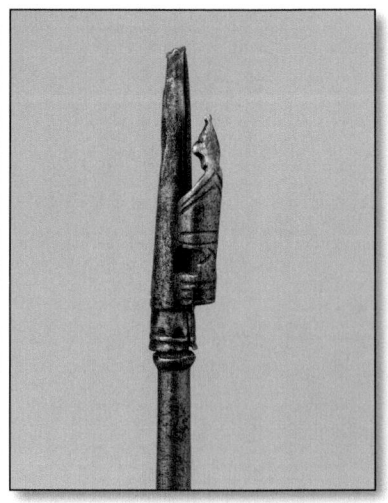

Based on contemporary pictorial evidence, this type of tall, pointed Eastern-style helmet was in common use in Russian lands throughout the Middle Ages, even though these are attributed to the period c. 1450–1550. Helmets of this type were customarily worn with a chainmail aventail to protect the face and neck, and adorned with feathers, plumes, or horse-tail hair arranged as a panache spreading outwards to the long finial, or in Persia, a small pennon. Height 46.7 cm, weight 1.56 kg. (Metropolitan Museum of Art, Object No. 04.3.208)

Plate A. King Valdemar of Denmark
(Illustration by Giorgio Albertini © Helion & Company)
See Colour Plate Commentaries for further information.

Plate B. Danish knight
(Illustration by Giorgio Albertini © Helion & Company)
See Colour Plate Commentaries for further information.

Plate C. German mercenary crossbowman and handgunner
(Illustration by Giorgio Albertini © Helion & Company)
See Colour Plate Commentaries for further information.

Plate D. Gotland rural militia officer
(Illustration by Giorgio Albertini © Helion & Company)
See Colour Plate Commentaries for further information.

Plate E. Gotland rural militia soldier
(Illustration by Giorgio Albertini © Helion & Company)
See Colour Plate Commentaries for further information.

Plate F. Gotland rural militia soldier
(Illustration by Giorgio Albertini © Helion & Company)
See Colour Plate Commentaries for further information.

Plate G. Visby burgher militia soldier
(Illustration by Giorgio Albertini © Helion & Company)
See Colour Plate Commentaries for further information.

Plate H. Visby mercenary and pirate
(Illustration by Giorgio Albertini © Helion & Company)
See Colour Plate Commentaries for further information.

Coats of Arms (illustrations by author)

King Valdemar of Denmark (Or three lions Azure crowned Or)

Duke Eric of Saxe-Lauenburg (Azure an eagle crowned Or)

Valdemar Sappi (Or eight water-leaves Gules)

Claus Limbek (Argent two bendlets enhanced Azure)

Henning Podebusk (Per fess, Or and Sable, in chief an eagle displayed of the second, in base chequy)

Duke Henry of Mecklenburg (Or a bull's head erased Sable, langued Gules, horned Sable, crowned Or)

Gotland Republic (Paly of eight Or and Purpure)

Coat of Arms and Standards

The Gotland Republic's seal, entrusted to the national lawspeaker, displayed a proud ram, the symbol of the Gotlanders, holding a standard. There is good reason to believe that the ram emblem was displayed elsewhere as well, perhaps on standards or shields. Gotland retains the ram symbol as provincial coat of arms into the present.

Fourteenth-century sources mention a Gotland standard or flag. The contemporary Eric Chronicle describes how the Gotland rural militia in 1313 flew a distinct (but not further described) standard when they confronted Sweden's King Birger Magnusson.[43] An anonymous mid- to late-fourteenth-century Castilian geographical and armorial manual, *El Libro del Conosçimiento de todos los rregnos* ('Book of Knowledge of All Kingdoms'), also mentions the Gotland Republic's flag, and even describes how the author of the book

The seal of the Gotland Republic. The seal displays a proud ram, the symbol of the Gotlanders, holding a standard. The text says †GUTENSES SIGNO XRISTVS SIGNATVR IN AGNO ('I sign for the Gotlanders, Christ is signed by the lamb'). (Gotland Museum, Visby; photo: Raymond Hejdström)

> … embarked upon a ship, and went on to an island they call Gotlandia, which is at the end of the Gulf of Alemana [German Gulf, that is, Baltic Sea]. On this island there is a great city they call Bisuy [Visby], in which there are ninety parishes, and the island is fully populated. After it is another smaller island, they call Oxilia [Ösel; modern-day Saaremaa]. And the king of these islands has for his insignia a flag with yellow and purple bars crossed (Spanish: *un pendon con vandas amarillas et cardenas atravesadas*).[44]

The comment that the ruler of Gotland also (at some point) controlled the island of Ösel in modern-day Estonia corresponds to Strelow's aforementioned reference to 'vassals' in Estonia and Livonia and need not surprise us. However, does this mean that the Castilian writer actually had seen the Gotland flag? Sadly, no description of it is known from other sources, and there is nothing to suggest that Gotland by this time had an official coat of arms. The Castilian may well have been aware of the texts by ancient geographers who mentioned an island in the Baltic Sea which they called Basileia ('royal land') and which became linked to the Goths. If the Castilian found it necessary to invent a Gotland flag, what would be more suitable than one which was based on gold (the heraldic term for yellow) and Imperial purple? As an educated Castilian, he was surely aware of the ancient Gothic kingdoms, not least Visigothic Spain which formed part of his own history.

Assuming that the Castilian's report nonetheless is correct, two difficulties remain with his description of the flag. First, what shade of purple was used? Assuming that the description refers to the original Tyrian imperial purple, the colour could range from dark reddish to deep blueish violet.

---

43 Jansson, *Erikskrönikan*, 143.
44 Translation based on *Book of the Knowledge of all the Kingdoms, Lands, and Lordships That Are in the World* (London: Hakluyt Society 2:29, 1912), 10, pl. 4; *El Libro del conoscimiento de todos los reinos: The Book of Knowledge of All Kingdoms* (Tempe, Arizona: Arizona Center for Medieval and Renaissance Studies, 1999), 16, 17, pl. 16a–c.

Second, what was the meaning of the author's word 'crossed'? Clearly, the illustrators of *El Libro del Conosçimiento* did not know either, when they drew heraldic coats of arms based on the text. The anonymous author was obviously interested in heraldry, but his descriptions are not always clear. Besides, the earliest reference to his book describes the author as a Franciscan Friar. This would make sense, since in the fourteenth century others of his order, too, worked to gather geographical data of the world. But this also means that he probably was not a professional herald.

Based on the anonymous author's description, the illustrators of his book drew the flag as a coat of arms – but each illustrator interpreted the design differently. The possibly oldest surviving, and certainly most complete, manuscript illustrates the bars as, in heraldic terminology, paly (vertical). Two others illustrate the bars as, in the same terminology, bendy (diagonal). Yet another manuscript combines the two, and includes both bendy and paly bars, crossed.

If interpreted as a flag, this might mean a square or rectangular flag with vertical bars, half of them yellow and half of them purple.

There is a high chance that the rural militia flew other standards as well. Each Third may have fielded its own standard. Based on later seals, it seems likely that the Southern Third had the ram as its symbol. Whether this ram was displayed similarly to the one on the seal which represented the entire Gotland Republic, or whether the Southern Third's ram in fact was the origin of the national seal, is unknown. The Northern Third displayed a tree on its seal, while the Middle Third was symbolised by a horse.

Defensive Buildings

Rural Gotland was a country of farmsteads, but even a first glance showed a traveller that many farmers were wealthy. We have already seen that prosperous merchant-farmers built large residences of stone. They also built large stone warehouses. In the fourteenth century, both types of buildings were typically covered in white plaster.

In addition, wealthy rural merchant-farmers built defensive stone towers for the protection of their goods and, in times of crisis, families. In the early Middle Ages, there was a persistent threat from Baltic raiders, who operated in much the same manner as the Viking Age Scandinavians had done before them. A defensive tower of this type is presently known as a *kastal* (from Latin: *castellum*, 'little fort'). Many wealthy merchant-farmers on Gotland with prosperous farmsteads accordingly built defensive stone towers for personal use, such as the one at Gammelgarn, constructed in the twelfth century. Others, however, were built next to parish churches. It is believed that they were used for the safekeeping of such valuables that could not rapidly be removed if raiders struck the shore. A small garrison could defend the tower for a few days, until the rural militia assembled and moved against the raiders.

The rural merchant-farmers also invested their profits in prestigious communal stone buildings, primarily parish churches. Construction of

THE GOTLAND RURAL MILITIA

stone churches only really got underway on Gotland when the threat from Baltic raiders was significantly reduced because of crusades and Christian proselytisation, and the defensive towers therefore had lost their defensive function. Many newly built churches reduced both visibility and field of fire from adjacent towers, which shows that the merchant-farmers assessed that there no longer was any real threat from outsiders.

When the Gotland trade declined in the fourteenth century, the merchant-farmers no longer had the same wealth at their disposal, so quite a number of rural Gotland churches show signs of ongoing additions and renovations from this time that were abandoned half-way through. The building and renovation of churches continued until about the mid-fourteenth century. The days of prosperous trade had by then already been over for some time. The Gotland merchant-farmers apparently continued the church-building projects as long as cash from the good old days remained, but from this time onwards, they lacked the means to continue such expensive projects.

One of the best-preserved stone warehouses is the three-floor warehouse in Lauks in Lokrume, once owned by Gervid Lauk, the first national lawspeaker whose name survived into the present. Gervid Lauk died in 1380 and was buried in Lokrume Church. The warehouse is believed to have been built in the late thirteenth century. A privy is built on the upper floor. In the fourteenth century, the Lauks farmstead also included a four-story residential house in which lived the Lauk family. At the time of the Danish invasion, another branch of the Lauk family lived in Visby as burghers, which illustrates the complex relationship between many burgher and merchant-farmer families. (Photo: author)

The stone barn at Kattlund farmstead, 26 m long, 10 m wide, and dated to the thirteenth century, is another example of the building activities of successful rural merchant-farmers. It is the only medieval stone barn preserved on Gotland. The barn was probably covered in white plaster in the fourteenth century. (Swedish National Heritage Board; photo: Carl Gustaf Rosenberg)

FALL OF THE MERCHANT-FARMER REPUBLIC

The Gammelgarn Defensive Tower is square, with each side nine metres in length. The defensive tower, 13 m high, has five floors, with stairs inside the wall and privies to enable the defenders to sustain a siege. The outer walls are two metres thick at the base. The defensive tower was probably originally covered in white plaster. (Photo: author)

Lärbro Church and Defensive Tower. Lärbro Defensive Tower, dated to the twelfth century, is older than Lärbro Church which was mostly built in the late thirteenth century, with the church tower added in the 1340s according to dendrochronological analysis. Many parish churches, including the one at Lärbro, had a nearby defensive tower for protection. The Lärbro Defensive Tower has six floors, with a stair inside the wall. The outer white plaster surface was renewed from time to time and gives a good idea of what a defensive tower originally looked like. (Photos: Arild Vågen (church) and Helen Simonsson (defensive tower))

6

The Visby Hanseatic League Burgher Militia

Visby was a great and prosperous city. While the city's population mostly spoke Low German, it was a cosmopolitan environment in which many languages could be heard on the streets, including Old Gutnish, Swedish, Russian, and no doubt others.

Visby and its immediate surroundings counted 17 churches, many of which, such as St. Mary's (Maria's) Church, frequented by Germans; St. James's (Jacob's) Church, frequented by Livonians; and the Orthodox St. Laurentius's (Lars's) Church, frequented by Russian merchants from Novgorod and Pskov, were associated with particular groups, or nationalities, of merchants. The city hosted Franciscan and Dominican convents, and the aforementioned Cistercian nunnery known as Solberga Abbey which operated just outside the city walls.

Visby had between 250 and 300 multi-floor houses of stone that functioned as combined offices and homes for the wealthiest merchants, who constituted the elite of the city and from whom city officials were elected. Each household also included junior employees and servants.[1] Most buildings had five floors and a basement. A few larger houses were built with up to seven floors. Each was the combined home and office of an average of four to five people, plus the same number of servants. This produced a merchant population of some 3,000 people, to which at least as many others (artisans, labourers, and so on) should be added. This produces a total population of at least 6,000 to 7,000 people. In reality, it is likely that the number was significantly higher.[2] Strelow claims a population of 12,000.[3] While the date of his information is uncertain, there is no doubt that Visby was by far the largest city of not only the Swedish realm but all of Scandinavia.

---

1 Westholm, *Visby 1361*, 16; Harrison, *Visby brandskattning*, 28.
2 In comparison, we have seen that Stockholm had an estimated 5,000 to 6,000 inhabitants. Copenhagen and Malmö, the two major Danish mercantile centres, had not yet reached this size and importance. In the early fifteenth century each had a population of some 5,000 inhabitants. Poul Grinder-Hansen (ed.), *Unionsdrottningen: Margareta I och Kalmarunionen* (Copenhagen: Danmarks Nationalmuseum, 1996), 29.
3 Strelow, *Cronica Guthilandorum*, 120.

The city was surrounded by a wall which was 3.44 km long and included the harbour. The city wall was built in two stages. The original wall was approximately five to six metres high with battlements and a wall-walk. The oldest known timber in the wall has been dated to 1281, with additional logs dated to 1287 and 1288. While work possibly began already during the 1270s, construction intensified in 1287–1288, which provoked the 1288 war. The architects did a rush job, so parts of the wall lack stable foundations and occasionally display poor workmanship. At ground level, the wall was between 1.3 and 2.3 m thick. In total, the wall had about 15 gates, of which eight led to the harbour. Three gates faced northern Gotland, two opened to the east, and two towards the south. The primary initial purpose of the wall was to mark the border between the Hanseatic city and the rural country and was possibly intended to force the rural farmers to pay customs duties when they brought produce and goods for sale inside the city.

Following the 1288 war, the city council reinforced the existing city wall. Dendrochronology shows that work on the additions began already in the 1290s. They added additional towers as well as saddle towers, and increased the height of the wall up to about 10 m. The saddle towers were a particularly poor technical solution. On those stretches where the wall because of the initial haste lacked proper foundations, the saddle towers occasionally collapsed. By 1361, the wall had 29 towers, the highest of which was the six-floor 'Tall Lisa' (Swedish: *Långa Lisa*), and 22 saddle towers. Only some battlements were built for combat purposes, and most do not connect with the towers. It accordingly seems clear that the burghers primarily expected to man the towers and gates, and not the walls, if war came.

Most of the additions were ready well before King Valdemar's invasion. Final work on the wall concluded soon after 1363.

The city wall as seen from the east. Most of old Visby was built in the thirteenth century. The stretch of wall and towers seen in this photograph are original, with only the roof of one tower added later. For reasons explained in this book, the mid- to late-fourteenth century marked the decline of Visby as a city of trade. This led to a reduction in population, which allowed the city to retain its thirteenth-century appearance. (Photo: Boberger)

THE VISBY HANSEATIC LEAGUE BURGHER MILITIA

Tower as seen from the outside. A saddle tower is visible to the left. (Photo: W. Carter)

Saddle tower. (Photo: W. Carter)

FALL OF THE MERCHANT-FARMER REPUBLIC

Only parts of the city wall were fitted with battlements. The wall-walk was probably covered by a wooden roof. (Hans Hildebrand, 1879)

Reconstruction of wall-walk. (Ture Carlsson, 1922)

We do not have any information on the strength or organisation of the burgher militia. Based on the city's population, we can estimate at most, some 600 men. The burgher militia was far from sufficient to man and defend the city's long curtain walls. However, it is unknown to what extent the city council would raise common labourers and sailors for war, and if such men would be entrusted with weapons. As noted, the city walls seem to have been built under the premise that the defenders would only man the towers and gates.

With no other information available, we must assume that the Visby burgher militia was organised according to the Continental model. This means that each quarter or guild likely raised a distinct contingent of the militia, under an officer appointed by the city council who on the Continent often went by the German title *viertelmeister* ('quartermaster'). He may have been assisted by other officers, and commonly a trumpeter who may have been a burgher or an employed professional. Each militia contingent likely fielded its own, distinct flag.

The burgher militia consisted of armoured men equipped and trained for close combat. Each brought his own arms and armament, but these must fulfil certain standards. Arms and armour would have been mostly identical to those used in Danish and German armies. Most would carry an early halberd of the German or Swiss type, or a guisarme, which most likely was a crescent-shaped double socketed axe on a long shaft. Many would have served as crossbowmen.

Most Visby burghers had the means to a acquire good arms and armour. It is unknown to what extent they trained for combat, either individually or in formation. Young merchants who went abroad to trade probably learnt the use of arms for self-defence, if no more.

Continental cities fielded both infantry and cavalry. Based on the aforementioned Hans Kosvelt's condition for donating a horse, a few wealthy and physically active Visby burghers may have trained as knightly cavalry.

The burgher militia was not the only armed force available to a Hanseatic city. Visby would also have a mercenary garrison. The wealthy city needed protection and could afford to pay for it. There is nothing in available source materials that allows us to base an estimate of the number, organisation, or background of mercenary soldiers on surviving documentation. A company-sized unit of from 100 to at most 150 men seems a likely garrison for Visby in 1361. Under normal circumstances, their job was to guard the port and the 15 gates, and to maintain public order.

Although Continental Hanseatic cities and towns primarily recruited mercenaries in an orderly manner from Hanover, Westphalia, Thuringia, and Saxony in central Germany, those who served in Visby mostly seem to have come from coastal Mecklenburg and Pomerania on the Baltic coast. Baltic mercenary companies commonly operated as amphibious pirates when unemployed by cities or rulers. Pictorial evidence from around 1400 suggests that they frequently dressed in garments that displayed Slavic influences. It accordingly seems likely that the Mecklenburgers and Pomeranians over time were joined by fighting men with some nautical experience from the entire Baltic region, including Poland, Livonia, and northwestern Russia.

Some mercenaries were probably artillerymen. Although unknown from the sources, it seems likely that Visby had cannons. Many Hanseatic League cities already had cannons by 1361. Lübeck was a pioneer in this field, with a 'fireweapon' (*vüerschütte*) for shooting arrows already in 1352. Eight years later, in 1360, the city hall in Lübeck was destroyed because of mistakes in the handling of gunpowder stored in its basement.[4] Since Visby was a leading Hanseatic city, it would be surprising had the city lacked cannons.[5]

---

4   David Nicolle, *Forces of the Hanseatic League 13th–15th Centuries* (Oxford: Osprey Men-at-Arms 494, 2014), 37.
5   The oldest surviving record of a cannon in Stockholm, the 'great gun' (Low German: *grote busse*), derives only from 1395, but the weapon had then already been in place for some time, and there is no reason to believe that Stockholm acquired artillery only decades later than its German trading partners.

7

King Valdemar Conquers Öland

In spring 1361, King Valdemar mustered his army and fleet on Zealand. He failed, or did not attempt, to hide his intention to move against the two wealthiest islands of the Baltic Sea, Öland and Gotland. We have seen that, according to Detmar's Lübeck Chronicle, he told his men that he would bring them to a place where there was so much gold and silver that the pigs dined from throughs made of silver.[1] Certainly, King Magnus of Sweden learnt of the Danish King's designs, because he apparently already on 14 February (the Saturday before Quadragesima or Invocavit Sunday) wrote to the city council in Visby, ordering it to muster men and ships for the defence of the country.[2] However, for practical reasons King Magnus only called up the *ledung* fleet in June.[3]

On 2 May 1361 (Saturday before Ascension Day), King Magnus sent a warning to the city council of Visby that 'some of our enemies' had entered into a secret alliance to attack Gotland with a strong army, and that they would surely do so, unless the Gotlanders 'day and night, carefully and diligently, watch all places where such a danger might emerge'. The King accordingly admonished them to 'maintain a vigilant watch in the harbour and on the walls day and night.'[4] King Magnus did not specifically mention King Valdemar. Perhaps he did not know exactly where King Valdemar would strike, or which, if any, allies of his might join the war. Yet, King Magnus began his letter to the Visby city council with the words 'You are aware that

---

1   Koppmann, *Die Chroniken der niedersächsischen Städte* 1, 529.
2   Strelow, *Cronica Guthilandorum*, 163–165. Although the seventeenth-century Visby historian Strelow had access to old letters in copy or even original, he describes this letter as sent by King Magnus from Hapsal (modern-day Haapsalu) in Estonia, which seems unlikely. Perhaps Strelow misread the letter or, possibly, only found incorrect references to it.
3   Based on a letter dated 4 July (Saturday before Saints Peter's and Paul's Day), which mentions the recent call-up. Swedish National Archives (RA), *Svenskt diplomatarium*, SDHK No, 7993. The letter's date is usually, but seemingly incorrectly, given as 3 July 1361.
4   Swedish National Archives (RA), *Svenskt diplomatarium*, SDHK No. 7962; Strelow, *Cronica Guthilandorum*, 166–167, who seems to have had access to an old copy or possibly the original letter, which is no longer preserved. The letter's date is habitually, but seemingly incorrectly, given as 1 May 1361.

... some of our enemies conspire...,' which strongly suggests that this was not the first exchange of letters about the impending war. Although only a copy of the letter to Visby has survived into the present, it is likely that he sent similar letters to others, including the national lawspeaker on Gotland and the commandants in Kalmar and Borgholm castles.

King Valdemar's army and fleet were ready to depart in late June or early July. The Danish fleet crossed the Strait and sailed north-eastwards along the Scanian coast, until it entered the Kalmar Strait, from which it easily crossed to the prosperous island of Öland. Like Gotland, Öland was wealthy, centuries earlier because of its then important position in Baltic trade but presently because of its good farmlands. However, Öland was smaller than Gotland, and the population correspondingly less numerous and well-prepared.

When King Valdemar in early July landed his army on Öland, the Ölanders raised the rural militia to resist. The odds were uneven, however, and King Valdemar's experienced knights and soldiers quickly defeated the Öland militia, killing 'more than 500' Ölanders in the process.[5] The only modern fortification on Öland, Borgholm Castle, fell soon afterwards. King Valdemar left a garrison in Borgholm Castle. He then embarked his men, and the fleet continued towards the next target. Having reached the northernmost promontory of Öland, the Danish fleet turned east for the shortest and safest crossing to Gotland.

---

5   *Libellus de Magno Erici Rege*, in Claudius Annerstedt (ed.), *Scriptores rerum Svecicarum medii ævi* 3:1 (Uppsala: Edvard Berling, 1871-1876), 12-16, on 15.

8

The Danish Fleet Lands on Gotland, 22 July

We do not know if the Gotlanders heeded King Magnus's warning earlier in the year. They likely took some precautions, including manning the beacons, chief of which was the important one on Stora Karlsö Island, an up to 52 m high rock about six km off Gotland's west coast, from which sentries were able to watch the surrounding sea for intruders.

Although little is known about specifically fourteenth-century beacons, the beacon system remained in operation into the eighteenth (and in northern Sweden, the mid-nineteenth) century, so we know quite a lot about how the system functioned as a whole. Beacons were erected on suitable high ground at regular intervals along the entire coast, so that warnings could be transmitted speedily. The same locations often remained in use for centuries. The one thing that we do not know is how the beacons were built in the Middle Ages. Possibly, they were built of logs raised against each other, up to nine or ten metres in height. If so, they could be expected to burn for only a short time, at most half an hour, before they collapsed. Based on eighteenth-century practices, the beacon may instead have consisted of two tar barrels raised high on poles. This system enabled speedy ignition and burned for a longer time. Or, the beacon was merely a high pile of flammable materials with a core of damp hay. This would have produced a fire that lasted for several hours and, more importantly in summer which was the primary raiding season, resulted in dense, black smoke that could be seen for long distances even on a sunny day. The beacons were frequently erected on a floor of flat stones for maximum ventilation and draught. Nearby was often built a covered lookout platform, and possibly a shed for overnight stays. Sentries were normally not posted in winter, since the threat of raiding then was small. However, in spring, and in particular after a warning had been sent out like the one provided by King Magnus, the local population was called upon to provide sentries according to a rotation system which was regulated by (but not described in) Guta Law.[1] There is thus little doubt that

---

[1] Christer Westerdahl, 'Försvar längs farlederna: Ledung, vårdkasar, farledsspärrar och borgar', Gerhard Flink (ed.), *Kung Valdemars segelled* (Stockholm: Streiffert/Riksantikvarieämbetet,

THE DANISH FLEET LANDS ON GOTLAND, 22 JULY

the lookout on Stora Karlsö Island and the chain of beacons were manned in July.

When the Danish fleet on 22 July approached the western coast of the island, the sentries on Stora Karlsö Island lit the beacon, the coastal Gotlanders sounded the alarm, and in all haste attempted to raise the local militia.[2] They had no more than a couple of hours before the Danes reached the shore. No ships were dispatched to confront the Danish fleet. Gotland had no warships. No standing unit was ready to contest the landing of the Danish army. The militia only mobilised when the alarm was sounded. Besides, the voyage between northern Öland and Gotland took at most 12 to 14 hours. Assuming that the Danes set out in the morning, they could land on Gotland around 6:00 p.m. on the same day. The sun did not set until 9:02 p.m.

The Danes almost certainly followed the customary sailing route from the northern promontory of Öland, which made landfall opposite Stora Karlsö Island. This route was easy sailing, if the winds were right. One only had to sail directly eastwards, and Gotland could be recognised from afar by the high clouds that often gathered over the island.

In ancient times, the Gotlanders had usually taken refuge, with their families and livestock, in large hill forts or similar fortified areas that had been prepared in advance for the contingency of an enemy landing. The enemy would then typically have raided the coastal settlements, burnt the wooden houses, and departed when no more plunder was available. However, such contingency plans no longer seem to have been in operation. Perhaps the many stone buildings erected by the Gotlanders since the early Middle Ages made the merchant-farmers reluctant to abandon their farmsteads to raiders.

By landing in the approximate centre of Gotland, King Valdemar managed to separate the militia contingents from the northern and

Stora Karlsö Island, the site for an important lookout and a key beacon on Gotland's west coast. (Photo: Stark)

  1995), 95–101, on 97–98; Guta Law 54 and 4, in Holmbäck and Wessén, *Svenska landskapslagar: Skånelagen och Gutalagen*, 238, 242; Westholm, *Visby 1361*, 137.

2 According to the Visby Franciscan Chronicle, King Valdemar's crossing from Öland to Gotland took place on Mary Magdalene's Day, that is, 22 July, a date which is plausible and generally accepted for lack of better documentation. Visby Franciscan Chronicle (Diarium Minoritarum Wisbyensium), in Ericus Michael Fant (ed.), *Scriptores Rerum Svecicarum medii ævi* 1:1 (Uppsala: Zeipel & Palmblad, 1818), 43.

southern parts of the island. This was probably by luck rather than design, since the customary sailing route from Öland led straight there. This meant that any landing would take place somewhere in Hejde Sixth, especially if the invaders headed towards Visby, or possibly northern Hoburg Sixth.

We can expect that the men of Hejde Sixth rapidly assembled in local contingents and marched towards the shore. They could not know where the enemy fleet would make landfall, so they would have to trust signals from the beacons and mounted messengers. Since most enemy ships were small, they could tentatively land almost anywhere on the long coast. Only the biggest cogs would need proper port facilities. The Gotlanders at least knew the terrain. With some luck, they might be able to anticipate the landing site and confront the intruders as they disembarked by small boats or by simply wading ashore through the shallow water.

The northern Gotlanders from Bro and Rute Sixths would be alerted by beacon, but they had no means of reaching the landing site in time to contest the landing. We can assume that they instead prepared to march towards Roma, where the National Assembly, the Gutnalting, was held, and which probably constituted the island's predetermined central assembly point.

Most southern Gotlanders from Hoburg Sixth and eastern Gotlanders from Burs and Kräklinge Sixths, too, would likely aim to march overland towards Roma. The militia units nearest to the enemy might instead march to join their compatriots in Hejde Sixth, if so, probably arriving on the following day. But then the contested landing would probably already be over.

Based on later events, it seems clear that many militia units assembled at the Hejde Sixth Thing site, located in Mästerby, a strategic location which on the western side of the island connected northern and southern Gotland. Mästerby housed a church and, possibly yet more importantly, the Hejde Sixth Thing site, which at least later also was known as the South Thing (Gutnish: Suderting). Nearby was the Suderthing Brook (Sudertingså, 'South Thing Brook') which flowed westwards from Fjäle Fen (Gutnish: Fjäle Myr), a group of surrounding wetlands that under most conditions were difficult to cross. The Suderthing Brook had steep banks and was probably wider and deeper in the fourteenth century then at present. For this reason, the Gotlanders had built a narrow causeway and a bridge over the brook. Presently known as Ajmund's Bridge, or only Ajmunds ('Eymund's'), it constituted one of few effective roads between north and south.

The Thing site was located immediately northeast of the bridge, which made it of key importance in case an invader came from the south.[3]

We do not know exactly where the Danes landed. Contemporary sources are silent on this point. The Danes would have been looking for a site that provided not only a safe landing spot for the ships, but also a location that

---

3 Ajmund's Bridge remained a strategic location into modern times. In spring 1808, a confrontation took place there between a Russian invasion force under Rear Admiral Nikolay Bodisko and a rural levy. The Gotlanders lacked both modern weapons and gunpowder, so the island's Vice Governor, Eric af Klint, negotiated a surrender. The brief campaign and subsequent Russian occupation of the island, which lasted less than a month, resulted in no casualties for either side.

still was undefended, perhaps because the local militia units had expected a landing elsewhere.

Many modern historians reckon that King Valdemar landed at Fröjel, where there was a well-known port. If so, the Danish fleet approached the coast at the fishing village Kronvall, but then continued northwards along the coast the slight distance to Fröjel. Or, possibly the Danes landed at Djupvik, about 4 km north of Kronvall and just south of Fröjel.

The fifteenth-century Link Poem, however, says the Danes landed at 'Garna haffn' (Garn Harbour), which likely refers to Västergarn significantly further to the north.[4]

The seventeenth-century Visby chronicler Strelow locates the landing to 'Chronevold'.[5] This was not the modern-day fishing village Kronvall, in sight of Lilla Karlsö Island but entirely inappropriate for disembarkation since there were no harbour facilities there.[6] By Chronevold, Strelow meant modern-day Vivesholm, further north and on the way to Västergarn. Strelow notes that by the late fourteenth century, the location was known as Landescrone. Vivesholm, although presently a peninsula north of modern-day Klintehamn, was then one of three small islands located about 100 m off the coast. It was a suitable location for an invasion fleet.[7] As long as the winds held, the Danish fleet would be able to reach Vivesholm before nightfall. Protected anchorage was available between the islands and the coast, and it was difficult for shore-bound defenders to interrupt a landing.

If Strelow can be trusted, a hastily raised local militia, perhaps a few men from Klinte parish, for whatever reason took it upon themselves to contest the landing. Their number is unlikely to have been more than about 100. Strelow, who because of his distance in time to the events is not always a reliable source, describes how a first skirmish was fought already where the Danes landed. The invaders were most vulnerable at the point of landing. However, the invaders were trained soldiers, and in addition clearly outnumbered the available defenders. The Danes easily cleared the shore, and the invasion army disembarked.

Whether some Klinte men actually opposed the landing is conjecture and only based on Strelow. Some may have chosen to defend themselves further inland, in Klinte Church or on the hill ('klint') behind the church. Or, perhaps they left their farmsteads to assemble with the others further north, if they considered it the strategically better choice. Because at this point in time, the main force of the Hejde Sixth militia was already on its way to the assembly point at Mästerby further north, where yet more contingents of militia probably arrived from other parts of the island to oppose the invaders.

---

4   G.E. Klemming (ed.), 'Svenska medeltidens rim-krönikor: Gamla eller Eriks-krönikan,' *Samlingar utgifna av Svenska Fornskrift-sällskapet* 17:1 (Stockholm: P. A. Norstedt & Söner, 1865), 171–192, on 183.
5   Strelow, *Cronica Guthilandorum*, 170.
6   Thordeman, *Armour from the Battle of Wisby, 19*; Bengt Hammarhjelm, *Gotländsk krigshistoria från Gutasagan till 1814* (Visby: Ödin, 1998), 74–75. The once-popular identification of Kronvall as the landing site is probably a late oral tradition, based on its similarities in names with Strelow's Chronevold.
7   Hammarhjelm, *Gotländsk krigshistoria*, 74–75.

FALL OF THE MERCHANT-FARMER REPUBLIC

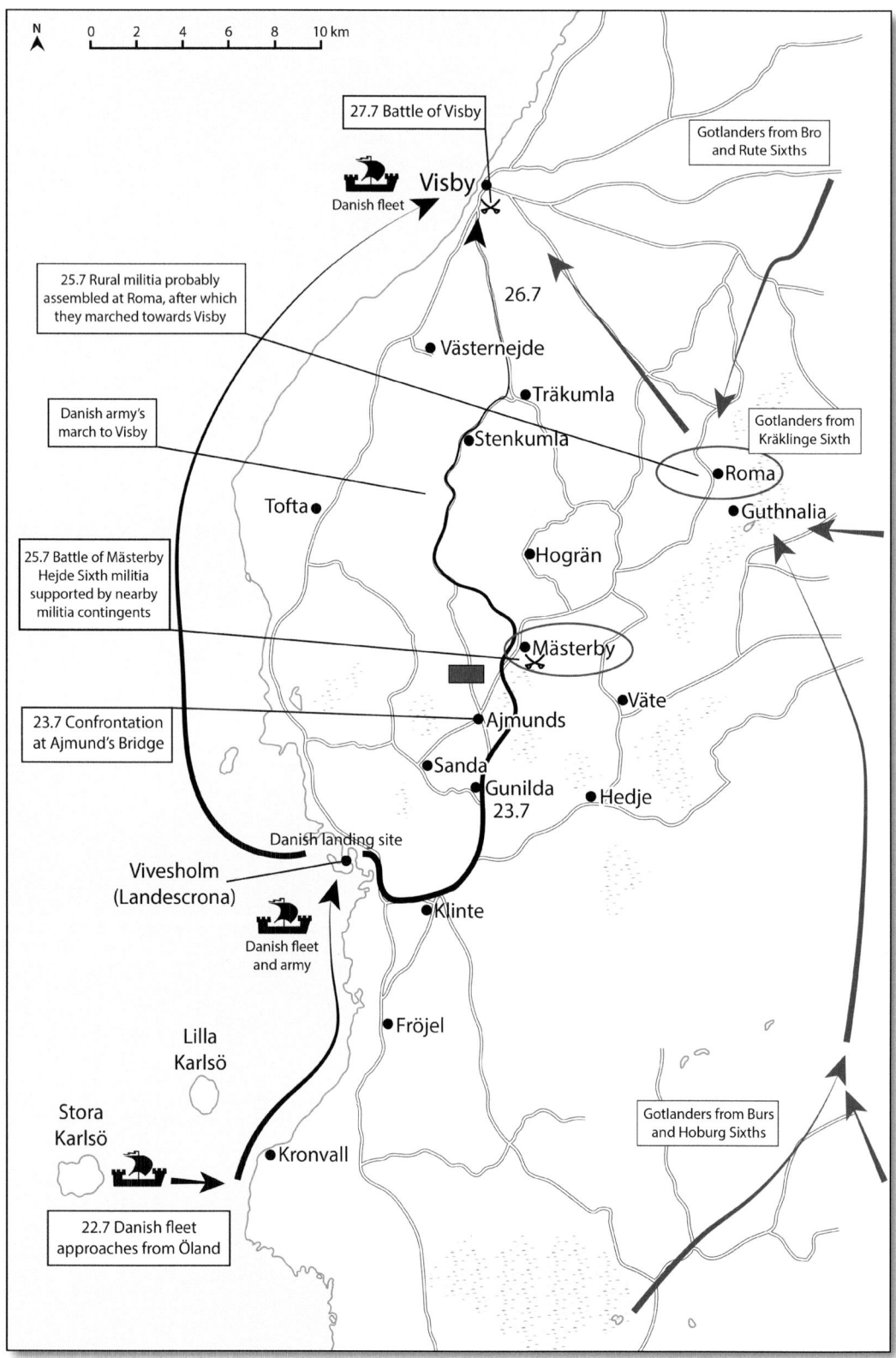

The Landing and March to Visby.

9

The Battle of Mästerby, 25 July

Having secured the landing site, King Valdemar immediately moved inland, to Klinte, and then marched northwards towards Visby along the inland road. The Danes marched by way of Gunilda farmstead, where local tradition holds that a skirmish of some kind took place, and where an old but undated memorial cross without text is linked to an oral tradition which informs us that King Valdemar spent his first night on Gotland there.[1] Gunilda was no more than 3 km from Ajmund's Bridge, not far from where the rural militia was assembling. There the Gotlanders confronted King Valdemar on 23 July.

Tactically, the Gotlanders had selected a highly defensible position. Marching overland, the Danes would almost certainly pass through this area to reach Visby. There were no roads along the coast, where the brooks reached the sea in wide deltas. Inland, it was even worse, with large marshlands that prevented traffic. The Danes had to march along the few lines of high ground that were used as inland roads. It was difficult, although by no means impossible, to cross the Suderthing Brook, except by the bridge, which the Gotlanders tore down. While the brook was neither deep nor wide, its banks were steep, which made it difficult for the heavily armed Danish infantry and cavalry to cross. The Gotlanders possibly also fortified the area with timber obstacles (abatis), a traditional northern method of war, or sharpened poles along the steep banks.

The militia at Mästerby and Ajmund's Bridge certainly included the men from Hejde Sixth, and quite possibly also contingents from Bro, Kräklinge, and Burs Sixths. The latter may have arrived only in the evening of 23 July. Technically, men from Hoburg Sixth did not have much further to travel than the men from Bro, Kräklinge, and Burs Sixths. Some were probably on their way to Mästerby. Possibly some 1,500 militia assembled at Mästerby. Any estimate of the strength of the Danish army must be equally imprecise. Some Danes were probably detached to guard the landing site. Others may have been foraging. Possibly, from 1,500 to perhaps as many as 2,500 Danes confronted the Gotlanders.[2]

---

1 Snöbohm, *Gotlands land och folk*, 144.
2 Lingström, *Mästerby, 1361*, 140.

FALL OF THE MERCHANT-FARMER REPUBLIC

The Danes may have found that the defensive position at Ajmund's Bridge was too strong. If so, any fighting that took place there was limited to exchanges of bow, crossbow, and gun fire. No archaeological battlefield remains have yet been found on this site.

A skirmish at Ajmund's Bridge would explain why the ensuing battle later was described as a two-day affair.[3] It would also explain why Ajmund's Bridge frequently recurred in oral traditions of the battle. However, it seems more likely that the two opposing forces merely confronted each other. King Valdemar must have been reluctant to send his men across the deep brook, and the Gotlanders did not intend to abandon their fortified line.

Unable to push back the militia head on, King Valdemar sent out scouts with orders to find an alternative route. Either on the same day, or more likely the next, they found one: across the Fjäle marshlands. The passage would be difficult but allow the Danes to attack the defenders in the flank. Fjäle marshlands was what can best be described as a fen, a wetland or very shallow lake, which reached from Ajmund's Bridge in the south to the Grens farmstead in the north, a distance of between four and five kilometres. The fen may have been mostly or in part covered in vegetation or may have consisted of open but very shallow water. The widest part of the fen was about 1,000 m, but the narrowest section was only from about 175 to 200 m, which made a crossing feasible, especially if the dry summer made parts of the marshlands passable. Dendrochronological analysis suggests that both the summer of 1360 and 1361 were unusually dry.[4] Possibly, the Danes attempted a first attack through Fjäle Fen already on 24 July but failed to break through. If no actual combat took place at Ajmund's Bridge, this might explain why the battle afterwards was described as a two-day affair. However, it seems equally likely that the Danes did not advance further on 24 July, instead awaiting the reports of their scouts.

Lina Fen, Härsne, the last great wetland on Gotland, before it was gradually drained from 1947 onwards. Fjäle Fen may have looked similar during normal conditions, but the summer of 1361 was unusually dry, which allowed the Danes to wade across. (Photo: Järnvägsmuseet)

---

3   Strelow, *Cronica Guthilandorum*, 170.
4   Lingström, *Mästerby, 1361*, 43.

THE BATTLE OF MÄSTERBY, 25 JULY

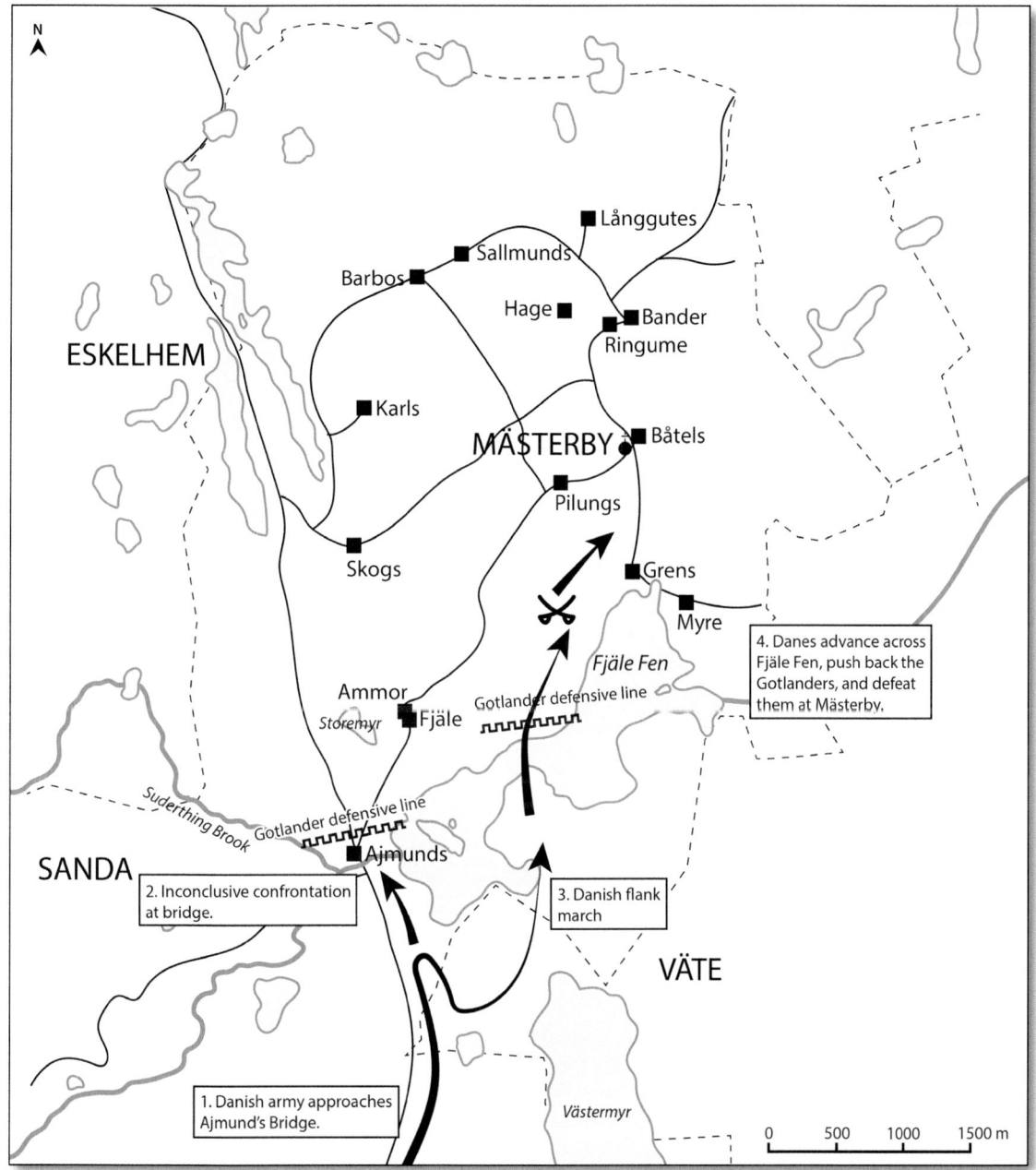

The Battle of Mästerby.

On 25 July, King Valdemar ordered a substantial force to flank march around the militia defences. Battlefield archaeology shows that the Danes advanced across the narrowest section of Fjäle Fen, and that the Gotlanders themselves moved into the fen to meet them there in a hard-fought engagement. When finally pushed back, the Gotland militia reformed further north, towards Mästerby, where there is evidence of another sharp fight.[5] Hence, Strelow reports the two-day battle as the Battle of 'Fjäle Fen in Mästerby'.[6] Ultimately, the Danes won the field.

The memory of the bloody battle survives in myths linked to nearby farmsteads. One such legend claims that King Valdemar brought a witch who somehow unnerved the Gotlanders and made them lose their courage (as noted, myths linking King Valdemar to witches and witchcraft abounded in Denmark, too). Another legend tells of a cavalryman who was cut in half in the battle, so that the horse walked into nearby Grens farmstead carrying only his lower abdomen and legs in the saddle. The legend relates to the name Grens (Gutnish: *Grains*, 'astride').[7] A memorial cross was later raised at the Grens farmstead, so certainly lives were lost there during the battle. In the mid-1980s, the sexton at nearby Väte Church claimed that they had previously discovered a mass grave near the church, similar to the ones outside Visby, but the locals had rapidly covered it up because they did not want their farmsteads disturbed by archaeologists or other outlanders.[8] Maria Lingström, who led the battlefield archaeology project in Mästerby, later discovered an inscription on the memorial cross, which reads Anno Domini MCCCLXI Iacobi, which gives St. Jacob' Day (25 July) 1361.

We do not know how many Gotlanders or Danes fell at Mästerby. The Link Poem claims 600 dead Gotlanders in a battle soon after the Danes landed. Possibly, this number refers to the battle of Mästerby.[9]

Battlefield archaeology excavations carried out by Maria Lingström discovered some 500 battlefield-related artefacts at Fjäle Fen and Mästerby. The finds included broken weapons, crossbow bolts, firearm munitions, chainmail, and pieces of lamellar armour, but also pieces of stirrups and spurs, which suggests that cavalry was used.[10]

After the Danish victory, the Gotlanders retreated. This time, they probably planned to assemble at Visby, where they expected to join forces with the city's burgher militia as well as with militia contingents from other parts of the island. However, we will see that some contingents, particularly those from southern Gotland, instead may have returned home to protect their own farmsteads.

---

5   Lingström, 'Fjäle myr 1361', 33–44; Lingström, *Mästerby, 1361*, 157–158.
6   Strelow, *Cronica Guthilandorum*, 170.
7   Snöbohm, *Gotlands land och folk*, 144.
8   Westholm, *Visby 1361*, 144.
9   Klemming, 'Svenska medeltidens rim-krönikor', 183–184.
10 Lingström, 'Fjäle myr 1361'; Lingström, *Mästerby, 1361*.

THE BATTLE OF MÄSTERBY, 25 JULY

Battlefield finds from Mästerby. (History Museum, Stockholm; photo: Katarina Nimmervoll)

10

The Battle of Visby, 27 July

The distance from Mästerby to Visby was just above 20 km, and the road passed through uninhabited forestland. It was an easy march.

On 26 July, the Danish army continued the march towards Visby in the footsteps of the retreating Gotlanders. In the evening, they made camp close to Visby. We do not know where, but it seems likely that at least King Valdemar and his close retainers moved into Nye farmstead, in Nygårds in Västerhejde, which was one of the largest farmsteads immediately south of Visby. The Danes almost certainly sent out foraging parties to loot the other farmsteads in the area.

On the following day, the Danish army reached Visby itself, where the Gotland militia awaited them, this time formed up to fight the Danish invaders under Visby's city walls.

There is some uncertainty about the date of battle. Most historians accept the date 27 July, which is the one indicated by the memorial cross at the Visby mass graves ('third day of St. Jacob', the first day of whom was celebrated on 25 July). The memorial cross was almost certainly raised before 1376, when the battle still remained in public memory.[1] The Visby Franciscan Chronicle, which is believed to have been written around 1420, mentions the battle twice, although on both occasions with obvious clerical errors with regard to the date. The first reference dates the battle to 'the eve before' (Latin: *in vigilia*) St. Jacob's Day, which would be 24 July. The second reference dates the battle as 'the morning after' (Latin: *in crastino*) St. Jacob's Day, which obviously would mean 26 July.[2] Clerical errors were fairly common when manuscripts were copied by hand, since under most conditions, the chroniclers used easily missed abbreviations for date references.

We have no contemporary written accounts of the battle. However, the archaeological data from the mass graves offer some clues for a reconstruction of what happened.

---

1. The cross is on stylistic grounds commonly dated to the 1370s or 1380s. Its text strongly suggests that it was raised by Gotlanders, not the Visby city council. The text also suggests that this must have taken place at a time when there were no Danish bailiffs on the island, and certainly before 1376, when Gotland swore fealty to the Danish Crown.
2. Visby Franciscan Chronicle, in Fant, *Scriptores Rerum Svecicarum medii ævi* 1:1, 34, 45.

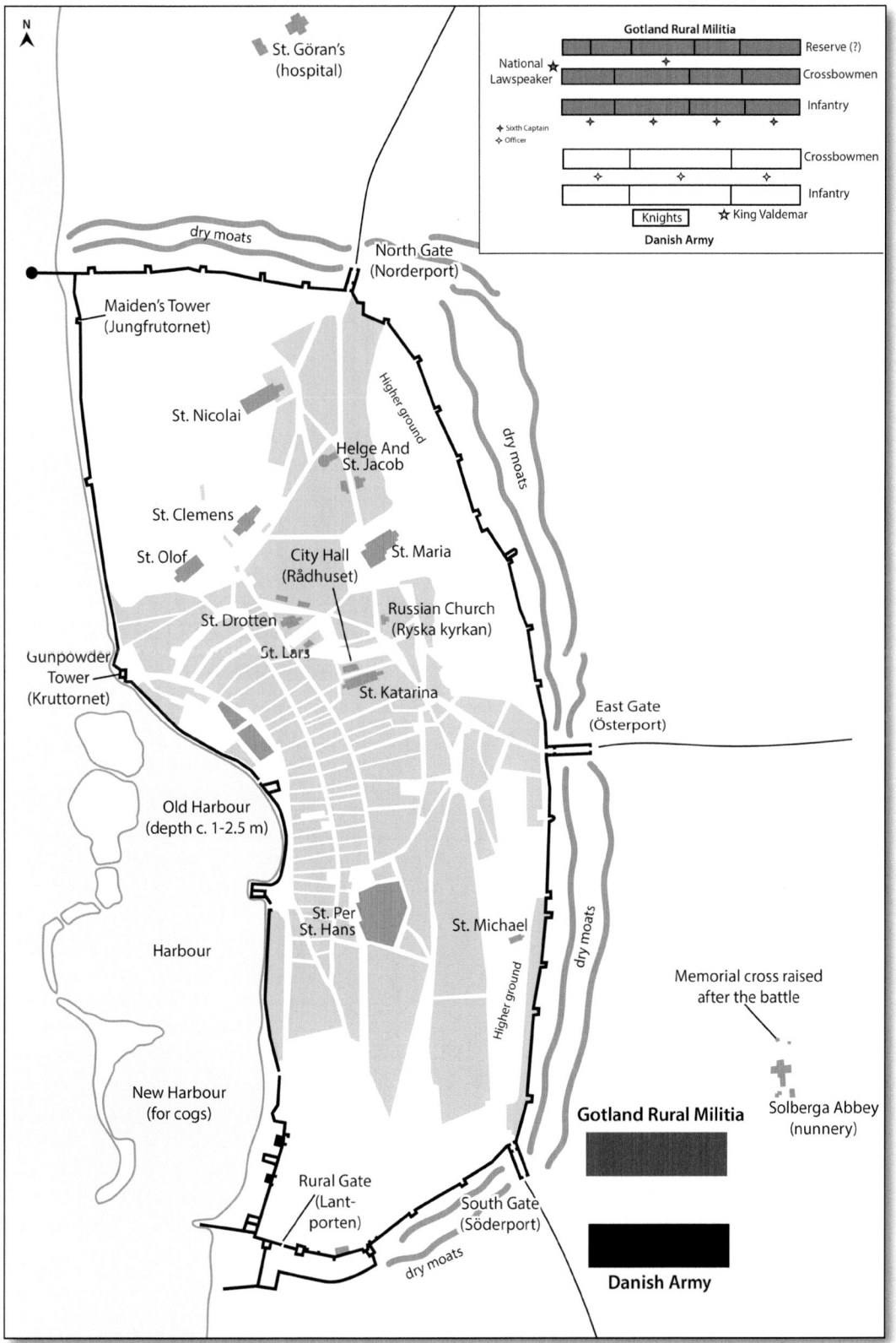

The Battle of Visby, with inset schematic of how the two armies possibly deployed.

It seems certain that the Gotlanders first assembled outside the city wall, specifically between South Gate (Söderport) and East Gate (Österport). In addition to the survivors from Mästerby, they arrived from the north, east, and probably southeast (Rute, Bro, Hejde, Kräklinge, and Burs Sixths). There was sufficient time even for the Gotlanders from distant Fårö Island in the north (about 65 km away) and Sundre and Fide in the south (about 90 km or more from Visby) to reach Visby in time for the battle, although we do not know if they did. Contingents from Hoburg Sixth may or not have participated. If not, they had retreated southwards after Mästerby to protect their own farmsteads.

When the Danes approached, the Gotlanders formed up for battle in front of the South Gate. To avoid another flank attack, they probably deployed in a dense formation, several ranks deep, between the city wall's dry moats and Solberga Abbey, which was located about 300 m east of the city wall.[3]

The Gotlanders possibly planned to prepare field defences outside the Visby curtain wall. There is no evidence of such plans, but similar tactics were used by militia units elsewhere at the time, particularly when they faced knightly cavalry.

Most militia were infantry, but the Gotlanders fielded a small cavalry as well. We do not know where they deployed, or whether they dismounted to fight in the line. Archers and crossbowmen probably deployed immediately behind the line, so that they could fire above their heads. There may have been an infantry reserve behind the line, presumably consisting of those deemed too young or too old to fight in the main line, and perhaps the survivors from Mästerby.

Upon arrival at the field south of Visby, King Valdemar, as was his habit, took the opportunity to dub many of his companions knights in order to raise their fighting spirit.[4]

It was earlier on hypothesised that the Danish army split into a smaller detachment which marched westwards against the sea gate, and a main force which continued towards north, east of the Gotlanders and the city wall until it formed up at East Gate. Possibly, there was also a yet smaller force which continued northwards to protect the army's northern (right) flank.[5] However, we have no way of knowing whether this was how King Valdemar deployed his men, or indeed whether he divided his units at all.

It seems that the Danes deployed their crossbowmen in the first line of battle. The battle likely began with both sides engaging the other with bows and crossbows. The militia surely included a number of crossbowmen and archers, but probably not as many or as well-organised as the professional German crossbowmen in King Valdemar's army, so their return fire was likely less effective. Crossbow bolts easily penetrated even good armour, so the effect was likely devastating. About 10 percent of the skulls found in the mass graves have holes that likely derive from crossbow bolts. Since

---

3   Thordeman, *Armour from the Battle of Wisby*, 24.
4   Detmar's Chronicle, in Koppmann, *Die Chroniken der niedersächsischen Städte* 1, 529.
5   Clason, 'Om i Korsbetningsgraven vid Visby funna skelett', 268; Harrison, *Visby brandskattning*, 113.

the head constitutes a minor part of the body, we can assume that many more casualties derived from crossbow fire than what we can detect from the osteological remains in the mass graves.

Possibly, the Gotlanders quickly realised that it was suicidal merely to stand still, taking casualties, and instead chose to charge. Or, perhaps, the Danish infantry moved in with polearms and swords when the Gotlanders were shaken by the crossbow fire. We can assume that the Danish cavalry, limited in number as it was, joined the battle, too. The archaeological finds show cuts against heads, arms, and legs. The wounds thus inflicted were grievous, with skulls splits and, in occasional cases, both lower legs broken, or possibly even cut off, by the same blow.[6] Based on the very large number of leg wounds found in the mass graves, attacks against the lower legs seem to have been a common tactics. Few Gotlanders wore leg armour, so a solid hit would down the man so struck. When on the ground, he was easier to kill. Of the skulls that show wounds from cutting weapons, a significant number shows cuts in the neck. Some may have been inflicted on fleeing men, but it is likely that many were so struck when already prone on the ground because of other wounds. Since the helmet still would have provided some protection for the head, it was easier to kill an enemy on the ground by aiming for his neck below the helmet.

Although the written evidence makes it certain that most of the fallen men were Gotlanders, the battle was not entirely one-sided. Some Gotlanders may have taken cover in or behind the dry moats, where they could only be engaged by infantry, not cavalry. Other contingents of Gotlanders perhaps arrived late. If the battle was still ongoing, they may have engaged the Danish army in the rear, inflicting some casualties before they were overwhelmed by the superior Danish numbers, or before they chose to abandon the fight and retreat (or flee). The mass graves contain Danish casualties, and not only those of common soldiers. We have already seen that heraldic devices on one cuirass (linked to the Roorda family), together with the presence of Danish coins, strongly suggest that some of the men buried in the mass graves were Danes.[7] While there is no reason to believe that the dead man linked to the Roorda family was a senior noble, neither was he a common soldier. We can probably assume that if the number of important Danish casualties had been limited to a handful, these dead would have been recovered and buried separately under more honourable conditions. Yet, these men, too, were dumped into the mass graves.

Modern isotope analysis, too, confirms that some of the dead were Danes. Preliminary data suggest that possibly as many as a third of the dead in the mass graves were Danes.[8] King Valdemar's soldiers probably found themselves fighting harder than they had expected when told that

---

6   Forensic analysis suggests that although both lower legs in these cases certainly were disabled by the blow, the fracture actually fully severed the bones only after burial, because of the weight of the soil. Clason, 'Om i Korsbetningsgraven vid Visby funna skelett', 287–288.
7   Thordeman, *Armour from the Battle of Wisby*, 143–145. The Danish civil war coins were so debased that they hardly were accepted as currency outside Denmark.
8   Neijman, *Gotlandic Rural Militia*, 70.

the enemy only consisted of rural levies. The outcome of the battle was not predetermined.

This leads us to the question of the Visby burghers.

Would the Visby burgher militia and mercenary contingent take action? For Hermann Munter and other prominent burghers, the decision was neither obvious nor easy.

Some burghers were Gotlanders or were related by marriage to men fighting among the rural militia outside the city walls. This provided strong motivation to join forces with the rural militia against the foreign invader.

On the other hand, the rivalry of the past between the Hanseatic city and its rural competitors were probably not completely forgotten. Possibly, some friction remained between burghers and rural merchant-farmers.

Besides, there was always the risk that a victorious enemy might take advantage of his position of strength by sacking the city and murdering its inhabitants. Visby's city walls were strong, but the burghers did not have enough men to man its entire length. The city would have been easier to defend, had they let in the rural militia. However, the city's depots of food supplies had not yet been refilled since last year, and remaining food would hardly have lasted long if both burghers and rural militia had to endure a long siege inside the city.[9]

Whatever option Munter and associates chose, and whatever the outcome, they would afterwards have to justify their decision. The issue of confronting the Danes or not was not merely a personal decision for the mayor and city council of Visby, but one that concerned the entire Hanseatic League. Moreover, the responsibility for taking the wrong decision would be terribly personal. Munter and the others knew and had probably personally witnessed, how in 1342 both Visby mayors, Hermann Swerting and Johannes Moop, and several members of the then city council were executed by beheading for acting against the interests of the Hanseatic League. The background was the war over Scania between King Valdemar, who enjoyed the backing of the League, and King Magnus of Sweden. As part of the hostilities, King Magnus imprisoned several merchants from Lübeck. At the same time, he also demanded a special monetary war contribution from his territories, including Visby. The two Visby mayors Swerting and Moop and the city council had not dared to refuse the war contribution, even though King Magnus then was engaged in hostilities against the Hanseatic League of which Visby was a leading member. However, when the burghers later learnt of the city council's decision, they deemed it treason. Swerting's and Moop's decision had cost the burghers money and, moreover, risked their status and future with the League. For this, the city officials had to pay the ultimate price.

And now, the two kings were at it again, for the same reasons as in the past. It is fair to assume that Munter and associates discussed their options with some trepidation. They surely would not have wished to share the fate of Swerting and Moop by turning against League interests, nor did they want to risk the enmity of King Valdemar and his battle-hardened soldiers. It is

---

9   Hammarhjelm, *Gotländsk krigshistoria*, 77.

even possible that they had been informed about the impending invasion not only in May from King Magnus – but also from their compatriots in the Hanseatic League, which as we have seen at this point supported the Danish King. No surviving documents mention it, but in this particular case, absence of evidence is not evidence of absence. We know from other sources that the Hanseatic cities frequently exchanged business and political information which they did not necessarily share with outsiders.

Had the well-armed Visby burghers and their mercenary soldiers at this point chosen to sally out, King Valdemar might have lost the day. Had the burghers opened the gates to let in the surviving Gotlanders, King Valdemar would have had to lay siege to the strongly fortified city, something for which he probably was poorly prepared. Besides, we know nothing about the supply situation in his army. The Danish army had been on the move for more than five days. Some food supplies from Öland must have remained on the ships, and others had presumably been taken from local farmsteads along the road to Visby, but was it enough?

Yet, the burgher militia neither sallied out, nor opened the gates for the rural militia. The city gates remained firmly closed. The easiest decision in a crisis is always to do nothing. Munter and the city council did exactly this. There is nothing to suggest that the burghers took any action, however slight, to support the Gotlanders.

The refusal of the Visby burghers to join the battle meant that the Gotlanders could have no hope of defeating the Danes. Soon, it must have been obvious to them how the battle would end. We do not know how long it took for the Danes to break the Gotlanders. Many probably attempted to flee the field, but since the city gates remained closed, they had nowhere to run. There is nothing to suggest that the Danes took prisoners. Danes and Germans regarded the rural militia as peasants of the kind they knew from their own countries, rustics who deserved no mercy, and they probably thought that even if taken alive, the Gotlanders lacked the means to ransom themselves. This, of course, was a faulty conclusion, since the financial circumstances of the prosperous Gotland merchant-farmers were quite dissimilar to that of oppressed and overtaxed Danish peasants. But can we expect the Danish and German soldiers to have known this? It is very likely that the Danes and their mercenary soldiers killed everybody who stood against them, or they could lay their hands on.

The result was disastrous for the Gotlanders. Approximately '1,800 peasants' fell in the battle, the Visby Franciscan Chronicle later claimed.[10] Hemmed in by Danish units, dry moats, and city walls, few managed to escape. At some point, the battle turned into a massacre of the surviving Gotlanders. Since nothing more is heard of the national lawspeaker, it seems likely that he perished, too. This would also explain why his name is lost to history.

---

10   Visby Franciscan Chronicle, in Fant, *Scriptores Rerum Svecicarum medii ævi* 1:1, 34, 45. The *Libellus de Magno Erici Rege* even claimed 2,000 dead Gotlanders. Annerstedt, *Scriptores rerum Svecicarum medii ævi* 3:1, 15.

FALL OF THE MERCHANT-FARMER REPUBLIC

In comparison, the Zealand Chronicle claims, King Valdemar's army won the day 'almost without loss' (Latin: *quasi sine lesione*).[11]

The memory of the 1,800 dead was probably roughly correct and may have derived from the labour to bury all of them after the battle. That many of the dead actually were Danes was not something that King Valdemar would have advertised at the time, and the information was later forgotten.

The dead were buried in mass graves within the outer walls of Solberga Abbey, so that they would rest on hallowed ground. Even so, the dead were unceremoniously dumped into the mass graves as they arrived, not side by side but helter-skelter in heaps. The battle took place in the heat of summer, so it was important to get the corpses into the ground as soon as possible to avoid the outbreak of disease. Burial must have taken several days. The need for haste seems to have been particularly important in what is believed to be the mass graves dug last. While the weapons and helmets of the dead were retrieved, many men were otherwise simply dumped into the graves with armour, clothes, personal belongings, and even cash in some cases. Many of the dead had been hit by crossbow bolts, and nobody took the time to remove them before burial. In some cases, the failure to remove the armour of the dead can be explained by it being damaged and not worth the trouble to retrieve. However, several cuirasses appear to have been perfectly usable when dumped into the mass graves.

A rough estimation based on the number of mail coifs and belt buckles suggest that about every sixth person in grave one, every fourth person in grave two, and every eighth person in grave three were buried in armour.[12]

Altogether, the archaeologists found 185 chainmail coifs, 25 complete cuirasses and numerous parts thereof, pieces of numerous armoured gauntlets (including two old-style gauntlets of chainmail), parts of a pair of sabatons (armoured shoes), shoulder plates, several elbow or knee cups, four knives, 38 crossbow bolts, hundreds of coins, six spurs or parts of spurs, and even seven horseshoes, six of which were small and thus most likely worn by Gotland ponies of the type used by most rural inhabitants.[13]

The face of battle. The human remains in the Visby mass graves have come to symbolise warfare in the Middle Ages, or indeed in any age. (History Museum, Stockholm; photo: Helena Rosengren)

---

11 Jørgensen, *Annales Danici Medii Ævi*, 188
12 Thordeman, *Armour from the Battle of Wisby*, 119.
13 Thordeman, *Armour from the Battle of Wisby*, 99, 110, 112–113, 115, 122–125, 143–145, 344–413, 414–434.

THE BATTLE OF VISBY, 27 JULY

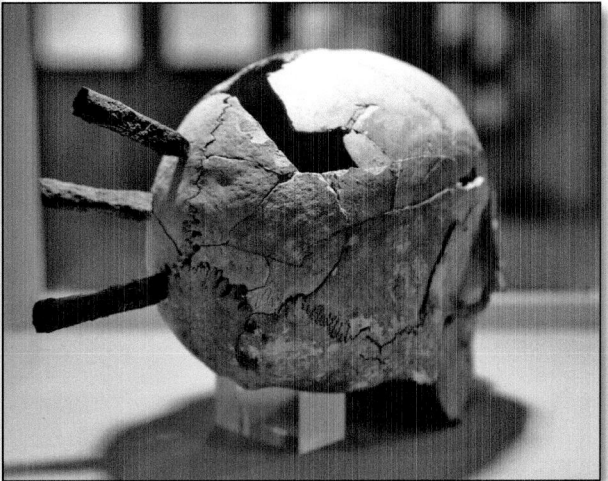

Gotlander or Dane? With three crossbow bolts lodged in the rear of the skull, it is easy to forget that it once was a living soldier. However, while the skull wounds are genuine, the crossbow bolts were placed there by a museum curator in the aftermath of the Second World War. The wounds were likely caused by a mace or morning star polearm. (History Museum, Stockholm; photo: Jenny Nyberg)

Within a generation after the battle, a memorial cross was raised on the battlefield. The Latin text translates: 'In the year of the Lord 1361 on the third day after Saint Jacob's fell outside Visby's gates by Danish hands the Gotlanders buried here. Pray for them' (ANNO D(OMI)NI M CCC LXI F(E)RIA III POST JACOBI / ANTE PORTAS WISBY I(N) MA(N)IB(US) DANOR(UM) CECIDERU(N)T GUT-ENSES / H(IC) SEP(UL)TI OR(ATE) P(RO) E(IS)). Note the abbreviated forms commonly used in Latin inscriptions. The place, previously a pasture, then received its present name Korsbetningen ('Pasture by the Cross'). (Photo: Medström)

FALL OF THE MERCHANT-FARMER REPUBLIC

The mass graves at Korsbetningen were found in 1905. The three excavated mass graves contained the remains of 1,185 men. However, an additional mass grave was also identified, but it was never properly excavated. In addition, one more mass grave was destroyed before it could be excavated and documented, when the Swedish Army built a gunpowder storage depot in 1811, and parts of yet another grave were destroyed without excavation as part of another construction project in 1903. The claim of 1,800 dead on the field outside Visby accordingly remains plausible. (Swedish National Heritage Board; photo: Nils Åzelius)

11

The Submission of Visby

After the battle, Munter and his associates agreed to open the city's gates to King Valdemar. A few days after the battle, King Valdemar had a letter of privilege prepared for the city of Visby. He guaranteed the city's traditional privileges and rights. Based on a surviving copy from 1425,

> We, King Valdemar, by the grace of God King of Danes and Wends, and Christopher, Our son, by the same grace Duke of Lolland, recognise and testify in public with this letter, that We guarantee all the rights and freedoms of the wise and honest men, mayor, councillors, and all burghers in Our city of Visby, Our beloved and loyal people, which they have enjoyed since days of yore.
>
> Further, We grant them Our special grace, that they will enjoy such freedoms on the shore in our realm Denmark, which Our other towns have, which are in the same realm.
>
> In addition, they and their people shall safely carry their goods in Our realm, and We guarantee them their coin, which they have used since days of yore. In testimony of these agreements: those who were present hereby, that is, His Highness Duke Eric of Saxe[-Lauenburg], Master Claus Limbek, Master Henning Podebusk, and Master Valdemar Sappi, Knights.[1] In testimony of all these written promises, which We henceforth firmly will adhere to, We the aforementioned Valdemar, King of Denmark, and Christopher, Duke of Lolland, have affixed Our seals under this letter, which is given and written in the year of the Lord 1361/five days after/holy St. Olaf's Day [3 August].[2]

The letter was also witnessed by selected representatives of Visby: Prior Henrik (Henricus) of the Dominican Convent, Custos Gottskalk (Gotschalcus) of

---

1   In German, Duke Eric's title was *Hochgeboren Fürst [und] Herzog*.
2   The date of the letter is disputed since the original is lost. The surviving copy from 1425 gives the date as St. Olaf's Day (29 July). Swedish National Archives (RA), *Svenskt diplomatarium,* SDHK No. 7999. However, both Arild Huitfeldt, *Danmarckis Rigis Krønicke* 1 (Copenhagen: Joachim Moltken, 2nd edn 1652), 525, and a few years later, Strelow, *Cronica Guthilandorum*, 174 states that the letter was signed five days *after* St. Olaf's Day, that is, on 3 August. Huitfeldt or Strelow, or both, may have had access to the original or earlier copies. Besides, since King Valdemar would have other things on his mind immediately after the battle, and since it is more likely that a few words were lost than added when a copy was made, we accept the later date.

the Franciscan Convent, and the aforementioned Hermann Munter, who as noted likely was the mayor of Visby.

From the perspective of the Visby burghers, the Letter of Privilege was all they might have hoped for. The letter guaranteed all the city's previous rights and privileges, including in the lucrative Denmark trade. Visby could even continue to mint its own coins. In short, King Valdemar informed the city that it henceforth belonged to the Danish, not the Swedish, Crown, but otherwise business would go on as usual. King Valdemar claimed no direct overlordship but stuck to the traditional form 'King of Danes and Wends'. There is nothing in the letter to suggest even the tiniest hostile act against Visby. And why should it have been? King Valdemar had already before the invasion concluded agreements with the Hanseatic League, of which Visby formed a part. One was the deal about Scanian market privileges, and the other was the non-aggression pact. While Visby surely was expected to provide supplies to the Danish army and rich gifts to King Valdemar, this was in line with customary contributions when a king and his army stayed in a merchant city. No plunder took place. A year later, on 15 December 1362, the Visby city council wrote to Lübeck and the Hanseatic cities that the goods in Visby owned by the other cities remained safe, 'since we last year in our plight safeguarded all such goods that was stored with us on behalf of the cities [together] with our own goods' (Low German: *wente wi overme jare alsodane gud, alse mit uns was van den steden, in unsen noden vrieden mit unseme gude*).[3]

We can assume that the Danish fleet at this point moved to Visby, to protect the city from possible Swedish reinforcements and, of no less importance, find safe shelter in case the weather deteriorated.

Hidden Hoards

Meanwhile, King Valdemar's men plundered rural Gotland. The immediate neighbourhood of Visby was the first to feel the onslaught. An archaeological excavation has showed that the farmstead Bingeby, about two kilometres east of Visby, was burnt and abandoned at some point in the mid-fourteenth century. Interestingly, the excavation of the farmstead found 13 crossbow bolts of the same type as the Danes employed in the Battle of Visby.[4] The high number of crossbow bolts suggests that a remnant of the rural militia

---

3   *Hanserecesse: Die Recesse und andere Akten der Hansetage von 1256–1430*, 221. Some translate the final words as 'safeguarded all such goods that was stored with us on behalf of the cities *by surrendering* our own goods'. Lindström, *Anteckningar om Gotlands medeltid* 1, 109, disagrees with this reading of the original text, since its primary focus lies on arguing the honour and dependability of the Visby burghers as a banking partner (all goods entrusted with us are safe), not the details of what happened in 1361 which everybody then already knew.

4   Anna-Lena Gerdin, 'A Coastal Farmstead in the Shadow of the City', *The Significant Detail: Europeanization at the Base of Society – The Case of the Baltic Rim 1100–1400 AD, Transactions of the CCC Workshops at Skäftekärr in Sweden 7–10 October 1999, and at Tukums in Latvia 15–18 April 2000* (Visby: Gotland University College, CCC Papers 9, 2007), 123–151.

THE SUBMISSION OF VISBY

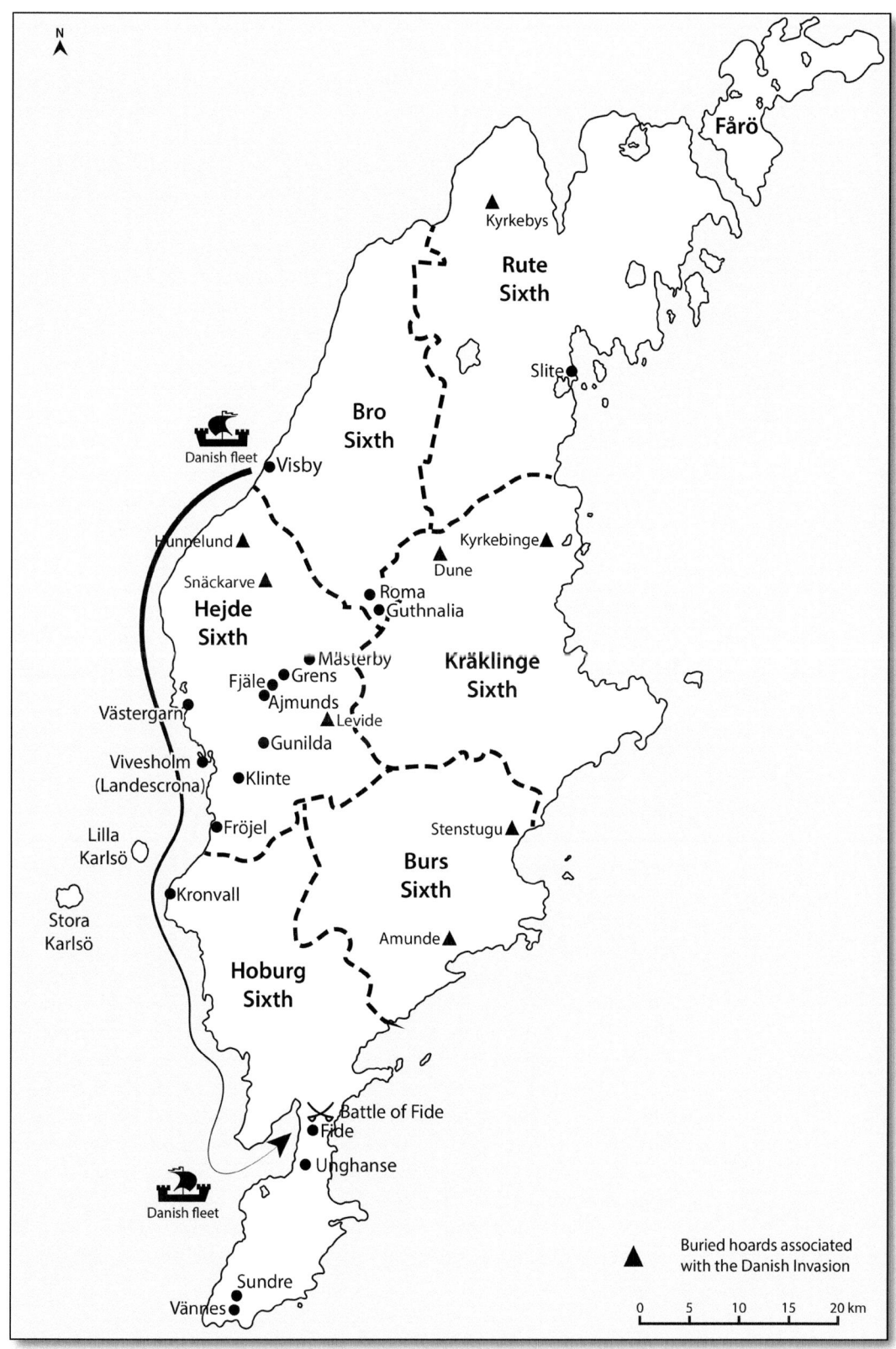

The Campaign on Southern Gotland and Battle of Fide.

had taken refuge on the farmstead after the battle and contested the Danish plunderers.

Although the full extent of the pillaging of rural Gotland remains unknown, it is certain from archaeological finds that many Gotland merchant-farmers had plenty of silver which they buried when the Danes arrived. Several hoards have been found throughout the island which because of the date of the coins were likely buried in the aftermath of the Danish invasion, as a means to keep them safe from Danish soldiers.

It is a sobering thought that the mere existence of such a hoard in an archaeological context indicates that the owner of the silver was unable to retrieve his valuables because he was killed, either in the battle of Visby or afterwards, when Danish soldiers ransacked any farmstead within reach. Some hoards were probably unearthed and seized by the Danes – after torturing any survivors found on the farmsteads. Yet others may have remained undiscovered, until survivors retrieved them after the Danes had left the island.

The most obvious riches were probably to be had on southern Gotland. Although surviving evidence is patchy and at times difficult to interpret, there is every reason to conclude that having received the submission of Visby, King Valdemar embarked upon a campaign to gain control over southern Gotland. Most likely, a part of his army immediately embarked on ships that then sailed south along the island's western coast, to southern Gotland.

This leads us back to the prosperous Unghanse farmstead in Öja on southern Gotland. Why is this farmstead pointed out in myth and legend in such strong terms as the one that betrayed the island to King Valdemar? There is no way of knowing for sure, but it has been suggested that the owner of Unghanse perhaps opened up his farmstead and freely shared his supplies with the Danes as a means to avoid plundering.[5] The Unghanse farm was wealthy, with a large and luxurious stone house that measured 10 x 8 m during the Middle Ages. If King Valdemar personally led the campaign on southern Gotland, he may well have chosen to make the Unghanse farmhouse his headquarters during the campaign. And with King Valdemar's amorous reputation being what it was, there may well have been a scandal with Unghanse's beautiful daughter at the time, just as the later legend suggested.

The most well known hoard from King Valdemar's time is the Dune Hoard, found in 1881 on the farmstead Dune in Dalhem parish, southeast of Visby. The hoard, the largest medieval buried treasure found in Scandinavia, was buried sometime in the second half of the fourteenth century. It consists of 122 objects of silver and gold, mainly bowls, spoons, necklaces, pendants, bangles, finger rings, loops, belt fittings, buckles, clasps, sequins, and knives with decorated handles. It lay under a small cairn in the remains of a wooden box. A broken scythe had been placed on the box to provide magical protection against discovery.

The oldest objects date to the mid-eleventh century and the newest from the mid-fourteenth century, that is, the time of the Danish invasion. The

---

5   Westholm, *Visby 1361*, 178.

objects originate from the Byzantine Empire, Germany, France, England, Norway and, unsurprisingly, Gotland. Several items of jewellery were made from coins of Spanish, Andalusian, Moroccan, German, and Russian origin. Several pieces carry inscriptions of ownership. Most ownership markings are believed to refer to Gotlanders, but the name Zalognev, which is found on one item, probably signifies the property of a Russian merchant.

The Dune farmstead is believed to have been one of Gotland's most important ones. We know that in 1252, the merchant Bartolomeus (Bartholomew) Dune sold wine to the English court. In 1412, the farmstead was owned by Botulf Dune, who functioned as lawspeaker for the Lina Thing. Present research suggests that one of the coins in the hoard date from the period after 1361. This suggests that the Dune family recovered the hoard after the departure of the Danes but then reburied it again during a later period of unrest, possibly after the taking over of Gotland by the pirate confederation known as the Victual Brothers in 1389 (more on which below). Perhaps the man who reburied the hoard then was killed before he could tell anybody about its location. Alternatively, perhaps Botulf Dune in the early 1400s still considered the times too perilous to unearth the family hoard. We will see that Botulf Dune's time was one of continued strife on Gotland. Or perhaps the hoard remained lost because the magical power provided by the scythe still remained operational …

Finds from the Dune Hoard. (Photo: Gunnel Jansson, History Museum, Stockholm)

> ### Did King Valdemar Plunder Visby?
>
> Much later, a legend arose about the plunder of Visby, which King Valdemar then was said to have ordered after the battle. However, the legend was an invention, introduced by descendants of Visby burghers who preferred to forget that their ancestors had retained their wealth and lives by not standing together with the rural Gotlanders in the battle.
>
> The legend may have arisen based on the Zealand Chronicle, compiled a few years after the events, which noted that King Valdemar 'took gold, silver, different kinds of furs, and excessive amounts of treasures from it [Visby]' (Latin: *auro, argento, pellibus uariis et aliis infinitis diu iciis exinde protractis*).[6]
>
> Other near-contemporary literary sources also mention the treasures from Gotland. In the words of the Franciscan Detmar in Lübeck, King Valdemar and his men 'got the land and took a great treasure of gold and silver from the burghers of the city' (Low German: *krech he dat land, unde nam van den borgheren der stad grote bescattinghe an gholde unde an sulver*).[7] The Visby Franciscan Chronicle, compiled a few years later but possibly based on earlier texts, noted, in part almost verbatim but in Latin, that King Valdemar carried home a 'vast treasure of gold and silver from the city and land' (Latin: *maximo thesauro de ciuitate et terra / maximum thezaurum auri et argenti ... de civitate ac terra*).[8] Unlike the overseas chronicles, the Visby Franciscan Chronicle noted that treasures also derived from rural areas.
>
> The same appears in the Link Poem: 'then he plundered the city and the land so thoroughly that they never recovered, and he got unimaginable amounts of gold and silver there' (Old Swedish: *sydhan skynnaden staden ok landeth j röther saa the fingo thes aldrey bother vsigelighet gull ok silff han ther fyk*).[9]
>
> In short, the Visby burghers certainly paid King Valdemar off with the customary contributions in supplies and coin demanded by successful armies in need of provisions. Later legends embellished this, claiming that King Valdemar threatened to burn the city, unless they paid him a huge ransom in gold and silver, to be collected within three days in three huge beer vats put in the main square.[10] There is no contemporary evidence to support this claim, and it is unlikely to be true, because of King Valdemar's treaty with the Hanseatic League.

---

6   Jørgensen, *Annales Danici Medii Ævi*, 188

7   Koppmann, *Die Chroniken der niedersächsischen Städte* 1, 529.

8   Visby Franciscan Chronicle, in Fant, *Scriptores Rerum Svecicarum medii ævi* 1:1, 34, 45.

9   Klemming, 'Svenska medeltidens rim-krönikor', 184.

10   Strelow, *Cronica Guthilandorum*, 172.

12

The Battle of Fide, 10 August

Our evidence for King Valdemar's campaign on southern Gotland is circumstantial, but persuasive. The evidence consists of several items: all related to Fide Church on southern Gotland.

The first clue is an early fifteenth-century fresco in Fide Church. The fresco includes a scroll (unreadable today but copied in the nineteenth century) with a verse from the Bible's Book of Lamentation, which sets the tone of the fresco which depicts a suffering Christ in front of a cross.

Christ's halo contains another set of presently unreadable letters, which in the nineteenth century was copied as D C C C D L I I I I I I I I I I I. When read as Roman numbers, they produce a sequence (500+100+100+100 +500+50+1+1+1+1+1+1+1+1+1+1+1), which gives the number 1361. The inscription accordingly forms a chronogram. In a chronogram each letter has a numerical meaning that, when read together, indicates a specific date, in this case 1361.

The halo chronogram is easy to crack and was probably intended to catch the reader's attention. Because there is more to find in the fresco. Above the suffering Christ, two surviving lines of a Latin poem give more information. The poem contains a hidden message, which only an educated man would understand. Literacy was high on Gotland, and both merchant-farmers and clergymen could be expected to solve the puzzle.

The two lines of the poem read: *Edes succe[n]se gens cesa dolens ruit ense …* ('The temples are put on fire, the suffering people is defeated, … attacks with the sword'). The text sounds like something from the Bible. However, the Roman numeric values (with the letter 'u' interpreted as 'v' in the customary manner) hidden in the text produces the sequence D V C C C D L V I (500+5+100+100+100+500+50+5+1) which again gives the number 1361. This inscription, too, accordingly forms a chronogram for the year 1361.[1]

The chronogram, when read in conjunction with the poem itself, is in itself evidence of trouble following King Valdemar's invasion. Gotlanders who read the Latin classics (and some certainly did) would know that *edes*

---

1   Snöbohm, *Gotlands land och folk*, 148.

(*aedes*) in classical Latin meant 'house' and not only 'temple'. Moreover, there was once a continuation of the poem, which probably was erased from the church wall at a crucial point. Tryggve Siltberg, ultimately found the rest of the text copied in a medieval manuscript from Vadstena Monastery (which was later brought to Uppsala). He found that the complete poem ends *[… ruit ense] emulus ecce canis capitur Gudlandia Danis* ('See, the like of a dog attacks with the sword, Gotland taken by Danes'). The poem definitely, and in no polite terms, alludes to King Valdemar's invasion. The complete poem accordingly reads, in Leonic hexameter:

> The houses are put on fire, the suffering people is defeated,
> See, the like of a dog attacks with the sword, Gotland taken by Danes.

Besides, the mocking rhyme *canis – Danis*, meaning 'dog – Danes' would be obvious to the reader.

And if this is not enough, the first three letters of the continuation of the poem produce the sequence M V L V C C C I (1,000+5+50+5+100+100+100+1), which again is a chronogram for 1361.[2]

The words 'The temples/houses are put on fire' have been interpreted as references to the Danes looting and burning houses and possibly churches on southern Gotland after the battle of Visby. There are indeed signs that Fide Church may have suffered fire damage at around the time of King Valdemar's invasion. A tentative interpretation is that the church and the surrounding farmsteads were ravaged very soon after the battle of Visby, and that the church was restored during the subsequent rule of Gotland by the Teutonic Order (see below) from 1398 to 1408. This date would correspond with the artistic style of the painting and was probably the time when the poem was painted in the church. But later the Danes returned, and the locals realised that they had better erase the final part of the poem which rudely and openly compared the Danish King to a dog. But they did not hide the first part of the text, with the hidden reference to 1361. The subterfuge with hidden numbers was prudent since Gotland then belonged to Denmark, and a Danish priest might be sent to the distant church. The locals must have assumed, probably correctly, that if the Danish Crown sent its own priest to the extreme south of Gotland, he would

The suffering Christ at Fide Church. (Photo: author)

---

2   Tryggve Siltberg, 'Hundens like' Bonderepublikens dom över Valdemar Atterdag i Fidedikten', *Fornvännen* 97 (2002), 25–43; Tryggve Siltberg, 'Talsymmetri i Fidedikten', *Fornvännen* 98 (2003), 219–220. Siltberg finds another year in the final three words, which he interprets as linked to the Artlenburg Treaty, which at the time was a well-known symbol for the Gotland Republic's independence.

likely not be highly educated and thus unlikely to discover the hidden date and message.[3]

The second clue consists of runes inscribed in Fide Church. Runes remained in common use in medieval Scandinavia. The runes include the three personal names Jacob (Jacobus), Lawrence (Laurentius), and Olaf.[4] Jacob and Lawrence are written in runes but with Latin spelling, which suggests that they refer not to individuals but to important dates in 1361. St. Jacob's Day (25 July) would signify the Battle of Mästerby. St. Lawrence's Day (10 August) may have been the day when the Danish army fought and defeated the southern Gotland militia at Fide.[5] Fide had a strategic location. From the church tower, one of few such locations, it was possibly to monitor the sea on both sides of the island.

The third clue consists of graffiti in Fide Church. Its presence suggests that foreign soldiers were stationed there at some point in the second half of the fourteenth century. Based on the style and content of the graffiti, it has been suggested that these men possibly were Danes from King Valdemar's army.[6]

Graffiti in Fide Church depicting knights in battle. The apparently crowned helmet of the victorious knight opens the possibility that the graffiti depicts King Valdemar and was made by one of his soldiers. Nearby is graffiti depicting a lion, which echoes the Danish King's coat of arms. Fide Church, Gotland. (Author's collection)

Based on these clues, it seems plausible that King Valdemar's men fought a battle at Fide, burned the neighbouring farmsteads, and for a while used the church as barracks and lookout point.

For the rest of the island, it is only the abandoned silver hoards and local legends that give evidence of Danish plundering. Yet, while details are lacking, it would have been highly uncharacteristic of a successful invasion army not to take advantage of the situation.

---

3 Bengt G. Söderberg, 'Fide kyrka och striderna 1361: En dateringsfråga för Gotlands muralmåleri', *Fornvännen* 30 (1935), 35–42.
4 Sven B.F. Jansson and Elias Wessén, *Gotlands runinskrifter* 1 (Stockholm: Kungl. Vitterhets Historie och Antikvitets Akademien, 1962), 36–37.
5 Westholm, *Visby 1361*, Appendix (rev. edition 2014). Westholm suggests that the name Olaf refers to St. Olaf's Day (29 July) which was the day when the mayor of Visby and others witnessed King Valdemar's Letter of Privilege. However, we have seen that there is reason to believe that this letter was dated several days later. Moreover, the date of Visby's surrender would mean nothing to rural Gotlanders. Besides, the name Olaf, which was very common, is inscribed next to a crude depiction of a man. Jansson and Wessén, *Gotlands runinskrifter* 1, 37, argues that an otherwise unknown Olaf simply inscribed his own name and image.
6 Uaininn O'Meadhra, 'Klotter i kyrkan! Gotländska ristningar från medeltiden', *Folkets historia* 22:4 (1994), 16–29, on 26; Uaininn O'Meadhra, 'Medeltida ristningar i Gotlands kyrkor', *Hikuin* 24 (1997): *Kirkearkeologi i Norden* 6 - Skåne, 227–236, on 231.

13

King Valdemar Departs

On 28 August (St. Augustine of Hippo's Day), King Valdemar embarked his army on his fleet and departed from Gotland.[1] Although we do not know his reasons with certainty, it seems highly likely that King Valdemar was concerned with the growing tensions with the Hanseatic League. The Scanian herring market had opened four days earlier, but without the Hanseatic Wendish-Saxon merchants, who had embargoed Danish ports three weeks before the market opened.

Munter and the Visby city council probably felt relief, when the Danish sails disappeared over the horizon. Doing nothing had been the right choice, after all. Their lives and wealth were safe, except for the, sadly expected, expenses invariably linked to having a powerful army quartered in the vicinity for a month.

Even so, there is reason to believe that some Visby burghers probably felt that perhaps they should have acted differently. Those with relatives among the rural merchant-farmer families may have felt this deeply. Unfortunately, this conclusion must remain conjecture. There is nothing that can be discerned in the admittedly scarce historical data from the time. However, three centuries later, when the local historian Strelow, a Visby native, wrote his Gotland Chronicle, he was obviously unhappy with the real, historical events which he had ascertained. To hide these uncomfortable facts, Strelow found it necessary to change and embellish the story to assuage the feelings of his fellow Visby burghers and save the reputation of the city. In his Chronicle, Strelow went so far as to claim that it was the men of the burgher militia, not the rural militia, who had fought and died outside the city walls – all 1,800 of them.[2]

Another legend, apparently introduced in the Swedish mid-fifteenth-century Link Poem but further propagated by Strelow, was that those Danish ships that carried the plunder from Gotland sank in a storm on the way back to Denmark.[3] Perhaps some of Strelow's readers found this thought reassuring

---

1   Visby Franciscan Chronicle, in Fant, *Scriptores Rerum Svecicarum medii ævi* 1:1, 45.
2   Strelow, *Cronica Guthilandorum*, 170.
3   Link Poem, in Klemming, 'Svenska medeltidens rim-krönikor', 171–192, on 184; Strelow, *Cronica Guthilandorum*, 173.

since it would have meant that there was justice, after all. Unfortunately, there is nothing to support this myth of divine retribution.

The Status of Gotland

Surviving sources shed little light on what happened on Gotland immediately after King Valdemar's departure. Nor do we know much about the island's status after the invasion. Did the Danish King leave a garrison on the island? Or bailiffs? Did Gotland and Visby become Danish territory, which King Valdemar seems to imply in his letter of privilege for the city of Visby? Did the island pay taxes, and if so, to whom?

We know far more about what happened on King Valdemar's other conquest, the island of Öland. The small Danish garrison in Borgholm Castle on Öland did not last long. Soon, the rural Öland militia rose, and killed the Danish bailiffs. King Magnus's men regained control of the island in early 1362, and Öland again swore fealty to the King of Sweden.

The surviving Gotlanders may have done the same, although contemporary sources are silent on this point. The Link Poem claims that the Gotlanders indeed killed the Danish bailiffs as soon as King Valdemar had departed and then resumed their oath of fealty to the Swedish King.[4] Perhaps they did. However, the poem was written at a time of significant Swedish-Danish rivalry, is highly tendentious, and its information on Gotland is unreliable.

King Valdemar did not immediately begin to call himself King of Gotland, nor did he, or as far as is known, his representatives, take part in any kind of governance of the island.

If King Valdemar's intention had been to transfer Gotland to Mecklenburg as part of the wedding of his daughter Prince Ingeborg to Duke Albert's eldest son Henry, which took place on or before 3 June 1362, this did not happen. If such a gift ever had been part of the marriage contract, King Valdemar presumably regarded the handover of Gotland as superfluous in light of his subsequent successes. Instead, we will see that King Valdemar in August 1362 himself finally assumed the title King of Gotland, more than a year after the invasion and after another successful war elsewhere (more on which below).

We do not know if the Danish Crown by then maintained a presence on Gotland or exercised any real governance there. It would take until 15 years after the conquest before we find any conclusive evidence on who then actually was in control of the island. The scattered evidence of the intermediate 15 years suggests a variety of interpretations, most of which are mutually exclusive and none of which goes beyond conjecture. If Gotland remained Danish, which is possible but by no means certain, then King Valdemar's power rested on the presumed loyalty of the Visby burghers, and the lingering military weakness of the King of Sweden.[5]

The island's presumed change of status did not, in any case, affect Visby. The Hanseatic League regarded, correctly, that there had been no significant

---

4   Klemming, 'Svenska medeltidens rim-krönikor,' 184.
5   Yrwing, *Gotlands medeltid*, 49.

FALL OF THE MERCHANT-FARMER REPUBLIC

change in the status of the city. Like Lübeck, Visby was regarded as a free city. Its burghers were members of the Hanseatic League, not subjects of the King of Denmark. The Hanseatic Diet meeting in Lübeck on 25 May 1364 re-confirmed the Visby burghers' status as members of the Hanseatic League, and not Danish subjects.[6] By then, Visby representatives had already attended several League meetings. Business did indeed continue as usual. Visby continued to lead the Gotland-Livonian *Drittel* after the submission to King Valdemar. In practice, Gotland remained as semi-autonomous under Danish rule as previously under Swedish, and perhaps because he had thoroughly plundered the island, King Valdemar made no attempts to increase taxation there.

Swedish knight, mid-fourteenth century. Swedish knights were not yet as up to date with developments on the Continent as their Danish counterparts. This knight wears a coat-of-plates cuirass of the same type as those found in in the Visby mass graves. Few great helms are known from Sweden, but based on surviving finds and pictorial evidence, they may have been lighter than those used in Denmark. (Tommy Hellman)

---

6   *Hanserecesse: Die Recesse und andere Akten der Hansetage von 1256–1430*, 280.

14

The League Goes to War

We have seen that the Hanseatic League by May 1361, after much haggling and some initial irritation, had agreed to pay as much as 4,000 marks to King Valdemar in exchange for his guaranteeing their trading privileges in Denmark, which by then again included the all-important Scanian herring market. The privileges would give the League an advantageous position in the market and bring significant profits, even though the League merchants also would have to pay the local fees and customs duties traditionally associated with the herring market. Which of course was the same fees and duties which League merchants in recent years sullenly had paid to King Magnus's bailiff and then complained bitterly about.

Then, somebody within the League got a bright but highly ambitious idea. Would not a full monopoly and complete market control be a far better deal than the traditional, merely most-favoured position? A hostile takeover would necessitate a significant outlay of initial expenses, but the high costs would in part be offset by avoiding future fees to King Valdemar, and in part by imposing the very same fees on non-League merchants. The name of the individual who proposed the project is lost to history, but soon the League councillors decided that this plan, the deal of a lifetime, was well worth embarking upon despite the associated risks. The League cities had already realised that when working together, they had the financial and manpower resources to project substantial influence on, and perhaps power over, monarchs of small countries. Why pay for market access that could be taken by force? Funding a mercenary army was merely the next step in business development.

The League accordingly abandoned its support for King Valdemar. Already on 1 August, the Hanseatic delegates, who in late July assembled in Greifswald, decided that the League henceforth would boycott Danish ports under threat of the death penalty.[1] The records of the meeting say nothing about King Valdemar's conquest of non-Hanseatic Gotland, the news of which had not yet reached Greifswald. Clearly, the League delegates were

---

1 *Hanserecesse: Die Recesse und andere Akten der Hansetage von 1256–1430*, 184–185.

concerned with other matters relating to Denmark, which meant the Scanian market.

At the same time, King Magnus sent not a Swedish fleet to retake Gotland, but envoys to Lübeck, the primary city of the Wendish-Saxon cities of the Hanseatic League. The emissaries would present a joint Swedish-Norwegian proposal (which made perfect sense because the two kingdoms were a family affair, since King Haakon of Norway was King Magnus's son).

King Valdemar's victories on Öland and Gotland made it prudent for King Magnus to resolve the differences that hitherto had upset his relationship with the League. He knew of the Danish invasions of Öland and Gotland no later than 15 August, when he referred to it in a letter.[2] On 22 August 1361, the Swedish emissaries arrived in Lübeck. They immediately declared that Sweden was open to resolve all previous disagreements. The Hanseatic representatives agreed, talks progressed rapidly, and an agreement about an anti-Danish alliance was concluded already on 8 September. The Hanseatic cities and towns that joined the alliance were Lübeck, Hamburg, Wismar, Rostock, Stralsund, Greifswald, Anklam, Stettin, Kolberg, Bremen, and Kiel, that is, essentially the Wendish-Saxon *Drittel* of the Hanseatic League, which as noted was headed by Lübeck.[3] The other cities remained cautious or even chose to stay neutral.

Traditional historiography tends to describe the alliance between the Wendish-Saxon *Drittel* of the Hanseatic League, King Magnus, and King Haakon as a reaction caused by the Danish invasion of Gotland and the alleged Danish sack of Hanseatic Visby (which as we have seen never took place). However, there is nothing in the objectives agreed upon by the allies to suggest that Gotland was the cause of war. First, it was only the Wendish-Saxon *Drittel* of the Hanseatic League which joined the coalition, not the Gotland-Livonian *Drittel* which in many ways relied on its leading city Visby and, had Visby been sacked, would have had the greatest incentive to right this wrong. Second, neither Sweden nor the League saw the need to reconquer Gotland, which had suffered but was not really lost to either party. Hence, the objectives of the allies did not at all include the liberation of Gotland but fully focused on one goal only: securing the Scanian herring market.[4]

In short, the League would help return the Scanias to Swedish rule. In return, the League would secure its interest in the Scanian herring market by receiving direct control over the castles and important towns along the Scanian shore: Helsingborg, Lund, Malmö, Skanör, and Falsterbo, the latter two of which as we have seen safeguarded the herring market, which was held on the coast between them. This would enable the League not only to secure its profitable trade privileges under a new regime but also gain full control over the market side of the Strait with all that this implied with regard

---

2   Swedish National Archives (RA), *Svenskt diplomatarium*, SDHK No. 8007.
3   *Hanserecesse: Die Recesse und andere Akten der Hansetage von 1256–1430*, 185–192.
4   The agreement mentions Gotland, but only in the context that the alliance is aimed against those (Danes and their supporters) who attacked Scania, Gotland, and Öland. It says nothing about recovering Gotland, and Öland had probably already shaken off Danish rule.

to rights of toll-free trade and also, we can assume, the imposition of fees and custom duties on rival merchants.

Full trading privileges coupled with direct control of the Scanian side of the Strait and its trade was a significant upgrade from the League's previous position, and certainly worth fighting for. The League would contribute a fleet of 62 ships of various tonnage and 2,730 fighting men (Table 3). In addition, the League would provide eight siege engines: five *blide* (trebuchets; Low German: *blida*) and three *werke*, a Low German term of uncertain meaning which most modern-day historians habitually interpret as ballistae. However, based on contemporary Swedish usage, which was indistinguishable from that of northern Germany, *blide* and *werke* were built and manned by separate groups of professionals. While the Master of Trebuchets (*blidhemester*) was responsible for trebuchets as well as any other kind of available non-gunpowder artillery including ballistae, the Master of Works (*werkmester*) was in charge of all breaching machinery such as rams (*arietes*), drills (*musculi*), and siege towers (*turres*).[5] It accordingly seems likely that the three *werke* which the League embarked on its fleet was some such kind of siege machinery. However, we will see that the League ships also carried cannons, and in light of the smaller number of *werke* as compared to *blide*, another possibility is that the three *werke* signified three stone-shooting cannons.[6]

Lübeck:	6 cogs	6 smaller vessels	600 soldiers	1 *werk*	1 *blida*
Hamburg	2 cogs	-	200 soldiers		
Rostock and Wismar	6 cogs	6 smaller vessels	600 soldiers	1 *werk*	1 *blida*
Stralsund and Greifswald	6 cogs	6 smaller vessels	600 soldiers	1 *werk*	1 *blida*
Kolberg, Stettin, Anklam	6 cogs	6 smaller vessels	600 soldiers	1 *blida* each from Kolberg and Stettin	
Bremen	1 cog	-	100 soldiers		
Kiel	1 ship	10 smaller vessels	30 soldiers		
Total: 27 cogs, 1 ship, 34 smaller vessels, 2,730 soldiers, 3 *werke*, and 5 *blide*					

Table 3. The planned strength of the Hanseatic expeditionary fleet, as agreed on 9 September 1361 (source: *Hanserecesse: Die Recesse und andere Akten der Hansetage von 1256–1430*, 191–192)

To support the venture, King Magnus and King Haakon would raise ships and an army of, in total, 2,000 knights and soldiers.[7] In the final analysis, the fleet apparently came to consist of 27 cogs, 25 smaller vessels, and from 2,040

---

5 Hedberg, *Kungl. Artilleriet: Medeltid och äldre vasatid*, 22, 23.
6 Possibly, a comparison can be made with French *engine a verge*, which meant any kind of artillery, including cannons.
7 *Hanserecesse: Die Recesse und andere Akten der Hansetage von 1256–1430*, 187-190, on 188.

to 2,540 fighting men.[8] The Counts of Holstein, Iron Henry of Holstein-Rendsburg and Adolph of Holstein-Plön, joined the anti-Danish alliance, too.

Unfortunately for the alliance, it soon turned out that the Swedish emissaries had vastly exceeded their authority when they promised to give away so many castles. Not only had the League demanded the Scanian castles; they had also asked for Bohus Castle and Marstrand in Norwegian Bohuslän. King Magnus refused to ratify the agreement, since he did not wish to surrender essentially all of Scania and furthermore had no intention to give away the important Bohus Castle. The resulting re-negotiations, ensuing disputes between the respective retainers of Kings Magnus and Haakon, and difficulties in raising the necessary men and ships delayed the war.

Nonetheless, in spring 1362 preparations were finally concluded. In May or early June, the Hanseatic fleet set sail towards Helsingborg Castle under the command of Johann Wittenborg, the Mayor of Lübeck. King Magnus and King Haakon contributed five ships, rented and manned in Lübeck, under the command of the aforementioned Iron Henry of Holstein-Rendsburg and Adolph of Holstein-Plön.

The original plan was first to seize Copenhagen, but King Magnus wanted the fleet instead to focus on Helsingborg Castle, which guarded the northern part of the Strait. The League representatives had no objections, since after all it was the Scanian coast which was their primary objective.

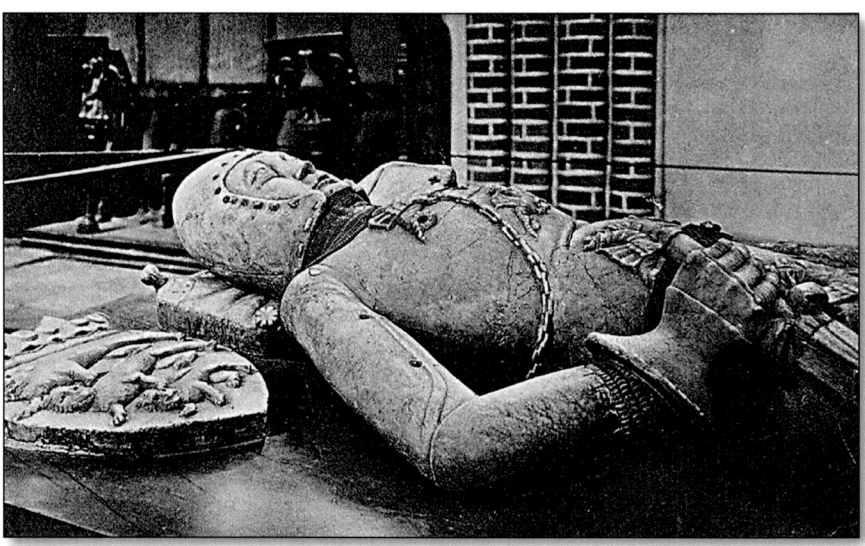

Effigy of Christopher, Duke of Lolland, from his tomb. (Roskilde Cathedral)

Unfortunately for the allies, King Magnus at the time faced growing opposition within Sweden, so ultimately was unable to join his forces to the allied army. King Haakon did lead an army of horse and foot south in support of the League offensive, but he reached no further than Varberg in

---

8   Schäfer, *Die Hansestädte und König Waldemar*, 281, 288–289, 299–301, 433; Lundbye, *Valdemar Atterdag*, 137; Tägil, *Valdemar Atterdag*, 317.

North Halland province. King Haakon then abandoned the offensive, instead returning north to raise more men.

Given the absence of the two kings, the remaining allies unsurprisingly gave the experienced Iron Henry overall command of the campaign. When the allied army disembarked to lay siege to Helsingborg Castle, the fleet barely had enough infantry left to guard the ships. Nonetheless, Iron Henry laid siege, and for days what the Zealand Chronicle described as 16 siege engines (*machinas*) bombarded the castle, which was ably defended by the Danish commandant, Peder Nielssøn (of the family known as Jernskjæg, 'Iron Beard', after its distinctive coat of arms).[9]

Meanwhile, King Valdemar assembled his fleet, and then set out towards Helsingborg Castle, in the hope of reaching it before any Swedish or Norwegian reinforcements might arrive.

On 8 July (St. Kilian's Day), King Valdemar in a surprise naval attack defeated the allied fleet off Helsingborg. It was a great victory, and a triumph for King Valdemar. He captured 12 cogs, loaded with food supplies and armaments. About six weeks later, on 21 August, he in a letter to the Dutch Hanseatic city of Kampen, in a triumphant mood for the first time referred to himself as 'King of the Danes, Slavs, and Goths' (Latin: *Danorum, Sclavorum Gothorumque rex*). The term Slav was merely the translation of Wend, the people which we have seen previously inhabited the northeastern German coast which Denmark once had controlled and which hosted many Hanseatic cities. The inclusion of the term Goths referred to Gotland, which he had not hitherto claimed. Perhaps King Valdemar had half-expected to abandon the island to King Magnus as soon as he left it. As we have seen, King Magnus had other things on his mind. But the Danish triumph contained a seed of bitterness. King Valdemar's only surviving son and heir-apparent, Christopher, Duke of Lolland, was grievously wounded, by a later account from a stone shot by cannon from one of the ships in the battle off Helsingborg Castle. The young man never recovered, and died a year later, in June 1363.

The League survivors entered into a truce with King Valdemar, which also bound King Magnus and King Haakon – who were informed of the truce only later. The two kings were upset, but the League representatives nonetheless continued negotiations, blaming the two kings for not sending the promised men to the joint campaign and for failing in their duties. On 28 September 1362, King Magnus had to give Öland and Borgholm Castle as a surety to the League.

When the defeated League fleet returned to Lübeck, the city council had Johann Wittenborg imprisoned. A year later, he was sentenced to death for his failure and executed by decapitation. The venture had been a total loss. The League had to pay a ransom of 202,000 marks silver to recover the men (and possibly ships) who had fallen into Danish captivity. But there was more, and we know it because the League accountants kept meticulous records. In addition to the ransom payments, there were the

---

9   Jørgensen, *Annales Danici Medii Ævi*, 188.

usual war-related expenses, which totalled 166,200 marks.[10] The Hanseatic ledgers went deeply into the red. These losses go a long way in explaining the harsh treatment of Wittenborg. While surviving records are silent, one may wonder if Wittenborg, Lübeck's mayor, also was the man who had come up with the plan to attack Denmark in the first place. As we have seen, the Hanseatic League was a corporate body that showed little mercy to officials who squandered the League's monetary resources, failed to reach expected objectives and, it follows, failed to reach the projected increase in profits that depended on reaching these objectives.

On 6 November 1362, the League entered into a full truce with King Valdemar until 6 January 1364 (Epiphany), again without informing King Magnus and King Haakon. This effectively ended the war. While King Magnus was displeased, King Haakon seems to have accepted realities on the ground. During the negotiations, he took the opportunity to make an individual and quite different deal with King Valdemar, namely, a marital alliance. As a result, King Valdemar on 9 April 1363 married his daughter Margaret to King Haakon in the presence of King Magnus and Queen Blanche. We will see that this wedding in time would have a crucial effect on Scandinavian history. However, for now Margaret was only 10 years old, so she remained with her parents for another three years, until 1366.

After the truce of November 1362 ended, fresh negotiations between the various parties resulted in another truce on 18 June 1364. King Valdemar and the League finally concluded a peace treaty on 3 September 1365 at Vordingborg Castle, in which King Valdemar restored the League's trading rights in the Scanian herring market.

King Valdemar had won the war. He had also made King Haakon of Norway an important ally.

---

10   Lundbye, *Valdemar Atterdag*, 141, 146, 157.

15

Swedish Turmoil

By then, King Magnus faced severe troubles at home. In 1363, a number of his nobles began to conspire to put Duke Albert of Mecklenburg the Younger (c. 1338–1412), the present ruling Duke Albert's second eldest son and King Magnus's nephew, on the Swedish throne. On 10 November 1363, the Duke of Mecklenburg embarked his army, which included his son, retinue, and 600 men, on a fleet and sailed to Kalmar and Öland, where he made a brief stop. Count Iron Henry of Holstein-Rendsburg, who since 1361 held the important Kalmar Castle, now joined forces with Duke Albert. So did Bernard of Werle-Waren and Lorenz of Werle-Güstrow, both of the princely House of Mecklenburg.[1] The fleet then continued towards the north. The Duke's ultimate destination was Stockholm, where he landed on 29 November, and claimed the throne.

King Magnus naturally fought back, assisted by his son King Haakon who henceforth held on to the throne jointly with his father, but the civil war went badly for them. On 18 February 1364, Duke Albert the Younger was formally elected and crowned King of Sweden, where he would reign, in a manner, until 1389. Since King Albert lacked funds to pay his men, he handed out promises and land. On 26 July 1364, he awarded Iron Henry the entire island of Gotland as indemnity for 4,000 marks silver. King Albert did then not control Gotland and apparently hoped that the reward would encourage Iron Henry to conquer the island.[2]

The civil war continued for several years. King Magnus and King Haakon were finally defeated in the Battle of Gata near the town of Enköping which is commonly believed to have taken place on 3 March 1365. While King Magnus was captured, King Haakon escaped, although wounded, from King Albert's men. King Magnus would remain in captivity until 1371 when a peace treaty finally was negotiated between him and King Haakon on the one side and King Albert on the other.

---

1 Lord Bernard II of Werle-Waren (c. 1320–1382) and Lord Lorenz of Werle-Güstrow (c. 1339 – c. 1393) were distant relatives. Lord Bernard was also the son-in-law of the late Count John the Mild of Holstein-Plön.
2 Schäfer, *Die Hansestädte und König Waldemar*, 407–408.

In spring 1366, King Valdemar ordered a Danish army under Duke Eric of Saxe-Lauenburg into Swedish territories presently held by King Albert. Duke Eric marched into Småland province on 1 May. He then also secured parts of Västergötland province including a wooden fort at Elfsborg (the future Elfsborg Castle) on the river Göta Älv, with easy access to the North Sea and thereby sea lines of communication with the rest of western Europe, and Varberg with North Halland province. At the same, King Haakon of Norway went on the offensive further east towards the Baltic Sea. King Haakon conquered Borgholm Castle on Öland (he managed to hang on to the island for a year), and unsuccessfully laid siege to the strongly built Kalmar Castle. Ostensibly, King Valdemar came to the rescue of his son-in-law King Haakon and his imprisoned father, King Magnus. Meanwhile, King Haakon continued to claim the Swedish throne jointly with his father, in opposition to King Albert.

King Albert's father, Duke Albert of Mecklenburg, on 28 July 1366 met King Valdemar to discuss a compromise. They signed a curious treaty, as if either was authorised to negotiate on behalf of the principal parties in the conflict, Kings Magnus, Haakon, and Albert. The treaty stated that King Valdemar would keep Gotland and Visby, as well as those territories recently conquered by Duke Eric (major parts of Småland, Elfsborg in Västergötland, and Varberg with North Halland), in exchange for King Albert retaining the rest of Sweden.[3]

Does this mean that the Danish Crown in 1366 still, or again, controlled Gotland (or, for that matter, Varberg)? This is far from certain. Two years previously, King Albert had given the island to Iron Henry. Had either man then controlled Gotland? This was unlikely, since Iron Henry remained in Kalmar, where Duke Albert on 5 February 1367 would give him an interest in Kopparberget copper mine as compensation for the 4,000 marks silver for which he in 1364 had been given, but apparently never held, Gotland.[4] Nor does it seem likely that King Valdemar's men in 1364 had maintained a firm grip on Gotland, since this would have precluded King Albert from giving away the island as surety. Perhaps no foreign bailiff of any allegiance was present on the island after King Valdemar's departure. Nobody knows for sure, and the documents may well refer to theoretical claims on the island rather than any form of actual possession. Besides, the notion that King Valdemar and Duke Albert (technically on behalf of his son) successfully could divide Sweden among themselves at the same time when King Haakon operated a successful army there seems unrealistic, too. Perhaps nothing at all should be read into the treaty. Based on later events, neither party took their counterpart seriously, the terms they agreed on were unrealistic, and the war continued.

---

3   Lundbye, *Valdemar Atterdag*, 165–167.
4   Schäfer, *Die Hansestädte und König Waldemar*, 417–418; Lundbye, *Valdemar Atterdag*, 170.

SWEDISH TURMOIL

Albert of Mecklenburg the Younger, as shown in a contemporary depiction on his grave monument in Bad Doberan, Mecklenburg. (Photo: Jacob Truedson Demitz)

Left: Albert of Mecklenburg the Younger, King of Sweden. Right: His father, Duke Albert II 'the Great' of Mecklenburg. As king of Sweden, Albert employed the three golden crowns on a blue field as Swedish coat of arms. A new coat of arms was necessary for Albert, who could not use the traditional golden lion emblem on a blue field of the previous dynasty, the Bjälbo ('Folkung') family, nor the crowned black bull's head of his father, who remained reigning Duke of Mecklenburg. It was long believed that Albert introduced the use of the three crowns emblem in Sweden. However, the three crowns emblem was by then a recognised Swedish symbol. Already in 1275, King Magnus Ladulås introduced three large crowns in his seal around the shield with the traditional 'Folkung' lion. His grandson King Magnus IV reintroduced the three crowns after his acquisition of Scania, when he began to refer to himself as King of Sweden, Norway, and Scania. Since Albert considered himself the successor of Magnus, it was natural for him also to assume the traditional emblem. Painting from the Mecklenburg Rhyme Chronicle of 1378. (Altes Archiv, Chroniken, Mecklenburgisches Landeshauptarchiv, Schwerin, Germany)

One of two battle shields dated to the 1380s from Kristdala Church, Döderhult, Småland Province. The wild boar image suggests that the shield probably belonged to either Lyder or Henrik Svinakula, members of a prominent local family. (History Museum, Stockholm; photo: author)

Gotland National Lawspeaker

The leader of the Gotland Republic, the National Lawspeaker, was a wealthy public official. In 1361, he was perhaps too old personally to fight in battle. This reconstruction is based on the dress displayed on the grave of the merchant-farmer Jacob and his wife Botvid from c. 1350 in Stenkyrka Church. An elegantly attired, affluent man, he wears a tunic under an outer garment of the type presently known as gardecorps, with voluminous but slit upper sleeves and close-fitting lower sleeves. The slit openings in the upper sleeves allowed the wearer to slip his arms through the sleeve in the manner of the outer upper garment later known as a casack. We can assume that the lawspeaker's dress was made of imported cloth, with edges trimmed with silver threads in twisted, braided, or woven styles. Golden trims were no longer permitted by sumptuary legislation in the Guta Law. He wears a chaperon over his head. The chaperon was a form of padded ring headgear with a fabric tube hanging to one side, which had developed from the common hood but in the fourteenth century was an elaborate type of headgear. (Illustration by Giorgio Albertini)

Visby burgher militia officer

The Visby burghers had the means to equip themselves with modern arms and armour. This burgher militia officer accordingly wears armour which is similar in style to that of professional German soldiers. He wears a bascinet over a chainmail coif on his head. In addition, he wears a coat-of-plates cuirass above a chainmail hauberk, which in turn is worn over a padded quilted *gambeson*. To this, he has added splinted arm and leg armour with elbow plates and iron *poleyns* covering the knees and *sabatons* over the feet. This officer wears gauntlets of small iron plates attached to an outer fabric or leather glove. He is armed with a broadsword and an early halberd. (Illustration by Giorgio Albertini)

16

The League Again Goes to War

Relations between League merchants and King Valdemar remained tense, despite the peace treaty of 1365. At the Hanseatic Diet meeting in Rostock on 16 December 1366, the Prussian League members complained that King Valdemar and his men imposed fees on League merchants and increasingly often seized their ships and goods. There were also complaints against the King of Norway, since League merchants faced difficulties there, too.[1]

On 11 July 1367, the Prussian and Dutch Hanseatic cities agreed, during a meeting in Elbing in Prussia, to cease all trade with Denmark and Norway, and then meet again on 11 November in Cologne to discuss a joint military strategy against Kings Valdemar and Haakon.

A meeting between King Valdemar and a delegation of League representatives under Jacob Pleskow, the aforementioned Visby merchant who presently served as mayor of Lübeck, took place at Falsterbo Castle on 22 August, two days before the formal opening of the Scanian herring market. It was customary for the King to open the herring market, so the time and place were appropriate. Pleskow presented the League's complaints. By all accounts, King Valdemar reacted with anger and then rode off to Malmö. The two sides continued the meeting on the following day, but this time, the Danish Crown was represented by Duke Eric of Saxe-Lauenburg. The two sides could only agree to meet again at Falsterbo on 13 October (14 days after St. Michael's Day), that is, four days after the herring market closed.[2]

The meeting in Cologne on 11 November (St. Martin of Tours's Day) was pivotal. As many as 43 members of the Hanseatic League were represented, either by delegates or by letters that authorised other members to speak for them. From the Wendish-Saxon *Drittel* came delegations from Lübeck, Wismar, Rostock, and Stralsund. The Westphalian-Prussian *Drittel* was represented by delegations from the Dutch members Kampen, Harderwijk, Elburg, Amsterdam, Brielle, and Bruges, and the Prussian towns Kulm, Thorn, and Elbing. The Gotland-Livonian *Drittel* was represented by Visby

---

1   Lundbye, *Valdemar Atterdag*, 173, 175.
2   Lundbye, *Valdemar Atterdag*, 177, 179–180.

THE LEAGUE AGAIN GOES TO WAR

and presumably others and seems to have co-ordinated their stance with that of the Prussian towns.[3]

On 17 November 1367, the delegates had agreed to declare war against the Kings of Denmark and Norway. The alliance became known as the Cologne Confederation, from the venue of the meeting. They also agreed on a demand of 150,000 marks silver in restitution from the Danish King, although they realised that he lacked the funds to pay this amount. The League would accordingly go to war, and they would raise a large fleet and army (Table 4).

German Baltic fleet:	
Wendish and Livonian towns	10 cogs, each with 100 armed men, and 20 smaller ships
Prussian towns (six in total)	5 cogs, each apparently with the same number of soldiers
In total	35 ships, with siege weapons and a planned total of 1,500 armed men (but ultimately only 12 cogs, an unknown number of smaller vessels, and some 940 Wendish, 100 Livonian, and 200 Prussian soldiers arrived)
Dutch North Sea fleet:	
Dutch Kampen	1 cog and 2 Rhine riverine craft with 150 armed men
Dutch Zuyderzee towns with Dordrecht, Amsterdam, Stavoren, and Harderwijk	1 cog, with 100 armed men
Dutch Zeeland towns	2 cogs, with 200 armed men
In total	6 ships, with a planned total of 450 armed men (but ultimately only around 425 soldiers arrived)
Mecklenburg and Sweden:	
Duke Albert and King Albert would together contribute 1,000 men	
Danish rebels:	
Claus Limbek would join with 80 or 100 men	
Grand total	21 ships, with a planned total of 1,950 armed soldiers (a fifth of whom should be crossbowmen), and land contingents of up to 1,100 men from Mecklenburg, Sweden, and Denmark

Table 4. The planned combined Hanseatic League-Mecklenburg-Swedish-Danish fleet (sources: *Hanserecesse: Die Recesse und andere Akten der Hansetage von 1256–1430*, 373–374, 382; Schäfer, *Die Hansestädte und König Waldemar*, 433, 465–468; Lundbye, *Valdemar Atterdag*, 184, 200; Tägil, *Valdemar Atterdag*, 315–317)

---

[3] Schäfer, *Die Hansestädte und König Waldemar*, 431–433.

FALL OF THE MERCHANT-FARMER REPUBLIC

The Wendish towns wanted to join forces with King Albert of Sweden, Duke Albert of Mecklenburg, Iron Henry of Holstein-Rendsburg, and other notables. The other members agreed to an alliance but said that they would not support these notables financially.

Those League members who had not agreed to the joint war were compelled to join, or face threat of expulsion from the League. This included Hamburg, which was located uncomfortably close to possible Danish retaliation. Only Bremen was excused, because of present internal problems in the city. Visby agreed to the joint war and the blockade that the meeting decided upon, promised that they would contribute to the cost, but said they would not participate in the fighting.[4]

The League then called King Valdemar to a final meeting in Lübeck on 2 February 1368.

The notables that the Wendish towns wanted to bring into the alliance were indeed in favour of a war against King Valdemar. Duke Albert and his son were already making plans, and on 25 January 1368 they were joined by Iron Henry of Holstein-Rendsburg – but also by Danish nobles such as Duke Henry of Slesvig (the son of the late Duke Valdemar) and the Lord High Justiciar, Claus Limbek. Their ambition was to divide Denmark between them. The plan was to give the entire Scanias and Gotland to King Albert. Duke Albert would receive the Danish islands of Zealand, Møn, Falster, and Lolland. Iron Henry and his fellow counts of Holstein would take over Jutland and the island of Fyn.[5]

The meeting in Lübeck between King Valdemar's representatives and the League on 2 February 1368 failed to resolve the tensions. King Valdemar refused all demands from the Hanseatic League.[6]

A final diplomatic coup was that the League managed to persuade Duke Eric of Saxe-Lauenburg to remain neutral in the forthcoming war. Neither side wanted the war to spread into Germany.[7] Besides, it is possible that Duke Eric already was seriously ill at the time. He died later in the year.

The coalition of League cities and disgruntled Danish nobles from primarily Jutland declared war on 19 March 1368, and attacked King Valdemar soon afterwards, in early April. The League fleet from the Wendish, Prussian, and Livonian cities joined forces, and then turned towards Copenhagen. Realising that both the Hanseatic League and his own nobles faced him, King Valdemar chose to go into immediate exile. On 6 April 1368, he left the country, bringing the royal treasury with him. King Valdemar hoped to get support from the German princes, who presumably would not sympathise with the socially inferior merchants of the League. And if, by chance, they did, King Valdemar brought sufficient funds to pay the princes for their support.

---

4   There is no evidence that Visby ever paid its dues. Lundbye, *Valdemar Atterdag*, 186; Yrwing, *Visby: Hansestad på Gotland*, 162, 171.
5   Lundbye, *Valdemar Atterdag*, 186; Yrwing, *Visby: Hansestad på Gotland*, 162–163.
6   Tägil, *Valdemar Atterdag*, 298–299.
7   Lundbye, *Valdemar Atterdag*, 188.

Copenhagen surrendered on 2 May 1368. The League turned the city into a base for further operations and then turned towards Malmö and the castles of Skanör and Falsterbo, all of which as we know were critical for the Scanian herring market. The League army seized all three strongholds without difficulties.

Meanwhile, King Albert led an army into the Scanias, where he took the town of Lund. However, he failed to conquer either Helsingborg or Varberg castles.

Meanwhile, the Dutch League fleet plundered and ravaged the Norwegian coast. They also burned Marstrand and its castle, and the settlements around Bohus Castle, which withstood the raiders.

The Dutch raiders caused significant problems for King Haakon, who hitherto had been busy fighting in Sweden in the attempt to liberate his father, King Magnus. He now had to return to Norway, where he already in June 1368 attempted to negotiate a ceasefire with the League (which they agreed later in the year).

Meanwhile, King Valdemar's attempts to raise support in Germany failed. The Hanseatic cities had more money than the King, and they wielded considerable influence. Although a few German princes expressed vague words of support of their Danish counterpart, none was immediately willing to go to war against the League on his behalf.

On 6 October 1368, League representatives met for a Hanseatic Diet meeting in Stralsund. Among other business, they sent a letter to the city council of Visby. The League representatives advised Visby to give their allegiance to King Albert, who fought on the League's side against King Valdemar.[8] Again, we learn little of Visby's and Gotland's status at the time. The letter could be interpreted as evidence that Gotland remained Danish territory. However, it could equally well mean that Gotland never had taken a formal position in the Swedish civil war.

Be that as it may, it seems quite certain the King Albert at this time, if not before, had gained a hold over Gotland. At least he felt sufficiently powerful there to issue a letter of protection in 1369 for the nuns of Solberga Abbey.[9] Since such a letter, if intended seriously, could only offer protection against men loyal to King Albert, it was likely written as a response to the activities of King Albert's associates on the island. We do not know who they were. However, it the light of later events it seems very likely that King Albert already at this time were enlisting pirates and freebooters as privateers to operate on his behalf (more on which below).

Meanwhile in Scania, the allied units of the League and King Albert increased their efforts to lay siege to the imposing Helsingborg Castle, ably defended by two Valdemar loyalists: the aforementioned knight Fikke Moltke and the squire Hartvig Kale.

King Albert's elder brother, Henry, the Hangman of Mecklenburg, brought his men to the siege, too. Ultimately Moltke and Kale agreed to surrender the

---

8   Lundbye, *Valdemar Atterdag*, 188.
9   Jöran [Georg] Wallin, *Gothländska samlingar* 2 (Göteborg: Lars Wahlström, 1776), 126–127; Strelow, *Cronica Guthilandorum*, 182 (with wrong date).

castle on 8 September 1369, had King Valdemar then not regained control over Denmark or agreed to a peace treaty. Moltke and Kale had little choice in the matter, since the castle by then were out of supplies. However, they also accepted a payment of 800 marks silver from the League, the first instalment of which was paid out on 29 September in the same year. Nor did the Allies manage to take the almost unassailable Lindholm Castle, which at this time was defended by the aforementioned Valdemar loyalist Peder Nielssøn (Jernskjæg). Lindholm Castle remained loyal to King Valdemar until the end of the war.[10]

Meanwhile, King Valdemar had taken refuge at the Imperial Court. There he finally managed to incite some German nobles against Duke Albert of Mecklenburg and the counts of Holstein. Their scheme did not end well. In October 1369, King Valdemar's German friends were defeated at Roggendorf near Gadebusch. This put an end to the attempt to support the Danish King from Germany.

Peace with the League was finally concluded with the Treaty of Stralsund on 24 May 1370, which the still loyal Henning Podebusk negotiated with the Hanseatic League and signed on the King's behalf. The League acquired the right to control, for 15 years, the castles at the Scanian market. League merchants also acquired exterritorial rights, henceforth being not subject to any Danish court, and could not even be called as witnesses. They also acquired the right to carry arms. If the King abdicated or died, no successor could be named before the League had approved him.[11] It was a total capitulation. The late Johann Wittenborg's dream had finally come true, seven years after he was beheaded by his own compatriots.

Having acquired this objective, the League dropped Duke Albert's plan to divide Denmark. The League had finally acquired the primary objective for which it had launched the invasion of 1362. But the rise of a powerful confederation of pirates in the Baltic Sea must have seemed ominous to the League merchants.

The League deliberately ignored the interests of their noble allies when they negotiated the treaty. None of the latter's grievances or demands were addressed. The nobles could damn the League, but this availed them nothing. Duke Albert of Mecklenburg had to negotiate a separate peace treaty with King Valdemar which was concluded on 30 October 1371. Duke Albert agreed to return the Danish territories which he had conquered.

By then, an agreement had also been reached between Kings Haakon and Albert. King Albert released King Magnus from captivity, who in return recognised King Albert as King of most of Sweden. King Magnus retained major parts of western Sweden.

Having agreed to the Treaty of Stralsund, King Valdemar could finally return to Denmark, where we again find him in mid-1372. On 24 January 1373, Duke Albert mediated a peace treaty between King Valdemar and his last domestic enemies, the counts of Holstein and the Jutland nobility. Again, all conquered territories were returned to the Danish Crown. Those who had abandoned the service of the King during the war lost much of their lands.

---

10   Lundbye, *Valdemar Atterdag*, 201.
11   Lundbye, *Valdemar Atterdag*, 203–204.

17

The Kalmar Union

King Magnus of Sweden died on 1 December 1374, when his ship sank in a storm off Bergen on the Norwegian coast.

King Valdemar died on 24 October 1375.[1] He was on 3 May 1376 succeeded as King of Denmark by King Haakon's youthful son Olaf II of Denmark (1370–1387; r. 1376–1387) with the boy's mother, Queen Margaret, as regent. The late King Magnus, who had lost his kingdom, would have been content to see his grandson assume the Danish Crown. But it was King Valdemar's daughter Margaret, Queen of Norway and henceforth regent of Denmark, who was the mainstay of the kingdom and the foundation on which to build.

King Valdemar's grave in Sorø Monastery. The effigy of King Valdemar shows how tall he was. The grave monument was later demolished, but a drawing was published in Peder Hansen Resen's *Atlas Danicus* of 1677.

---

1   Over time, his memory transformed into legend. At midnight, the ghost of King Valdemar is said to ride through the forests at the ruins of Gurre Castle with his hunting party and ferocious black dogs. We have seen that this was also the eternal fate of the King's sometime associate, sometime enemy Claus Limbek and his formidable wife. As for King Valdemar, the story goes that at the end of his life, he defied the Almighty: 'God can keep Heaven, if I can keep Gurre'. Other versions of the story attribute King Valdemar's wish to Vordingborg Castle, Helsingør Castle, or even all three of them.

FALL OF THE MERCHANT-FARMER REPUBLIC

In August 1376, Queen Margaret demanded that Gotland and Visby swear fealty to King Olaf, rightful and hereditary King of Denmark. As a result, Gotland and Visby acknowledged Olaf as rightful heir and ruler. Clearly, the island then was under some level of Danish control or at least influence. Queen Margaret also demanded that Visby forgive all those who assisted King Valdemar in his conquest of the island.[2] For the first time in the 15 years since King Valdemar's conquest, we actually have unambiguous documentary evidence of who ruled the island: Queen Margaret on behalf of young King Olaf. In 1380, the child-king Olaf inherited the Norwegian throne as well (as Olaf IV), again with Queen Margaret as regent. This resulted in a union of crowns between Denmark and Norway which in one form or another would last until 1814. King Olaf died in 1387, only 17 years old. Henceforth, Queen Margaret ruled both kingdoms as 'regent lady and master' (Danish: *fuldmægtig frue og husbond*). Two years later, at Falköping in 1389, her armies defeated and captured King Albert of Mecklenburg. This terminated the reign of King Albert and made Queen Margaret regent of Sweden in addition to Denmark and Norway. Peace talks finally took place in 1395. Ex-King Albert accepted the termination of his rule but demanded and received the right to Visby, which he claimed based on recent possession. Meanwhile, rural Gotland remained under Queen Margaret's rule under a Danish governor, Sven Nilsson Sture (c. 1370–1424). Sven Sture earlier in the same year built three forts on Gotland, from which he attempted to control the island.[3]

In 1397, Queen Margaret had her adopted heir, Eric of Pomerania (1382–1459), elected to the kingship of all three kingdoms. By this means, Margaret united the three kingdoms of Denmark, Sweden, and Norway as a union of crowns under a single monarch: her adopted son and proxy ruler. Real power remained in Queen Margaret's capable hands.

Formally confirmed in a meeting in Kalmar in 1397, the three-state union, known as the Kalmar Union (Latin: *Unio Calmariensis*), for the first, and so far, only time united the Scandinavian kingdoms – Denmark, Sweden (which included Finland), and Norway (which included its overseas possessions of Iceland, Greenland with possibly a slice of North America, the Faroe Islands, and the Northern Isles of Orkney and Shetland) – under a single monarch. The Kalmar Union laid the foundation for early modern northern Europe. The three Union kingdoms retained separate identities and separate governments, each known as a Council of the Realm.

From 1397 to 1523 the three Scandinavian kingdoms where thus formally united – by a combination of luck, marital arrangements, and shrewd politics.

Queen Margaret. Convinced of the need to form a powerful Nordic counterbalance against the manifold threats from the monopolistic Hanseatic League, the militaristic Teutonic Order, and the opportunistic and within the Empire well-connected Mecklenburg, Queen Margaret succeeded in uniting the unruly Scandinavian kingdoms – the only ruler in history to achieve this feat. (Roskilde Cathedral)

---

2 Yrwing, *Visby: Hansestad på Gotland*, 337.
3 Yrwing, *Visby: Hansestad på Gotland*, 175–176.

18

Piracy

Meanwhile, the followers of the deposed King Albert of Mecklenburg turned to piracy. They had already in 1389 made Gotland their base. Among them was Albert's son, Duke Eric (1367/1368–1397), who landed on Gotland in the summer of 1396, in the wake of the recently concluded treaty between Queen Margaret and his father.[1]

King Albert and his Mecklenburg supporters had at some point organised freebooters with ships which he employed, in lieu of a navy, as privateers. It was probably through this force that King Albert had controlled Gotland in and possibly around 1369. Twenty years later, the organisation of freebooters had acquired a life of its own, and grown into a confederation of pirate captains, known as the Victual Brothers (German: *Viktualienbrüder*, *Vitalienbrüder*). Most came from northern Germany, primarily Mecklenburg itself, but freebooters from throughout the Baltic region joined the confederation.[2]

In 1391, two years after King Albert fell into captivity, Queen Margaret's men laid siege to Stockholm. The siege would last until 1395. King Albert's cousin, Duke John II of Mecklenburg-Stargard (d. 1416), sent a fleet towards Stockholm, which on the way also plundered coastal settlements on Gotland. In addition, he hired the Victual Brothers. The Mecklenburg ports of Ribnitz and Gollwitz offered to supply all pirates who were willing to act as privateers against Queen Margaret's ships and essentially blockade her ports. Rostock and Wismar joined the alliance against Queen Margaret. The Victual Brothers were also tasked to function as blockade runners, and to supply besieged Stockholm by sea. The traditional explanation is that this task gave the freebooters their name, after the Latin word *victualia* ('provisions'), which in Low German became *vitalie*, with the same meaning. However, by then the name had already appeared in France (French: *vitailler*, *vitailleur*), where it was used for those pirate ships that functioned as blockade runners at Calais

---

1 Yrwing, *Visby: Hansestad på Gotland*, 177.
2 Many Scandinavian knights and nobles found it lucrative to operate as pirates. From 1377 to 1389, one of the most notorious was the commandant of Lindholm Castle in Scania, Jacob (Jep) Muus of Ellinge (c. 1340–1394), who at least in words pledged his support to Queen Margaret. He particularly preyed on Hanseatic ships in Scanian waters. Queen Margaret was not slow to take advantage of the situation and soon hired pirates to further her cause.

in 1347. The name also appeared, in a German context, in Hamburg expense accounts from 1390, already before the siege of Stockholm.³ It was thus not the blockade running to besieged Stockholm that gave the freebooters their collective name. In fact, by this time the term *vitailleur* or *vitalie* seems merely to have meant marauder, a raider for food supplies. But the Victual Brothers were far more than mere marauders. The pirate confederation at some point chose a self-designation which they also used as a battle cry: 'Friends of God and enemies of all the world' (German: *Gottes Freunde und aller Welt Feinde*). This clue suggests that in their own eyes, they were a free company of mercenaries. Already in around 1362, the well-known mercenary Jean de Gouges called himself, in French, *l'ami de Dieu et l'ennemi de tout le mond*, with this very same meaning.⁴ When a cash-paying patron hired their services, the confederation was ready to operate as a joint force. When no such patron could be found, the individual components of the confederation separated to operate as pirates.

In short, it seems that what had begun as King Albert's privateers and amphibious mercenaries (because they also fought on land), in time grew into pirates who might accept to carry out the occasional assignment for ready cash but otherwise plundered independently. In the process, the captains ceased paying their men the customary wages expected by mercenaries. By 1398, after another decade of raiding, the pirates had begun to call themselves the *Likedeeler* ('equal sharers'), which referred to their custom of sharing all plunder in lieu of receiving wages.

By then, the pirates were led by a number of infamous freebooter captains whose names acquired legendary qualities that resonate through history. Many were minor nobles and knights. Most notorious was the semi-mythical Claus Störtebeker (c. 1360–1401), whose name can mean 'Down the beakerful'. Captain Störtebeker allegedly received his nickname because of his feat of swallowing four litres of beer without once taking the beaker from his mouth.

As mercenaries and pirates, the Victual Brothers grew into a significant force. Their fleets at times consisted of from 900 to perhaps 2,000 men and up to 100 ships.⁵ The highest reported number was 2,000 men, in a report from the Master of the Livonian Order dated around 1397. The highest reported number of ships was 108. Duke Eric in 1397 led a fleet of 1,200 men in 42 ships.⁶ Most of their fighting men wore some armour and carried crossbows. By 1410, a few carried firearms instead. In 1410, a contingent of 400 of them

---

3   Karl Koppmann, *Kämmereirechnungen der Stadt Hamburg* 1: *Kämmereirechnungen von 1350–1400* (Hamburg: Hermann Grüning, 1869), 474.

4   Hans Christian Cordsen, 'Beiträge zur Geschichte der Vitalienbrüder', *Jahrbücher des Vereins für Mecklenburgische Geschichte und Altertumskunde* 73 (Schwerin: Verein für Mecklenburgische Geschichte und Altertumskunde,1908), 1–30.

5   Sibylla Haasum, 'Medeltida seglatser: Båtar och navigation', Gerhard Flink (ed.), *Kung Valdemars segelled* (Stockholm: Streiffert/Riksantikvarieämbetet, 1995), 85–93, on 92; Lars Ericson Wolke, *Kapare och pirater i Nordeuropa under 800 år: Cirka 1050–1856* (Lund: Historiska Media, 2014), 89.

6   Friedrich Benninghoven, 'Die Vitalienbrüder as Forschungsproblem', Sven Ekdahl (ed.), *Kultur und Politik im Ostseeraum und im Norden 1350-1450: Visby-symposiet för historiska vetenskaper 1971* (Visby: Museum Gotlands Fornsal, Acta Visbyensia IV, 1973), 41–52, on 49.

hired as mercenaries by Danzig carried poleaxes, which they used to deadly effect against the Polish-Lithuanian army. On land, they typically served on foot, although by 1433 some of their crossbowmen could operate just as well on horseback, including firing their weapons while mounted.[7] They operated as easily on land as on sea, which they showed in, for instance, Livonia against the Teutonic Order in 1396, on Gotland from 1394 to 1398 and in 1404, and from 1391 to 1395 in Sweden. Interestingly, they maintained permanent residents or liaison officers in selected ports, which accepted their presence. One such port was Bremen, which in return took a third of the residents' plunder, and half of any ransoms raised.[8]

For a while, the link to Mecklenburg retained some potency among the pirates. Albert's son, Duke Eric, led them for a while from Gotland. The Baltic pirates began to call him their 'king'.[9] When Duke Eric died prematurely in 1397, apparently from the plague, his enterprising young widow Sophie (c. 1380 – c. 1408), the daughter of Duke Bogislaw VI of Pomerania-Wolgast, took over the business. Sophie appointed a governor, the aforementioned Sven Sture who two years previously was sent to the island as Queen Margaret's commandant but soon joined the pirates. Through him, Sophie offered all pirates the freedom of the island, as long as they gave her and Sven half of their plunder. For a while, Sophie and Sven in all but name ruled as queen and king of the Baltic brotherhood of pirates.[10] The entire Baltic Sea, and in particular the ships of the Hanseatic League, suffered greatly from their depredations.

After a year of pillage, the Hanseatic cities in Prussia turned for help to their protector, the Teutonic Order. In March 1398, Konrad von Jungingen (1355–1407), the Grand Master of the Teutonic Order, ordered the Order's army to Gotland, together with an artillery train. Altogether, the Teutonic Order expeditionary force included 84 ships with 4,000 soldiers (including 50 knights) and 400 horses under Johann von Pfirt.[11] Taking the hint, most pirates drifted away from the island as the Order's soldiers landed. Sven Sture withdrew into two Visby towers with a few men but soon had to surrender his control of the island and depart. Duke John of Mecklenburg-Stargard, who had already entered the city in a hitherto failed attempt to safeguard the late Duke Eric's claim, took formal control, and then returned home.[12] When

---

7   Sven Ekdahl, '"Schiffskinder" im Kriegsdienst des Deutchen Ordens: Ein Überblick über die Werbungen von Seeleuten durch den Deutschen Orden von der Schlacht bei Tannenberg bis zum Brester Frieden (1410–1435)', Sven Ekdahl (ed.), *Kultur und Politik im Ostseeraum und im Norden 1350–1450: Visby-symposiet för historiska vetenskaper 1971* (Visby: Museum Gotlands Fornsal, Acta Visbyensia IV, 1973), 239–274, on 247–248, 250, 251, 260, 273.
8   Benninghoven, 'Die Vitalienbrüder as Forschungsproblem', 51.
9   Yrwing, *Visby: Hansestad på Gotland*, 177.
10 Contemporary sources give no further information about their relationship, or details of their activities, so as with all things piratical, then and later, the reader is free to let his or her imagination run wild.
11 Yrwing, *Visby: Hansestad på Gotland*, 181–182.
12 Sophie returned to Mecklenburg with Duke John. She ultimately married Lord Nicholas V of Werle-Goldberg and Waren (d. 1408), the grandson of the aforementioned Bernard II of Werle-Waren. Sven, by then a fugitive from the Queen's justice because of his crimes, led 400 pirates north into the Gulf of Bothnia, from which he began to negotiate a pardon which Queen

FALL OF THE MERCHANT-FARMER REPUBLIC

Soldiers armed with a falchion or possibly a sabre (which by this time disseminated from the south all the way to Novgorod) and a poleaxe, dressed respectively in cap, kettle hat, and conical helmet of Slavic style as depicted in late fourteenth or early fifteenth-century frescoes in Bunge Church, Gotland. While these men were depicted as cavalry, the combat scenes bring to mind the turbulent fighting on Gotland involving the Victual Brothers of Baltic mercenaries and pirates. (Photo: Wolfgang Sauber)

Albert of Mecklenburg, who still claimed ownership, heard the news, he entered into negotiations and in May 1399 agreed to give Gotland as indemnity to the Teutonic Order in exchange for 10,000 English gold nobles, the equivalent of almost 80 kg of gold or about 4,000 marks silver.[13]

The pirates left Gotland for a while, but they did not disappear. Many relocated to the North Sea. Some of them henceforth raided Bergen, the Norwegian coast, and the waters around Iceland and Greenland, all of which was claimed by the Kalmar Union and believed to lie directly to the north.[14] Piracy was rampant there, and already King Haakon had dispatched warships to Greenland to deal with the situation. Henceforth, the problem grew worse and would continue into the sixteenth century.[15] Others instead hired out their services as mercenaries – in particularly to the Teutonic Order. Known as 'ship children' (German: *Schiffskinder*), they became a noted force in Prussia. The 'ship children' were highly regarded as seasoned mercenary soldiers and accordingly highly paid, so 'ship lads' would perhaps be a better modern translation.[16] By 1433, they were commonly paid one mark each per week plus provisions and plunder, which was the same rate as for mercenary cavalry. They then demanded, and received, one and a half mark each per week plus provisions and plunder – a knightly rate.[17]

Margaret granted in 1398. He then returned into Danish service, was dubbed knight in probably 1406, and married a respectable but not further identified lady.

13 Yrwing, *Visby: Hansestad på Gotland*, 183.
14 Fourteenth-century geographers had not yet learnt to differentiate between the geographic north pole and the north magnetic pole, which is not stationary over time. Nor had they devised a map projection capable of displaying simultaneously the layout of both hemispheres. Hence, early compass navigators believed that the course to Greenland and beyond led straight to the north, for which reason early maps of the north Atlantic (as well as the description of Norway by the aforementioned Philippe de Mézières) indicate Iceland, Greenland, and the North American coast as located directly north of Scandinavia. Gunnar Thompson, *The Friar's Map of Ancient America 1360 AD: The Story of Nicholas of Lynn and the Franciscan Map of America* (Seattle: Laura Lee, 1996). The migration of the north magnetic pole in previous centuries was after the publication of Thompson's work computed based on both the iterative method and paleomagnetic records. While the two methods do not give identical results, they confirm that the north magnetic pole was located significantly further south in the fourteenth century.
15 Olaus Magnus, *Historia de gentibus septentrionalibus* 2: 9, 11. For a Swedish translation, see Olaus Magnus, *Historia om de nordiska folken* (Hedemora: Michaeliisgillet/Gidlund, 2010), 92, 94–95.
16 Ekdahl, '"Schiffskinder" im Kriegsdienst des Deutchen Ordens', 239–274.
17 Ekdahl, '"Schiffskinder" im Kriegsdienst des Deutchen Ordens', 253, 269, 271.

PIRACY

Comparable headgear style from the fifteenth-century collection of illuminated manuscripts known as the Radziwiłł Manuscript, Codex, or Chronicle, alternatively the Königsberg Chronicle. The illuminated manuscript is believed to be a copy of a late thirteenth-century original. The artist of Bunge Church must have made his drawings of enemy soldiers based on either an illustration such as this, or far more likely, real soldiers dressed in garments and armour of Slavic styles, which in his time meant Victual Brothers. Elongated hats of this type were in Russian lands originally associated with Cumans (known to Russians as Polovtsians) but soon disseminated widely through Slavic society. (Radziwiłł Manuscript, Library of the Russian Academy of Sciences, St. Petersburg)

Russian helmets from the Crypt of the Annunciation Cathedral in Moscow, dated to the fourteenth to fifteenth centuries. Slavic helmets of this type seem to have inspired the artist of Bunge Church. (Photo: Shakko (Sofia Bagdasarova))

FALL OF THE MERCHANT-FARMER REPUBLIC

Russian kettle hat, attributed to the time of Dmitriy Donskoy, fourteenth century. Less tall versions, too, were commonplace in Slavic lands. (Kremlin Armoury, photo: Shakko (Sofia Bagdasarova))

Although presently little studied, Slavic influences in dress and military equipment almost certainly reached Gotland. These styles may have influenced rural militia and mercenary companies such as the Victual Brothers alike. (Radziwiłł Manuscript, Library of the Russian Academy of Sciences, St. Petersburg)

19

The End of a Golden Age

Gotland and Visby were controlled by the Teutonic Order from 1398 to 1408. Their presence was against the wish of Queen Margaret who by various means attempted to recover Gotland for the Union.

In December 1403, Queen Margaret sent an army to the island. In January 1404, her soldiers laid siege to Visby. They attempted to storm the city, but the Teutonic Order garrison repelled the attackers. In March, the Order garrison was reinforced by yet more men. The Union supply line went by way of Kalmar. At this point, an Order fleet under Ulrich von Jungingen, the Grand Master's brother, suddenly attacked and captured or burned 160 of the Union transports that had assembled at Kalmar to supply Queen Margaret's army on Gotland. In May, Ulrich von Jungingen brought yet more reinforcements to Visby. The two parties negotiated a truce in July 1404, after which Queen Margaret's men left the island. It was not a favourable agreement for the Union. In forts such as Slite, they had to leave any trebuchets, crossbows, and firearms.[1] The Union only recovered Gotland in 1408, and then by purchase. Queen Margaret first paid Albert of Mecklenburg 8,000 marks silver for ownership of the island and then paid the Order 9,000 English gold nobles ostensibly for the work done to build a castle at Visby but, in reality, to leave the island.[2] The latter was the equivalent of 70 kg of gold or about 3,600 marks silver – less than the Order had given, or promised to give, to Albert.

The return of Queen Margaret's soldiers sealed the fate of Visby and Gotland. Her adopted son, King Eric of Pomerania, arrived in Visby in 1411. He had a strong castle, Visborg, built on a foundation already laid by the Order next to the city, which first Queen Margaret and, after her death from natural causes, King Eric henceforth ruled through a bailiff in Visborg Castle. Henceforth, Visby must promise to support the King in his wars. Both burghers and rural Gotlanders were unhappy about the change and would rather have remained under the rule of the Teutonic Order. In 1412, King Eric decided it was time to reduce the status of the island's free rural population to the level of the much-oppressed Danish peasantry. King Eric

---

1 Yrwing, *Visby: Hansestad på Gotland*, 183–184; Hedberg, *Kungl. Artilleriet: Medeltid och äldre vasatid*, 22.
2 Yrwing, *Visby: Hansestad på Gotland*, 187, 369–370.

raised taxes more than ten-fold, in coin but with additional duties in the form of provisions and supplies, and in addition demanded that all peasants provide eight days of forced, unpaid labour per year to Visborg Castle. The new regime badly impacted upon trade. Visby ceased developing. Prosperous merchants abandoned the city, and few new houses were built. Business stagnated, and the formerly leading Hanseatic city gradually turned into a provincial backwater and small town. This, incidentally, explains why modern-day Visby still retains its character as a fourteenth-century fortified city. Nobody any longer had the incentive, or means, to pay for the construction of new buildings, fortifications, or churches in the city.

Meanwhile, the Kalmar Union suffered from internal discontent. King Eric's tendency to appoint Danish and German commandants and bailiffs soon became a source of dissatisfaction in Sweden and Norway. His tax increases, intended to finance a military takeover of the Duchy of Slesvig, were unpopular. Besides, his attempts to seize Slesvig failed.

Besides, overfishing and possibly changes in spawning patterns may ultimately have taken its toll of the Scanian herring market. Some believe that in about 1425, a significant stock of herring instead took to spawning in the North Sea, off the coast of the Netherlands. Whether this actually happened is uncertain, because no real data has survived into the present. Besides, if so, this was in any case a temporary fluctuation. By the end of the century the herring stock had recovered, at least for the time being. Meanwhile, much of the trade moved from the annual market into Scanian mercantile centres such as Malmö.

A greater problem was King Eric's ongoing disputes with the Hanseatic League. In 1426, King Eric introduced the Sound Toll as a means to disrupt League trade and as an alternative income to that from the Scanian herring market. Whoever controlled the Strait, or Sound, also controlled the means to raise customs revenue there. These revenues, which became known as the Sound Toll, accrued not to the Kingdom of Denmark but to the King personally, for whom it soon became a key source of income. However, the introduction of the Sound Toll was a slap in the face to the Hanseatic League. The League cities of the Wendish-Saxon *Drittel* responded by declaring war. But the League no longer acted in unison. The cities of the Westphalian-Prussian *Drittel* stayed neutral, and the non-Hanseatic Dutch towns instead joined the war on King Eric's side. The introduction of the Sound Toll also caused great losses to Swedish mining enterprises, which exported iron and copper through the Strait. Taking advantage of popular discontent, Engelbrekt Engelbrektsson, a wealthy mining entrepreneur, in 1434 became the leader of a major Swedish revolt against Union rule.

Over time, the Kalmar Union gradually fragmented as a polity. While many leading Danish, Swedish, and Norwegian noble families were connected by marriage, owned lands in more than one kingdom, and accordingly were in favour of the Union, they wanted a union founded on negotiations between the councils of the realm, in which they held important posts. This vision was not shared by those nobles who were less well-connected, lacked lands overseas, and accordingly depended on royal service in which they could gain personal advancement by winning the King's favour. They wanted a

THE END OF A GOLDEN AGE

union based on the principle of direct royal rule.³ In Sweden there were also nobles who wished to detach Sweden from the Union. While there always was discontent in Denmark and Norway, opposition was particularly virulent in Sweden, where a series of strongmen each henceforth strove to claim rule over Sweden and, perhaps ultimately, kingship. Civil strife and rebellions made King Eric's position untenable, so in 1436 he took refuge on Gotland, basing his remaining, waning power on the strength of Visborg Castle. With all other sources of income denied him, Eric again made Gotland a centre for piracy, on which he now depended for a living. Again, pirate captains flocked to Gotland and made Visby their base of operations.

This situation remained unchanged until July 1448, when a newly elected Swedish king, Charles VIII, sent an army of 2,000 men with orders to retake Gotland.⁴ King Charles's men took Visby in December, and in January 1449 the rural Gotlanders swore fealty to him and, as in times past, to the Swedish Crown.⁵ Meanwhile, Eric of Pomerania was bottled up in Visborg Castle and could do nothing. However, by then Denmark too had elected a new king, Christian I of Oldenburg, who sent his army to the island.⁶ Suddenly, there were three armies on Gotland: Swedes, Danes, and Eric's pirate confederation. This situation could not last. In April, Eric handed over Visborg Castle to the Danes and departed. Negotiations between Sweden and Denmark followed, until the Danish King himself arrived with a fleet, and disembarked yet more soldiers on the island. With Visborg Castle in Danish hands and superior Danish forces on the island, there was little the Swedes could do. In late July 1449 the Swedish army agreed to withdraw from the island.⁷ Henceforth, Gotland was a Danish possession.

Cannon ball made of stone for a 160-pounder, found at Visby. Although this cannon ball possibly was made for the fourteenth-century operations on Gotland, it more likely derives from one of the fifteenth-century sieges of Visby. (Army Museum, Stockholm; AM.062529)

---

3   In modern historiography of the Kalmar Union, rule by council of the realm is called *regimen politicum*, while direct royal rule is referred to as *regimen regale*. Although based on fourteenth-century theoretical concepts, neither term featured prominently in fifteenth-century political discussions.
4   King Charles VIII Canutesson (1408 or 1409–1470; King of Sweden 1448–1457, 1464–1465, and 1467–1470; also, King of Norway 1449–1450), known in Swedish as Karl Knutsson Bonde, in June 1448 had himself elected King of Sweden based on his army from Finland, where he probably was born and his family enjoyed much support. Later in the year, King Charles had himself elected King of Norway as well.
5   Yrwing, *Gotlands medeltid*, 57; Yrwing, *Visby: Hansestad på Gotland*, 202, 337.
6   Christian I of Oldenburg (1426–1481) was King of Denmark 1448–1481, King of Norway 1450–1481, and King of Sweden 1457–1464, which meant that he, for a while, restored the Kalmar union. Christian was the first king of the House of Oldenburg which henceforth would provide many Danish king.
7   Yrwing, *Visby: Hansestad på Gotland*, 202–201; Dick Harrison, *Karl Knutsson: En biografi* (Lund: Historiska Media, 2004), 168, 171–176.

FALL OF THE MERCHANT-FARMER REPUBLIC

Civilisations seldom fall overnight. More commonly, they first decline and then gradually merge into something entirely different. This was the fate that awaited the merchant-farmer republic and indeed all of Gotland. Because of the many wars, the island's rural economy was in shreds and henceforth limited to small-scale agriculture. Economic development had practically ceased. Population numbers had declined. While the Gotlanders collectively still retained ownership of the trade factory in Novgorod, by the 1390s they had it rented out to German merchants from the Hanseatic League. Henceforth, the national lawspeaker or his representative, the Cistercian abbot of Guthnalia, would occasionally travel to Reval or even Novgorod to collect rent for the factory, but no Gotlanders seem to have traded there anymore. Soon after the 1449 withdrawal of the Swedish army, the Danish governor of Gotland claimed ownership of the Novgorod factory. Faced by the opposition of the League merchants, his repeated attempts to gain control failed, and the factory remained under the formal control of the national lawspeakers for another century, until 1552 when it finally passed into Danish hands. However, because of shifting trade patterns the factory was by then of little utility or value, and the Danish governor received his final rent payment already in 1557.[8]

Visby suffered a similar fate as rural Gotland, but for a while resisted the winds of change. As late as in 1460, Visby sent a total of 32 merchant ships to Danzig, presumably a similar number to Lübeck, and some ships to other cities, too. Yet, by 1476 the comparable figure for the Danzig trade had fallen to 21 ships. Population numbers declined in the city too, not least because of the exodus of those merchants who had the means to move their business elsewhere. Visby participated for the last time in a Hanseatic Diet meeting in 1447 and lost its status as a member of the Hanseatic League soon after 1476.[9]

Gotland would remain Danish territory for two centuries – until 1645, when Sweden regained the island in the Treaty of Brömsebro.[10] The re-acquisition was an afterthought in the peace agreement, since the war between Denmark and Sweden primarily was fought in Denmark. Earlier in the year, a Swedish fleet had landed on Gotland, and Swedish soldiers easily moved into Visby. Gotland was merely informed of its change in status after the Treaty was already concluded. The little Danish garrison then left the island.

By then, descendants of the merchant-farmer chiefs of old still lived on their traditional farmsteads, which often were passed down within the same families into modern times. But henceforth, these Gotlanders were farmers, not international merchants or ruling chiefs.

---

8 Yrwing, *Gotlands medeltid*, 135–137; Frithiof Hall, *Bidrag till Cistercienserordens historia i Sverige* (Hernösand, dissertation, 1898), 171.
9 Yrwing, *Visby: Hansestad på Gotland*, 204–207, 286.
10 Michael Fredholm von Essen, *The Lion from the North 2: The Swedish Army during the Thirty Years War, 1632–1648* (Warwick: Helion, 2020), 122.

THE END OF A GOLDEN AGE

The 1905 excavation of the first mass grave at Visby gained worldwide attention. The mass grave was first identified by Visby archaeologist and archivist Oscar Vilhelm Wennersten, who also carried out the initial excavation with little funding and only those means available locally. (Photo from Nils Johan August Lagergren's collection, Swedish National Archives – Regional State Archives in Visby.)

On 25 July 1905, Kaiser William II of Germany visited the Visby excavation during a summer cruise around the Baltic with his yacht, the Hohenzollern. When the Kaiser peeked down into the open pit, Wennersten, working down there, famously looked up and reportedly told the Emperor: 'Here Your Majesty observes war's horrible consequences. I hope that you will remember it!' The Kaiser took the admonition with good grace and awarded the archaeologist a medal. Wennersten wore the decoration for a while, until he realised that rural Gotlanders interpreted the blue ribbon as a sign of membership in the Blue Cross Society, an international temperance movement, hence no longer offered him alcoholic drinks. (Photo: Knut Falck, Antikvarisk-topografiska arkivet (ATA), Swedish National Heritage Board)

Appendix I

Pictorial Description of Cuirasses Excavated at Visby

Bengt Thordeman, who documented the excavated armour at Visby, divided the reasonably complete 25 excavated cuirasses into a typology consisting of six main types. The first five consisted of coat-of-plates armour, while the sixth type consisted of lamellar armour. It seemed to Thordeman that with the exception of the lamellar type, a sequence could be determined, from presumably older cuirasses with many plates to more recent ones with fewer plates. The exception was perhaps Type 5, by which Thordeman labelled the single lamellar cuirass (No. 24) modified into a coat-of-plates cuirass. Thordeman, and most later scholars, accordingly, interpret the reduced number of plates as a chronological development. While this interpretation can neither be proven or disproven, this Appendix displays the variety of coat-of-plates cuirasses found at Visby.

All photographs in this section are by Victoria Dabir, History Museum, Stockholm, except those of the lamellar cuirass (No. 25) which are by Bengt Thordeman and his team.

Type 1

Cuirass No. 1

PICTORIAL DESCRIPTION OF CUIRASSES EXCAVATED AT VISBY

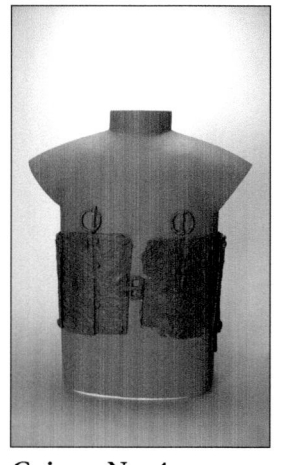   

Cuirass No. 4

  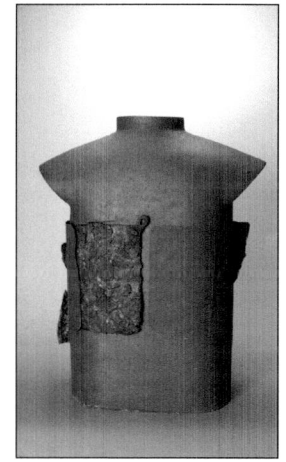 

Cuirass No. 6

Cuirass No. 7

FALL OF THE MERCHANT-FARMER REPUBLIC

Type 2

Cuirass No. 8

Cuirass No. 12

Cuirass No. 13

PICTORIAL DESCRIPTION OF CUIRASSES EXCAVATED AT VISBY

  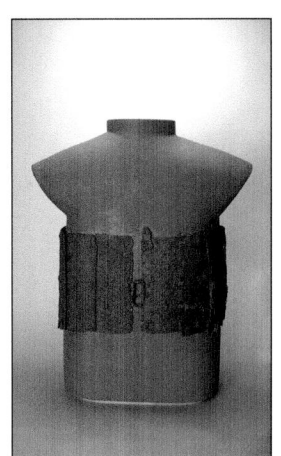 

Cuirass No. 15

Type 3

  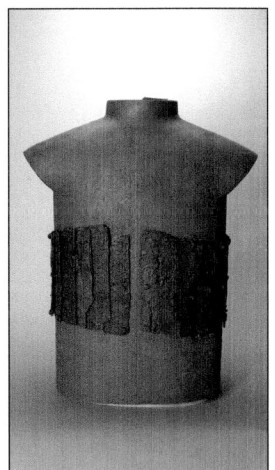 

Cuirass No. 16

Cuirass No. 17

FALL OF THE MERCHANT-FARMER REPUBLIC

Cuirass No. 18

Type 4

Cuirass No. 19

Cuirass No. 21

PICTORIAL DESCRIPTION OF CUIRASSES EXCAVATED AT VISBY

Cuirass No. 22

Cuirass No. 23

Type 5

Cuirass No. 24

175

Type 6 (Lamellar)

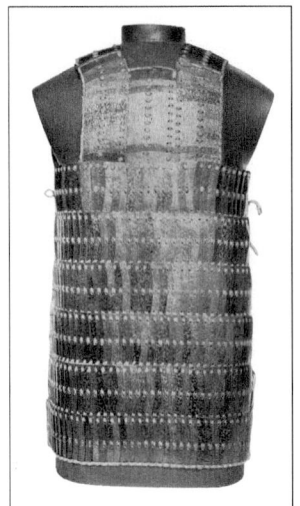   

Cuirass No. 25

Appendix II

North European Currency

The value of goods and services was measured in marks. This was a North European unit of weight of unknown origin, first mentioned in a written source in 857 AD. The mark could be either pure silver to the weight of one mark (mark silver; German: *Mark lötig*; Swedish: *mark lödig*), or a coin with a nominal value of one mark (mark coin; Swedish: *mark penning*). Although there were some regional variations, the mark was the common currency of exchange in Scandinavia and Germany in the fourteenth century. At first, the relationship between the mark silver and mark coin was 1:1, but rulers had a habit of reducing the silver content in the coins they issued, thus depreciating the value. The relationship thus changed to 1:2, 1:3, and so on. As a result, the mark silver retained its value over time, while the mark coin was debased and over time lost much of its value.

In the fourteenth century, the regional differences in the mark can be summarised as follows:

- A Swedish mark silver equalled 210.6 g,
- A Norwegian mark silver equalled 214.5 g (1329),
- A Danish mark silver equalled 210.47 g (1332–1333).

In comparison, the Cologne mark silver, which equalled 233.856 g, was the most common unit of weight outside Scandinavia and would ultimately become the basis for the Imperial currency. Over time, the Cologne mark silver for this reason grew to dominate Baltic trade, but it had not yet reached this status in King Valdemar's time.

Naturally, smaller denominations were also needed for the calculation of financial transactions. These denominations were the *öre*, the *örtug* (pl. *örtugar*), and the *penning* (pl. *penningar*). From about 1290 onwards, the calculation in mainland Sweden was 1 mark = 8 *öre*; 1 *öre* = 3 *örtugar*; and 1 *örtug* = 8 *penningar*. Gotland used the same calculation, except that on this island, 1 *örtug* = 12 *penningar*. Most of these denominations were issued as coins only from the late fourteenth century onwards.

Coins were in circulation, but their use remained limited in rural areas. Gotland was an exception. Because of the island's widespread trade, coins from a vast range of countries were commonplace. However, because of this diversity most were treated as having a value equal to the silver content of the coin rather than its nominal value.

The only coin issued on Gotland before about 1340 was the silver *penning* ('coin'; German: *Pfennig*, pl. *Pfennige*), a name that incidentally also was the origin of the English term penny. The *penning* minted on Gotland could be double- or one-sided (that is, a bracteate).

At around 1340, Gotland issued a higher denomination of coin known as the *gote* ('Gotlander') which equalled 12 *penningar*. Sweden employed a corresponding silver *penning* which was the only coin issued before about 1370. Then, in about 1370, Sweden introduced an additional coin, the *örtug* (corresponding to the Gotland *gote*). The *örtug* had already existed for some time as a unit of calculation, but it was then never minted.

At first, the Swedish mainland employed separate economic systems in the southwest (Götaland), which developed early because of the region's close links to the British Isles and the Continent, and the east (Svealand), which saw little economic development before the second half of the thirteenth century but then rapidly turned itself into the dominant political and economic centre of the Swedish realm. While the Swedish territories had separate economies, in Svealand 1 mark coin equalled 192 *penningar*. In comparison, in Götaland 1 mark coin equalled 384 *penningar*. Götaland adopted the Svealand, that is Swedish, monetary system in the late thirteenth century. The more developed monetary system of Gotland and Öland did not change, however, so their 1 mark coin continued to equal 288 *penningar*. In comparison, in Norway 1 mark coin equalled 240 *penninger*, while in Cologne 1 mark coin equalled 256 *pfennige*.

In northern Germany, a higher denomination of coin was introduced in around 1365. This was the *Witten*, which equalled 4 *Pfennige*.

Although the mark silver, and especially the Cologne mark silver, was the primary exchange currency in the Baltic region, merchants occasionally made large-scale payments in other currencies, based on gold instead of silver.

The 24-carat gold florin (3.53 g) was commonly employed as a base currency. The florin (Italian: *fiorino d'oro*; Latin: *florenus aureus*) was, as the name suggests, minted in Florence. It was as pure as a gold coin could be. In 1346, the exchange rate was 1 Cologne mark silver = 5.5 florins.

The 23-carat Rhenish gulden (1386: 3.54 g), a gold coin minted in Hanseatic cities, was the principal trade coin of Germany. It had roughly the same value as the florin.

The 24-carat Venetian ducat (3.545 g) dominated in the Near East but at this time was rare in northwestern and particularly northern Europe. It, too, was comparable to the florin.

A smaller gold coin was the 24-carat English gold noble, introduced in 1344 (8.97 g) but gradually growing lighter until 1351 (7.776 g). The gold noble was common in western Germany but in the Baltic region was primarily used within the Teutonic Order's territory. The exchange rate was about 1 Cologne mark silver = 2.5 nobles.

The English gold sterling (1351: 23.21 g) should also be mentioned, since it in written sources is often confused with the earlier English silver sterling (323.7 g), which often was brought to Gotland in large quantities.

Colour Plate Commentaries

Plate A. King Valdemar of Denmark

This depiction of King Valdemar of Denmark is based on a contemporary fresco in St. Peter's Church, Næstved, Denmark. The depiction shows King Valdemar in full armour including a crowned bascinet helmet worn over a chainmail coif. Graffiti in Fide Church, Gotland, shows a knight who possibly wears the same type of crowned bascinet and may represent the Danish King.

King Valdemar wears a tight surcoat with wide, elbow-length sleeves, under which he wears a coat-of-plates or, possibly, plate cuirass. He wears a long-sleeved chainmail hauberk beneath the cuirass for additional protection. The lower arms are protected by iron vambraces. His hands would normally be protected by iron gauntlets over the soft leather gloves. He wears armoured *cuisses* to protect the thighs, iron *poleyns* covering the knees, and greaves for the lower legs. His feet are protected by *sabatons* made from small overlapping iron plates. In addition, legs and feet are very likely protected by chainmail chausses (leggings) under the greaves and *sabatons*, although these are not visible here. The King is armed with a broad, knightly broadsword and a ballock dagger.

King Valdemar's personal coat of arms showed three blue, crowned lions on a yellow (gold) field. At least in later years, the field was covered with red hearts or water-leaves. The same pattern of hearts or water-leaves appears on his surcoat.

Plate B. Danish knight

This depiction of a Danish knight is based on the effigy of Prince Christopher, Duke of Lolland, on his tomb in Roskilde Cathedral. The colours have been reconstructed according to recent analysis.

Interestingly, Prince Christopher is depicted as wearing more modern and up-to-date armour than his father, in fact following the very latest in German armour design and fashion. His bascinet comes with a turnbuckle above the forehead to secure a visor of the up-to-date dog-faced or 'houndskull' (*Hundsgugel*) type. But he also carries a traditional great helm with a horned crest of the type that remained popular in Germany. A separate chainmail coif, worn under the helmet, provides additional protection for the face and neck.

Prince Christopher wears a tight, sleeveless surcoat of very modern style, embroidered with heraldic dragons, under which an unseen modern plate cuirass provides added protection. It was the development of the old coat-of-plates into a single plate cuirass in the mid-fourteenth century that made it possible for a knight on the battlefield to follow the tight-fitting civilian fashion then in vogue, which gave the appearance of a wasp-waist. Plate cuirasses were just becoming common in Germany but had not yet made a major impression on Scandinavian chivalry. Three iron chains from the cuirass secure his broadsword, ballock dagger, and whatever additional item he wished to keep handy (likely the great helm or shield). Prince Christopher wears a long-sleeved chainmail hauberk beneath the cuirass for additional protection. The cuirass seems to come with attached shoulder pieces, which add to the protection provided by the iron rebraces that cover the outsides of the upper arms, to which they are secured by buckled straps. The lower arms are protected by hinged and buckled iron vambraces. However, despite the modern armour, he lacks *couters* to provide additional protection to the elbows, which were becoming increasingly common, but not yet universal, in Germany. His hands are protected by iron gauntlets over soft leather gloves. Prince Christopher wears armoured *cuisses* with scalloped fringes to protect the thighs, hardened leather greaves reinforced with studded iron straps down the front, and iron *poleyns* over the knees. His feet are protected by *sabatons* made from small overlapping iron plates. In addition, legs and feet are protected by unseen chainmail chausses under the greaves and *sabatons*.

Prince Christopher carries a broad, knightly sword in a sword belt hung low around the hips, and a ballock dagger similar to the one carried by his father.

Plate C. German mercenary crossbowman and handgunner

This German mercenary crossbowman is typical of the professional soldiers available at the time. He wears armour that is almost as complete and just as functional as that of a knight, even though it is not quite as decorative. He wears a broad-brimmed kettle hat over a chainmail coif, and a sturdy coat-of-plates cuirass over a chainmail hauberk, which in turn is worn over a padded quilted *gambeson*. Armoured cuisses protect the thighs, with iron *poleyns* strapped over the knees, iron greaves over the lower legs, and iron *sabatons* which cover the top of the feet. In addition, the soldier wears gauntlets made of iron plates riveted to leather gloves.

This soldier draws ('spans') the crossbow with the help of the stirrup and a hook attached to his belt. He turns the crossbow with the groove towards himself, places one foot in the stirrup, then bends over or goes down on one knee, until he can hook the claws of the spanning hook over the string. He then straightens or stands up using his body to pull the string back. This method of spanning was efficient and remained common throughout the fourteenth and fifteenth centuries.

While most soldiers armed for projectile combat carried crossbows, by this time a few carried handguns instead. As noted, handguns were used in the Gotland campaign.

This crossbowman carries a falchion as a sidearm. The falchion was a heavy straight sword or cleaver with a single cutting edge, which easily cut through fabric or chainmail armour.

Plate D. Gotland rural militia officer

This officer is the commander of a section of the rural militia, or possibly even the entire militia. When not in command of the militia, he would be a prosperous merchant-farmer who likely also functioned as local chief in his area.

We know that the East influenced armour and fashion on Gotland, even though we do not know how widespread these influences were. As a prosperous merchant-farmer who likely made his fortune in the Novgorod trade, this officer accordingly wears a tall, pointed kettle hat of Slavic style over a chainmail coif. Note the rectangular lower edge of the coif, which was typical for Gotland, and the plate shoulder armour pieces reminiscent of a modern epaulette. His other armour and equipment are similar to that worn by German infantrymen: a coat-of-plates cuirass over a chainmail hauberk, which in turn is worn over a padded quilted *gambeson*. He wears soft quilted or padded leather *cuisses* over thighs and knees, with domed iron *poleyns* to provide additional protection to the knees, and splinted armour greaves consisting of strips of metal attached to a fabric or leather backing to protect the lower legs.

The officer is armed with a spear, broadsword, dagger, and mace, the latter of which was a sign of command. His shield displays the emblem of Gotland, a white (silver) ram with a gold-and-red flag on a red field.

Plate E. Gotland rural militia soldier

The majority of the rural militia had the means to arm and equip themselves with weapons and armour that were no less functional that those used by professional soldiers. Yet, being non-professionals, we probably should expect a slightly more eclectic choice of gear. This militia soldier wears a broad-brimmed kettle hat over a chainmail coif with the rectangular lower edge, which was typical for Gotland, and the plate shoulder armour pieces reminiscent of a modern epaulette. He also wears an Eastern lamellar cuirass over a chainmail hauberk, which in turn is worn over a padded quilted *gambeson*. The lamellar cuirass is not an antique, even though it likely derives from earlier in the century, when the Gotlanders more frequently traded in the East. Lamellar armour of this type remained in common use in both the Russian principalities and in the Byzantine Empire.

However, the militia soldier's lower legs are unarmoured. Based on both contemporary effigies and forensic examination of the dead found in the Visby mass graves, many rural militia soldiers lacked leg armour. We do not know if this was because of personal choice, for instance to enable easier cross-country movement, or a lack of gear. Certainly, there seems to have been no shortages with regard to other items of arms and armour.

The militia soldier is armed with a morning star, a spiked club which, in similarity to the Flemish *goedendag*, had a sharp metal spike inserted in and extending out of the head, like a short pike. The morning star was a weapon popular with militia units and would remain in service with Scandinavian militias for centuries.

By this time, the buckler had already replaced earlier, larger types of shields. This flat wooden buckler is typical of the style, with a large, round iron boss which covers the fist-grip bar. The buckler's face and edge are reinforced with iron.

Plate F. Gotland rural militia soldier

Although the majority of the rural militia had access to chainmail and coat-of-plates or lamellar cuirasses, we can assume that some of the men raised for militia service were somewhat less well equipped. Guta Law stated that every free man aged 20 and above must have a full set of weapons at home and be willing to fight when mobilised. To own a full set of weapons was both a right and an obligation for a free man. However, as far as we know the law did not stipulate that the full set necessarily include a coat-of-plates or lamellar cuirass. This militia soldier indeed owns a full set of weapons, but he has satisfied himself with a broad-brimmed kettle hat and a quilted *gambeson*. His primary weapon is a crossbow, so he perhaps prefers the increased mobility that comes with lighter armour. In addition, this militia soldier carries a long axe, a knife or dagger, and likely a buckler on his back.

He wears a loose-fitting, thigh-length tunic and fairly loose hose (trousers), all made of natural woollen fabric. He might also carry a cloak of the same material, but if so, he removed it before the battle. His head is covered by a long-tailed hood (gugel) with a 90 cm long and 2 cm wide trailing tail (liripipe). His dress is based on that of the so-called Bocksten Man, the remains of a medieval man's body found in a bog in Varberg Municipality, Sweden. Generally dated to the fourteenth century, his garments constitute one of the best-preserved finds of medieval garments in Europe. We know from numerous pictorial sources that this style of dress was commonplace in Scandinavia at the time. By 1361, fashion prescribed a shorter tunic and tighter hose, but loose-fitting garments were easier to work in, so survived (or made a comeback) in rural areas into the sixteenth century.

COLOUR PLATE COMMENTARIES

Plate G. Visby burgher militia soldier

Although the Visby burgher militia did not consist of professional soldiers, the burghers certainly had the means to equip themselves with modern arms and armour. This militia soldier accordingly wears armour which is similar in style to that of the professional German soldier already illustrated. He wears a broad-brimmed kettle hat over a chainmail coif to protect his head, and a coat-of-plates cuirass over a chainmail hauberk, which in turn is worn over a padded quilted *gambeson*. However, like the rural militia he has not provided himself with any kind of leg armour or iron gauntlets.

This burgher militia soldier is armed with an early halberd of what is customarily called the German or Swiss type. He brings no shield, since the halberd requires the use of both hands, but carries a proper broadsword as sidearm.

Plate H. Visby mercenary and pirate

Visby hired mercenaries for protection, but we know nothing of those who served there in 1361. They may have been well-ordered professionals from central Germany, similar to those men who fought for King Valdemar. However, they may alternatively have belonged to one of those far more disreputable shipborne Baltic mercenary companies which fought for anybody who was willing to pay – and who turned pirates as soon as they had no paying customers. Such companies sold their services to Hanseatic cities including Visby, the Duchy of Mecklenburg, and (from the fifteenth century onwards) the Teutonic Order.

This man is essentially a pirate. We do not know if he is a Swede, Gotlander, Mecklenburger, Pomeranian, or Slav, but he has adopted the very long hair and beard customarily worn by Slavs in the Baltic. Perhaps he did so to look more intimidating. This soldier also wears a tall, pointed cap of Slavic style. In a fight, he would instead put on his pointed kettle hat, also of Slavic style, which he kept close at hand. An alternative would have been a pointed helmet with a chainmail aventail to protect the face and neck. Men of means would attach feathers, plumes, or horse tail hair arranged as a panache spreading outwards from the top of the helmet.

A soldier would typically have worn his coat-of-plates cuirass over a chainmail hauberk, but those of lesser means might have worn it directly over a padded quilted *gambeson* instead. This man has eschewed the use of the heavy chainmail hauberk. Evidence from previous and later centuries show that sailors in the Baltic knew how to swim, so there is reason to believe that many discarded truly heavy armour when at sea.

This mercenary is armed to the teeth with dagger, knife, and most importantly, a long poleaxe. Some of his colleagues would have carried a crossbow as well. The Baselard dagger was very popular in the fourteenth century. Commonly known as *basler*, it may have been Swiss in origin and named after the city of Basel. When used by soldiers, they were generally slung on the right hip.

Further Reading

The written sources to the battles on Gotland are few, brief, and often unreliable. A total of 24 contemporary or near-contemporary letters, chronicles, and inscriptions relate directly to King Valdemar's military campaign on Gotland.[1] Certain echoes of the battles seem to resonate in saga and myth. And that is essentially what is available.

The situation is slightly better with regard to royal affairs, the strategic context, and broader descriptions of ongoing events. Nonetheless, contemporary and near-contemporary primary sources are limited both in number and with regard to the information therein. The exception is the contemporary documentation archived by the Hanseatic League, which is published in Volume 1 of *Hanserecesse: Die Recesse und andere Akten der Hansetage von 1256–1430* (1870).

The earliest primary source to King Valdemar's campaign is the letter, dated a few days after the battle, in which King Valdemar confirmed Visby's privileges. A few other royal letters have been preserved, although often only as later copies.

The battle is mentioned in old chronicles, but most were written years, or even centuries, after the battle. The Zealand Chronicle (*Chronica Sialandie*, also known as the Younger Zealand Chronicle, or *Continuatio Chronice Sialandie*), was compiled a few years after the battle.[2] It notes briefly that the King in 1361 first conquered Öland, and then landed on Gotland, where he was victorious in three battles and took a rich plunder.

Then came the *Libellus de Magno Erici Rege* ('Little book of King Magnus Ericsson'), a defamatory propaganda piece written at some point between 1365 and 1371 based on St. Bridget's angry outbursts from Rome but compiled in Sweden to mock King Magnus.[3] The Zealand Chronicle and the *Libellus de Magno Erici Rege* agree that three battles were fought during

---

1   Christian Tortzen, *Gotland 1361: Forudsætningerne, overleveringen* (Copenhagen: Gyldendal, 1961), 62–63, lists the 23 literary sources known in his time. In addition, a text was discovered on the memorial cross at Grens farmstead in 2011. Lingström, *Mästerby, 1361*, 129–130.
2   Jørgensen, *Annales Danici Medii Ævi*, 163–188. Research suggests that the Chronicle's data for the years 1360 and later were actually added as a separate product and accordingly does not qualify as an independent source. Tage E. Christiansen, 'Yngre sjællandske krønikes sidste aar', *Scandia* 40:1 (1974), 5–33.
3   *Libellus de Magno Erici Rege*: Claudius Annerstedt (ed.), *Scriptores rerum Svecicarum medii ævi* 3:1 (Uppsala: Edvard Berling, 1871–1876), 12–16.

FALL OF THE MERCHANT-FARMER REPUBLIC

Of high birth, the outspoken St. Bridget of Sweden (c. 1303–1373) was related to the royal family through her mother, which gave her a high degree of latitude. She married early and gave her husband eight children. Interested in religion since childhood, St. Bridget had visions which she claimed revealed Christ's instructions to her. After her husband's death in 1344 she accordingly proclaimed herself bride and mouthpiece of Christ. Two years later, she pestered King Magnus and Queen Blanche into providing lands for a monastery under her control in Vadstena. In 1349, she relocated to Rome, from which she continued to harass King Magnus and indeed anybody whom she found less than faultless. St. Bridget accused King Magnus of a wide range of shortcomings, which rendered him the derogatory nickname Magnus Smek ('Magnus the Caresser'). Some modern-day writers have interpreted her writings as suggestions that the King was homosexual. However, it seems more likely that St. Bridget's complaint related to King Magnus's loss of the Scanias to the silver-tongued King Valdemar, whom she also despised. St. Bridget's numerous visions were later collected and published. In 1999, St. Bridget was named one of Europe's patron saints, perhaps an appropriate choice for somebody who unremittingly criticised all who fell short of her impossibly high standards. This statue, probably consecrated in 1392, is believed to have been made in Italy by an artist who had met St. Bridget in life. (Vadstena Monastery; photo: Håkan Svensson)

the campaign, which corresponds to our interpretation that battles were fought at Mästerby, Visby, and Fide.

Next in time is the memorial that finally gives the date of the battle. It was raised next to the Visby mass graves at some point apparently before 1376, based on its style of ornamentation and the obvious absence of Danish representatives on the island when the memorial was erected.

Later chronicles are increasingly fanciful and contradictory. The Franciscan monk Detmar in Lübeck in the final few years of the century mentioned the battle in his chronicle, but he was far away and incorrectly dated it to 1360.[4]

The Visby Franciscan Chronicle is believed to have been written around 1420, although based on earlier notes in the convent's possession at the time.[5] The Visby Chronicle locates the place of battle to the field outside South Gate, but surprisingly, since the memorial by then already was in existence, gives contradictory information about the date of battle.

Then there are the Swedish rhyme chronicles. Of particular interest for our purposes is the Link Poem (*Förbindelsedikt*).[6] This rhyme chronicle covers the Danish invasion but was written close to a century after the event. It was produced to describe the period not covered by the Erik Chronicle

---

4   Koppmann, *Die Chroniken der niedersächsischen Städte* 1, 187–597, on 529.
5   Fant, *Scriptores Rerum Svecicarum medii ævi* 1:1, 32–47.
6   Klemming, 'Svenska medeltidens rim-krönikor', 171–192.

(*Erikskrönikan*) and the Charles Chronicle (*Karlskrönikan*). The Eric Chronicle was written in the 1320s as a piece of entertaining political propaganda, produced possibly upon orders from the Lord High Justiciar (Swedish: *drots*), Mats Kettilmundsson, who headed the regency government under King Magnus's childhood. The chronicle covers the period from about 1230 to 1320 and is preserved in several later copies.[7] In the mid-fifteenth century, King Charles VIII ordered the production of a rhyme chronicle about his own time, the so-called Charles Chronicle, which covers the period from 1389 to 1452. In conjunction with this, he had the Link Poem produced to link the other two chronicles.

Finally, the Visby seventeenth-century historian Hans Nielssøn Strelow wrote his Gotland Chronicle (*Cronica Guthilandorum*), first published in 1633. Strelow incorporated various popular sagas and myths into the narrative. In addition to such endearing stories, Strelow introduces numerous confirmed errors, primarily that it was the burghers, not the farmers, who fell in the battle, and claims that King Valdemar after the battle tore down a part of the city wall so that 11 men could march abreast through the breach into Visby. Strelow also claims that the Danes looted churches and monasteries (possibly true but not in Visby) and as we have seen ordered the burghers to fill three large beer barrels with silver as a contribution to the Danish King in order to retain their trade privileges (disproven as untrue). As noted, Strelow also reports that most of the treasure was lost in one of King Valdemar's ships which was shipwrecked off the Stora Karlsö Island when the expedition returned home. We have already seen that Strelow is not a credible witness when he felt it necessary to save the reputation of his fellow Visby burghers and of the city whose obvious decline had begun with the understandable but fateful decision of Hermann Munter and his associates to submit to the Danish invaders.

The archaeological remains of the battle of Visby have been thoroughly described, fill volumes, and are second to none in early European battlefield archaeology. The mass graves were excavated in 1905, and the results were spectacular. The archaeological finds, in particular items of armour, are authoritatively described by Bengt Thordeman in the unsurpassed two-volume work *Armour From the Battle of Wisby* (1939–1940). Thordeman published in English because of the worldwide attention that the excavations had gained. His volumes also contain all relevant primary sources in the original language (but not in translation).

Readers of Swedish may notice how Thordeman's description of the battle subtly changed because of events during the Second World War. In the pre-war English-language *Armour From the Battle of Wisby*, he presented statistics and conclusions in what might be described as a disinterested and somewhat detached academic manner. In the Swedish-language book *Invasion på Gotland* (1944), Thordeman instead emphasised a storyline of how a professional invasion army slaughtered poorly armed civilians. Which proves that academics, too, have human emotions.

---

7   Sven-Bertil Jansson (ed.), *Erikskrönikan* (Stockholm: Tiden, 1987).

The two most extensive modern narrative works are both in Swedish. These are Gun Westholm's *Visby 1361* (rev. edn 2014) and Dick Harrison's *Visby brandskattning* (2020), both of which successfully sort myth from fact and provide a good narrative history of the events. Both also rely heavily on Thordeman's work. Maria Lingström's dissertation *Mästerby, 1361* (2025) focuses on her archaeological excavations at Mästerby, but also offers a brief yet more up-to-date narrative, and it is available online in English. As a further boon, she provides translations into English of key primary sources and oral legends that arose from King Valdemar's campaign.

Biographies of King Valdemar Atterdag include Peter Lundbye's passionate but slightly dated *Valdemar Atterdag* (1939) in Danish, and Sven Tägil's *Valdemar Atterdag och Europa* (1962) in Swedish. For a biography of King Magnus of Sweden, there is Michael Nordberg's *I kung Magnus tid* (rev. edn 1997).

Finally, the reader may wish to visit Visby to see the medieval city. Every year, Visby hosts a medieval festival which includes battle reenactments and all the pageant that can be expected from a Danish invasion, except the bloodshed.

Bibliography

Primary Sources and Compilations

Bjurling, Oscar. *Das Steuerbuch König Eriks XIII: Versuch einer Rekonstruktion.* Lund: Ekonomisk-historiska föreningen 4, 1962.

Blatt, Franz (ed.). *Danmarks riges breve 3:5: 1357–1360.* Copenhagen: Det danske sprog- og litteraturselskab/Munksgaard, 1967.

Blatt, Franz (ed.). *Danmarks riges breve 3:6: 1361–1363.* Copenhagen: Det danske sprog- og litteraturselskab/Munksgaard, 1969.

Book of Knowledge: *Book of the Knowledge of all the Kingdoms, Lands, and Lordships That Are in the World.* London: Hakluyt Society 2:29, 1912. Edited and translated by Clements Markham.

Book of Knowledge: *El Libro del conoscimiento de todos los reinos: The Book of Knowledge of All Kingdoms.* Tempe, Arizona: Arizona Center for Medieval and Renaissance Studies, 1999. Edited and translated by Nancy F. Marino.

Bosworth, Joseph (ed.). *King Alfred's Anglo-Saxon Version of the Compendious History of the World by Orosius.* London: Longman, Brown, Green, and Longmans, 1859.

Detmar's Chronicle: Karl Koppmann (ed.). *Die Chroniken der niedersächsischen Städte 1: Lübeck.* Leipzig: S. Hirzel, Die Chroniken der deutschen Städte 19, 1884: 187–597.

Diplomatarium Danicum. Danish National Archives. Web site, https://tekstnet.dk/books/dipdan.

Grönlands historiske Mindesmærker 3. Copenhagen: Det kongelige nordiske oldskrift-selskap, 1845.

Jansson, Sven-Bertil (ed.). *Erikskrönikan.* Stockholm: Tiden, 1987.

Jansson, Sven Birger F. and Elias Wessén. *Gotlands runinskrifter* 1. Stockholm: Kungl. Vitterhets Historie och Antikvitets Akademien, 1962.

Hanserecesse: Die Recesse und andere Akten der Hansetage von 1256–1430 (Vol. 1). Leipzig: Duncker & Humblot, 1870.

Holmbäck, Åke; and Elias Wessén (eds). *Svenska landskapslagar* 4: *Skånelagen och Gutalagen.* Stockholm: AWE/Gebers, 1979.

Huitfeld, Arrild [Arild Huitfeldt]. *Danmarckis Rigis Krønicke.* Copenhagen: Joachim Moltken, 2nd edn 1652. First published in 1603.

Jónsson, Finnur (ed.). *Det gamle Grønlands Beskrivelse*. Copenhagen: Levin & Munksgaard, 1930.

Koppmann, Karl. *Kämmereirechnungen der Stadt Hamburg 1: Kämmereirechnungen von 1350–1400*. Hamburg: Hermann Grüning, 1869.

Libellus de Magno Erici Rege: Claudius Annerstedt (ed.). *Scriptores rerum Svecicarum medii ævi* 3:1. Uppsala: Edvard Berling, 1871–1876: 12–16.

Link Poem (*Förbindelsedikten*). G.E. Klemming (ed.). 'Svenska medeltidens rim-krönikor: Gamla eller Eriks-krönikan'. *Samlingar utgifna av Svenska Fornskrift-sällskapet* 17:1. Stockholm: P.A. Norstedt & Söner, 1865: 171–192.

Mézières, Philippe de. *Le Songe du Viel Pelerin*. Cambridge: Cambridge University Press, 2 vols, 1969. Edited by G.W. Coopland.

Mézières, Philippe de. *Songe du Viel Pelerin: Édition critique*. Geneva: Librairie Droz, 2 vols, 2015. Edited by Joël Blanchard with Antoine Calvet and Didier Kahn.

Olaus Magnus. *Historia de gentibus septentrionalibus*. Rome: Johannes Maria de Viottis, 1555.

Olaus Magnus. *Historia om de nordiska folken*. Hedemora: Michaelisgillet/Gidlund, 2010. Swedish translation of the above.

Olaus Petri. G.E. Klemming (ed.). *Olai Petri Svenska krönika*. Stockholm: H. Klemming, 1860.

Olearius, Adam. *Ausführliche Beschreibung Der kundbaren Reyse Nach Muscow und Persien, So durch gelegenheit einer Holsteinischen Gesandschafft von Gottorff aus an Michael Fedorowitz den grossen Zaar in Muscow, und Schach Sefi König in Persien geschehen*. Schleswig: Johan Holwein, 1663.

Schäfer, Dietrich. *Das Buch des lübeckischen Vogts auf Schonen*. Lübeck: Hansischer Geschichtsverein, 2nd edn 1927.

Snöbohm, Alfred Theodor. *Gotlands land och folk: Hufvuddragen till en teckning af Gotland och dess öden från äldre till nuvarande tider*. Örebro: Abraham Bohlin, 1871.

Steffen, Richard. 'Länsarkivets aktpublikationer 4: Handlingar rörande Visby domkyrka, dess jordar och inventarier'. *Gotländskt Arkiv* 5 (1933): 45–60.

Storm, Gustav (ed.). *Islandske Annaler indtil 1578*. Christiania: Det norske historiske Kildeskriftfond, 1888.

Strelow, Hans Nielssøn. *Cronica Guthilandorum*. Copenhagen: Melchior Martzan, 1663.

Svenskt Diplomatarium. Swedish National Archives. Website, https://sok.riksarkivet.se/sdhk.

Taxa procurationis noctium in visitatione insulæ Gotlandiæ: Claudius Annerstedt (ed.) *Scriptores rerum Svecicarum medii ævi* 3:2. Uppsala: Edvard Berling, 1871–1876: 290–293.

Valk, S.N. (ed.). *Gramoty Velikogo Novgoroda i Pskova*. Moscow: Izdatel'stvo Akademii Nauk SSSR, 1949.

Visby Franciscan Chronicle (Diarium Minoritarum Wisbyensium): Ericus Michael Fant (ed.). *Scriptores Rerum Svecicarum medii ævi* 1:1. Uppsala: Zeipel & Palmblad, 1818: 32–47.

'Visbyfranciskanernas bok: Handskriften B 99 i Kungliga bibliopteket – Latinsk text med översättning, inledning och register. *Arkiv på Gotland* 5. Visby: Landsarkivet i Visby/Gotlands kommunarkiv, 2008. Edited by Eva Odelman and Evert Melefors. Expanded and translated version of the above.

Wallin, Jöran [Georg]. *Gothländska samlingar* 2. Göteborg: Lars Wahlström, 1776.

Zealand Chronicle (*Chronica Sialandie*): Ellen Jørgensen (ed.). *Annales Danici Medii Ævi*. Copenhagen: Selskabet for utgivelse af kilder till Dansk Historie, 1920: 163–188.

Later Studies

Åkerlund, Harald. *Fartygsfynden i den forna hamnen i Kalmar*. Stockholm: Sjöhistoriska samfundet, 1951.

Åkeson, Petter. 'De begravda vid Korsbetningen: Individperspektiv på skelett från 1361'. *Arkeologi på Gotland 2: Tillbakablickar och nya forskningsrön*. Uppsala universitet, Institutionen för arkeologi och antik historia, Visby: Uppsala University, Campus Gotland, Department of Archaeology and Ancient History/Gotland Museum, 2017: 275–284.

Anon. '12 norske middelalderbuklere'. *Middelalder, Våpen og rustning og merket skjold*, 4 December 2021 (https://hoveloghage.wordpress.com/2021/12/04/12-norske-middelalderbuklere/; https://hoveloghage.wordpress.com/tag/skjold/).

Åselius, Gunnar. 'Visby 1361: Bönder mot knektar'. Lars Ericson, Martin Hårdstedt, Per Iko, Ingvar Sjöblom, and Gunnar Åselius. *Svenska slagfält*. np: Wahlström & Widstrand, 2003: 20–25.

Atmore, Lane M.; Lourdes Martínez-García; Daniel Makowiecki; Carl André; Lembi Lõugas; James H. Barrett; and Bastiaan Star. 'Population Dynamics of Baltic Herring since the Viking Age Revealed by Ancient DNA and Genomics'. *PNAS* 2022, 119: 45 (https://doi.org/10.1073/pnas.2208703119).

Benninghoven, Friedrich. 'Die Gotlandsfeldzüge des Deutschen Ordens 1398–1408'. *Zeitschrift für Ostforschung* 13 (1964): 421–477.

Benninghoven, Friedrich. 'Die Vitalienbrüder as Forschungsproblem'. Sven Ekdahl (ed.). *Kultur und Politik im Ostseeraum und im Norden 1350–1450: Visby-symposiet för historiska vetenskaper 1971*. Visby: Museum Gotlands Fornsal, Acta Visbyensia IV, 1973: 41–52.

Blomkvist, Nils. 'Folk och gårdar på medeltidens Gotland: En nyckelfråga för östersjöforskningen'. *Från Gutabygd 2010*. Visby: Gotlands Hembygdsförbund, 2010: 61–126.

Bracke, Niels. *Die Regierung Waldemars IV: Eine Untersuchung zum Wandel von Herrschaftsstrukturen im spätmittelalterlichen Dänemark*. Frankfurt am Main: Peter Lang, Kieler Werkstücke, Reihe A: Beiträge zur schleswig-holsteinischen und skandinavischen Geschichte 21, 1999.

Brobäck Alnehill, Valdemar. *De järnklädda stupade: En studie av rustningsplagg från Korsbetningen via arkeologiska, skriftliga och bildliga källor*. Visby: Uppsala University, Campus Gotland, Department of Archaeology and Ancient History, Bachelor's thesis, 2022.

Clason, Edward. 'Om i Korsbetningsgraven vid Visby funna skelett'. *Kungl. Vitterhets Historie och Antikvitets Akademiens Handlingar* 28: 3 (1925): 257–297.

Cordsen, Hans Christian. 'Beiträge zur Geschichte der Vitalienbrüder'. *Jahrbücher des Vereins für Mecklenburgische Geschichte und Altertumskunde* 73. Schwerin: Verein für Mecklenburgische Geschichte und Altertumskunde, 1908: 1–30.

Christiansen, Tage E. 'Yngre sjællandske krønikes sidste aar'. *Scandia* 40:1 (1974): 5–33.

Ekdahl, Sven. '"Schiffskinder" im Kriegsdienst des Deutchen Ordens: Ein Überblick über die Werbungen von Seeleuten durch den Deutschen Orden von der Schlacht bei Tannenberg bis zum Brester Frieden (1410–1435)'. Sven Ekdahl (ed.). *Kultur und Politik im Ostseeraum und im Norden 1350–1450: Visby-symposiet för historiska vetenskaper 1971*. Visby: Museum Gotlands Fornsal, Acta Visbyensia IV, 1973: 239–274.

Ericson Wolke, Lars. *Kapare och pirater i Nordeuropa under 800 år: Cirka 1050–1856*. Lund: Historiska Media, 2014.

Flemström, Marie; Jessica Larsson; and Petter Åkeson. 'Hic sepulti: En förnyad analys av skelettmaterial från Korsbetningen'. *Gotländskt arkiv* 79 (2007): 151–158.

Fredholm von Essen, Michael. *The Lion from the North* 2: *The Swedish Army during the Thirty Years War, 1632–1648*. Warwick: Helion, 2020.

Fredholm von Essen, Michael. *The Goths* 1: *From Berig to the Battle of Adrianople*. Wonersh: Society of Ancients, 2021.

Fredholm von Essen, Michael. *The Goths* 2: *From Alaric to Theoderic the Great and Beyond*. Wonersh: Society of Ancients, 2022.

Gannholm, Tore. *Gotland och den tyska Hansan: 1300-talets Europamarknad*. Stånga, Gotland: Tore Gannholm, 1994.

Gannholm, Tore. *The Gotlandic Merchant Republic and Its Medieval Churches*. np: Stavgard förlag, 2015.

Gerdin, Anna-Lena. 'A Coastal Farmstead in the Shadow of the City'. *The Significant Detail: Europeanization at the Base of Society – The Case of the Baltic Rim 1100–1400 AD, Transactions of the CCC Workshops at Skäftekärr in Sweden 7–10 October 1999, and at Tukums in Latvia 15–18 April 2000*. Visby: Gotland University College, CCC Papers 9, 2007: 123–151.

Grieg, Sigurd. 'Skjoldene i middelalderen'. Bengt Thordeman (ed.). *Nordisk kultur 12B: Vapen*. Stockholm: Albert Bonnier, 1943: 67–89.

Gutarp, Else Marie. *Medieval Manner of Dress: Documents, Images and Surviving Examples of Northern Europe, Emphasising Gotland in the Baltic Sea*. Visby: County Museum of Gotland, 2001.

Grinder-Hansen, Poul (ed.). *Unionsdrottningen: Margareta I och Kalmarunionen*. Copenhagen: Danmarks Nationalmuseum, 1996.

Haasum, Sibylla. 'Medeltida seglatser: Båtar och navigation'. Gerhard Flink (ed.). *Kung Valdemars segelled*. Stockholm: Streiffert/Riksantikvarieämbetet, 1995: 85–93.

Hadenius, Stig (ed.). *Historia kring Stockholm*. Stockholm: Wahlström & Widstrand, 1967.

Hall, Frithiof. *Bidrag till Cistercienserordens historia i Sverige*. Hernösand, dissertation, 1898.

Hammarhjelm, Bengt. *Gotländsk krigshistoria från Gutasagan till 1814*. Visby: Ödin, 1998.

Hammarhjelm, Bengt. *Gotländsk krigshistoria*. Visby: Gotlands militärkommando, 8 vols., 1993–1995. Earlier edition of the above.

Hansen, Paul-Erik. 'Skaanemarkedet'. *Handels- og Søfartsmuseets årbog* 1945: 17–90.

Harrison, Dick. *Jarlens sekel: En berättelse om 1200-talets Sverige*. Stockholm: Ordfront, 2002.

Harrison, Dick. *Karl Knutsson: En biografi*. Lund: Historiska Media, 2004.

Harrison, Dick. *Visby brandskattning*. Lund: Historiska Media, 2020.

Hedberg, Jonas (ed.). *Kungl. Artilleriet: Medeltid och äldre vasatid*. Stockholm: Militärhistoriska Förlaget, 1975.

Heinänen, Juha. 'On German Knights in Denmark during the Reign of Valdemar Atterdag 1340–1375'. *Ennen ja nyt* 4, 2004 (http://www.ennenjanyt.net/4-04/heinanen.pdf).

Hellman, Tommy. *Ringbrynjehuvor från massgravarna vid Korsbetningen: Några frågor rörande deras konstruktion samt en jämförelse med en i England återfunnen, som äkta betraktad ringbrynjehuva*. Stockholm: Stockholm University, Department of Archaeology, 1995.

Hildebrand, Hans. *Sveriges medeltid: Kulturhistorisk skildring*. 4 vols. Stockholm: P.A. Norstedt & Söner, 1879-1903.

Huldén, Lena. *Krigen kring Östersjön 1: Med blod och svärd, 1000–1520*. Helsinki: Schildt/SMB, 2008.

Huldén, Lena. *På vakt i öster 1: Medeltiden*. Np (Helsinki): Schildt, 2004.

Ekdahl, Sven (ed.). *Kultur und Politik im Ostseeraum und im Norden 1350–1450: Visby-symposiet för historiska vetenskaper 1971*. Visby: Museum Gotlands Fornsal, Acta Visbyensia IV, 1973.

Kirpichnikov, Anatoliy Nikolayevich. *Drevnerusskoye oruzhiye 2: Kop'ya, sulitsy, boyevyye topory, bulavy, kisteny IX–XIII vv*. Moscow: Nauka, 1966.

Klavsen, S.H. *Ved Lillebelt, eller Middelfartsunds Historie*. Middelfart. Claudius Madsen, 1867.

Lagerlöf, Erland. *Gotland och Bysans: Bysantinskt inflytande på den gotländska kyrkokonsten under medeltiden*. Visby: Ödin, 1999.

Lagerqvist, Lars O.; and Ernst Nathorst-Böös. *Vad kostade det? Priser och löner från medeltid till våra dagar*. Stockholm: LT, 4th edn 1997.

Lindström, Gustaf. *Anteckningar om Gotlands medeltid 1*. Visby: Hanse-Production, 1978. First published 1892.

Lingström, Maria. 'Fjäle myr 1361: Arkeologiska undersökningar av slagfältet från dagarna före slaget vid Visby ringmur'. *Fornvännen* 104 (2009): 33–44.

Lingström, Maria. *Mästerby 1361: 2011 års resultat*. Mästerby: Forskningsgruppen Mästerby 1361, 2012.

Lingström, Maria. *Mästerby, 1361: Battlefield Archaeological Perspectives on the Danish Invasion of Gotland*. Uppsala: Uppsala University, Department of Archaeology, Ancient History and Conservation, dissertation, Aun 56, 2025.

Lundbye, Peter. *Valdemar Atterdag: Danmarks riges genopretter*. Copenhagen: Ejnar Munksgaard, 1939.

Lundmark, Efraim. 'Bilefeld, Strelow och de gotländska kyrkornas kronologi'. *Fornvännen* 20 (1925): 162–180.

McLachlan, Sean. *Medieval Handgonnes: The First Black Powder Infantry Weapons*. Oxford: Osprey, Weapon 3, 2010.

Neijman, Thomas. *The Gotlandic Rural Militia: A Study of the Invasion of Gotland 1361 in Response to a Modern Narrative*. Stockholm University Department of History, thesis, 2017.

Neijman, Thomas; and Magnus Mårtensson. 'Rustningshandske 17 från Korsbetningen'. *Fornvännen* 114 (2019): 28–35.

Nicolle, David. *Forces of the Hanseatic League 13th–15th Centuries*. Oxford: Osprey Men-at-Arms 494, 2014.

Nordberg, Michael. *I kung Magnus tid: Norden under Magnus Eriksson, 1317–1374*. Stockholm: Norstedt, rev. edn 1997.

Ödman, Anders. *Borgar i Skåne*. Lund: Historiska Media, 2002.

O'Meadhra, Uaininn. 'Klotter i kyrkan! Gotländska ristningar från medeltiden'. *Folkets historia* 22:4 (1994): 16–29.

O'Meadhra, Uaininn. 'Medeltida ristningar i Gotlands kyrkor'. *Hikuin* 24 (1997): *Kirkearkeologi i Norden* 6 – Skåne: 227–236.

Östergren, Majvor. 'Silverskatternas fyndplatser: Farmännens gårdar'. Ingmar Jansson (ed.). *Gutar och vikingar*. Stockholm: SHM, 1983: 34–48.

Östergren, Majvor. *Mellan stengrund och stenhus: Gotlands vikingatida silverskatter som boplatsindikation*. Stockholm: Stockholm University, Institute of Archaeology, dissertation, 1989.

Schäfer, Dietrich. *Die Hansestädte und König Waldemar von Dänemark: Hansische Geschichte bis 1376*. Jena: Gustav Fischer, 1879.

Siltberg, Tryggve. 'Gotlands bebyggelse 1614: Gårdar, människor och organisation', *Gotländskt Arkiv* 62 (1990), 125–152.

Siltberg, Tryggve. '"Hundens like": Bonderepublikens dom över Valdemar Atterdag i Fidedikten'. *Fornvännen* 97 (2002): 25–43.

Siltberg, Tryggve. 'Talsymmetri i Fidedikten'. *Fornvännen* 98 (2003): 219–220.

Siltberg, Tryggve, 'Gotlands gårdssamhälle 1413–1900 och ödegårdsfrågan 1514–1750'. *GUSEM* 2 (Gutilandorum Universitas Scholarium et Magistrorum, 2011). Högskolan på Gotlands historiska förening: 233–277.

Söderberg, Bengt G. 'Fide kyrka och striderna 1361: En dateringsfråga för Gotlands muralmåleri'. *Fornvännen* 30 (1935): 35–42.

Söderberg, Nils V. 'Hur gick det till?' *Gotländskt Arkiv* 33 (1961): 21–26.

Steffen, Richard. 'Valdemarssägnerna och Jungfrutornets gåta'. *Gotländskt Arkiv* 16 (1944): 49–70.

Svedjemo, Gustaf. 'Gårdar byar och social struktur på Gotland under järnåldern och medeltid'. *Arkeologi på Gotland* 2. Visby: Uppsala University & Gotland Museum, 2017: 183–190.

Svedjemo, Gustaf. *Landscape Dynamics: Spatial analyses of villages and farms on Gotland AD 200-1700*. Uppsala: Uppsala University, dissertation, 2014.

Tägil, Sven. *Valdemar Atterdag och Europa*. Lund: CWK Gleerup, Bibliotheca historica Lundensis 9, 1962.

Thompson, Gunnar. *The Friar's Map of Ancient America 1360 AD: The Story of Nicholas of Lynn and the Franciscan Map of America*. Seattle: Laura Lee, 1996.

Thordeman, Bengt. *Armour from the Battle of Wisby 1361*. 2 vols. Stockholm: Kungl. Vitterhets Historie och Antikvitets Akademien, 1939-1940.

Thordeman, Bengt (ed.). *Nordisk kultur 12B: Vapen*. Stockholm: Albert Bonnier, 1943.

Thordeman, Bengt. *Invasion på Gotland 1361: Dikt och verklighet*. Stockholm: Hugo Geber, 1944.

Tortzen, Christian. *Gotland 1361: Forudsætningerne, overleveringen*. Copenhagen: Gyldendal, 1961.

Weibull, Curt. *Lübeck och Skånemarknaden: Studier i Lübecks pundtullsböcker och pundtullskvitton 1368–1369 och 1398–1400*. Lund: CWK Gleerup/Fahlbeckska Stiftelsen 2, 1922.

Weidhagen-Hallerdt, Margareta. 'Med byssa och kanon: Om Stockholms medeltida försvarsvapen visade på Stockholms medeltidsmuseum'. *Stadsvandringar* 14. Stockholm: Stockholms stadsmuseum, 1991.

Wessén, Elias. 'Nordiska folkstammar och folknamn: En översikt'. *Fornvännen* 64:1 (1969): 14–36.

Westerdahl, Christer. 'Försvar längs farlederna: Ledung, vårdkasar, farledsspärrar och borgar'. Gerhard Flink (ed.). *Kung Valdemars segelled*. Stockholm: Streiffert/Riksantikvarieämbetet, 1995: 95–101.

Westholm, Gun. *Visby 1361: Invasionen*. Stockholm: Prisma, 2007.

Westholm, Gun. *Visby 1361: Invasionen*. Visby: Gotlands Museum Fornsalens förlag, 2014. Identical edition to the above but with an added appendix with new information.

Yrwing, Hugo. 'Valdemar Atterdags gotlandståg 1361: Kritiska synpunkter på bakgrund och följder'. *Gotländskt Arkiv* 33 (1961): 7–20.

Yrwing, Hugo. *Gotlands medeltid*. Visby: Gotlandskonst, 1978.

Yrwing, Hugo. *Visby: Hansestad på Gotland*. Stockholm: Gidlund, 1986.

About the author

Professor Michael Fredholm von Essen is an historian and former military analyst who has published extensively on the history of Eurasia, and lectured, during conferences or as a visiting professor, around the world. He has published a large number of books, including *The Goths 1–2* (Society of Ancients, 2021–2022); *Afghanistan Beyond the Fog of War* (NIAS Press, 2018); *Transnational Organized Crime and Jihadist Terrorism: Russian-Speaking Networks in Western Europe* (Routledge, 2017); numerous articles in *Slingshot*, the journal of the Society of Ancients, and *Arquebusier*, the journal of the Pike and Shot Society; and many books for Helion and Company Publishing.

About the artist

Giorgio Albertini was born in 1968 in Milan where he still lives. After studying Medieval History at the University of Milan, he became involved in archaeology and has been involved in several excavations for European institutions. He was responsible for the graphic depiction of archaeological sites and finds. He also works as an historical and scientific illustrator for many institutions, museums, and magazines such as *National Geographic Magazine*, *BBC History*, and *Medieval Warfare*. He has always been interested in military history and is one of the founders of *"Focus Wars"* magazine.